To Bunny Taussig Hertzberg
with God's Blessings and
much Love!

Dr. George Hetherington

p.s. Rindy & I most thoroughly
enjoyed our visit recently
with you, Lyle & company!

The Soul
of the Rav

The Soul of the Rav

SERMONS, LECTURES, AND ESSAYS

by

RABBI SAMUEL E. KARFF

EAKIN PRESS ◆ Austin, Texas

I am drawn to understand both sides of an issue and can often at least partially validate even the point of view with which I must ultimately disagree. For better or worse I have an eye for the grays, the ambiguity, the unresolved tensions in life and in the quest for truth.

Samuel E. Karff
"You're Also Right"
Rosh Hashanah Morning
September 21, 1998

FIRST EDITION
Copyright © 1999
By Samuel E. Karff
Published in the United States of America
By Eakin Press
A Division of Sunbelt Media, Inc.
P.O. Drawer 90159 🖾 Austin, Texas 78709-0159
email: eakinpub@sig.net
🖳 website: www.eakinpress.com 🖳
ALL RIGHTS RESERVED.
1   2   3   4   5   6   7   8   9
1-57168-384-4

For CIP information, please access:
www.loc.gov

Table of Contents

Preface

The words included in these pages reflect my preaching and teaching life during the last thirty-one years—from my ordination address to new colleagues when I was thirty-six years old to my last High Holy Day messages to Congregation Beth Israel before becoming its Rabbi-Emeritus.

Allowing these sermons, addresses, and essays to be collected and preserved stirred some ambivalence. Words prepared for oral communication are intended to be heard rather than read. Many of these entries pre-date my own sensitization to the need for gender inclusive language. Inevitably, especially in the case of some earlier entries I might now have expressed my thoughts differently.

On the other hand these words accurately reflect the tone and substance of my teaching rabbinate. So I feel enormously grateful for the opportunity to see this retrospective sampler available in more permanent and accessible form. At this juncture in my life when I have retired from leading a congregation to embark upon a new but related vocation (part-time) as Visiting Professor of Society and Health at Houston's University of Texas Health Science Center, I feel very blessed by God for the privilege of having served as a congregational rabbi for over forty years. I am especially grateful to the leaders and members of Beth Israel and my former congregation, Chicago Sinai, for being so supportive and encouraging during the years when these sermons and essays germinated.

This volume would not have been possible without a generous grant from Ambassador Arthur Schechter and his wife Joyce, whom I am delighted to claim as congregants and dear friends. I am also much indebted to Ira Black who assumed the demanding responsibility of editing this collection in collaboration with Dr. Harvey Gordon. Each has sifted through and agreed upon the final selections on the basis of familiarity with my teaching as congregants and cherished friends.

My warm appreciation is extended as well to Catherine Beer and Vickie Burnett who have been the most diligent and devoted secretaries anyone could hope for, and whose familiarity with these thoughts is the fruit of many hours of typing and retyping.

I dedicate this volume to Joan Mag Karff, my beloved life partner over these forty years—and also my closest friend and most honest critic.

I pray that the years ahead will enable me not only to continue to learn and teach but that I will now have more time for my family, including my seven wonderful grandchildren, and live to see the Houston Astros in the World Series.

—Samuel E. Karff
February 16, 1999—30 Shevat 5759

Editor's Note

*The test of a first-rate intelligence is the ability to hold
two opposed ideas in the mind at the same time,
and still retain the ability to function.*
—F. Scott Fitzgerald

When one has spent any time at all in the company of Rabbi Samuel Karff, whether he is speaking from the *bimah* or teaching Torah or sharing a quiet moment of conversation, one is struck by a recurring phrase—"creative tension." It is a crucial thread, he would ask us to understand, which runs through Torah, through the teachings of the great rabbis of the Talmud, and, as you will see in this brief volume, throughout the rabbinate of Sam Karff.

I have spent a considerable amount of time with Sam Karff over the past twenty years, almost since the beginning of his tenure as Senior Rabbi of Houston's Congregation Beth Israel. My introduction to Sam Karff was to his voice. I was assigned to produce his weekly radio program, new to the air-waves, and record the sermons that were the cores of each program. His voice is itself a model of "creative tension." It is rich with rabbinic authority and equally rich in human compassion and humor; a voice of reason and of emotion. It is a voice at once

direct and subtle, as are the ideas it expresses. It is a voice of
forthrightness, not stridency. The voice reflects the man.

Reading through forty years' worth of essays, articles, lectures and sermons, one discovers a remarkable consistency in
thought and expression. Harvey Gordon and I made our selection, not so much because of the thoughts expressed—any random collection would have been an accurate representation of
Sam Karff's rabbinate—but to try to capture for the reader the
voice of Sam Karff. To this end—and to recognize that Sam
Karff has been, above all his other job descriptions, a "pulpit
rabbi"—we have chosen rather more sermons and addresses
than articles and essays. We suggest that those, like us, who have
heard him speak these words will use those memories to fill out
this printed approximation of his presence. For those who have
not heard him speak, we ask you to use your imagination.

The title of this book is taken from the last selection in this
collection, an address given before the Central Conference of
American Rabbis over which Rabbi Karff has served as
President. We have chosen to conclude with it, along with the
three final High Holy Day sermons of his tenure at Beth Israel,
because it defines so clearly what the life of the rabbi means and
encapsulates so well all the threads presented in the other chapters, you might suppose it had just been written as a summation
rather than fifteen years ago.

The selections are not in chronological order but rather
divided into chapters focusing on a particular aspect of Sam
Karff's rabbinic persona. The first chapter presents eight varia-
tions of the theme of creative tension—the yardstick by which
Rabbi Karff measures the lives we lead as Jews among non-Jews
and among our co-religionists. You will find echoes and sugges-
tions of that theme throughout this volume.

The second chapter, its title the first words of our prayer of
affirmation, explores a subject about which Sam Karff has been
passionately vocal—restoring the word "faith" to the Reform
Jewish vocabulary.

Each time a Torah has been held before the congregation,

Rabbi Karff has intoned, "Behold a good teaching has been given to you—do not forsake it." Each Shabbat morning a group of congregants has gathered with Rabbi Karff or one of his colleagues to study Torah. These always-exciting and often excited discussions remind us, perhaps, of Yavneh and that the rabbi's traditional role is that of teacher. Chapter Three presents Sam Karff as *rebbe*—teacher. The first selection is a special story, created by Rabbi Karff, which has been a feature of the Yom Kippur Morning Children's Service—there is not a child or parent who doesn't look forward to sharing it again with Rabbi Karff, however often they have heard it.

As Sam Karff has been teacher to his congregations, so too has he been rabbi to his colleagues. As Orthodox and Conservative Judaism are called Halachic Judaism for their adherence to the primacy of Law, Sam Karff has become renowned throughout the Reform movement for advocating that, while we too recognize the role of Law—of *Halacha*—in our Jewish lives, our strength is in our understanding of the power of *Agada*—the legendary and on-going stories of our people. Chapter Four's title was chosen consciously to echo our traditional appellation for the foremost human in our tradition—*Moshe Rabenu*, Moses our Teacher.

The rabbi is minister and counselor. The fifth chapter, its title a translation of *refu'ah sh'laymah* from our prayer addressing God the Healer, explores four different aspects of the healing theme.

In the years that I have been a Beth Israel member, Sam Karff and I have shared a wide variety of each other's life cycle events, from which he has always been able to glean the Godly dimension and raise each from isolated event to integral part of the Divine continuum. The sixth chapter focuses those moments in our lives that remind us that being Jewish is an intergenerational matter.

The final chapter takes its title from the purpose of Rabbi Karff's last three High Holy Day sermons before his retirement. They are a valedictory—a word of farewell.

I would like to take this opportunity to thank Vickie Burnett, Rabbi Karff's Executive Assistant for preparing all the typescripts, both proposed and finally selected, for editing. Especially, my thanks to Harvey Gordon for assisting in the selection and editing of the material for this book. Without his moral support and critical second-guessing, I would not have attempted the task.

Above all, my deepest appreciation to Sam Karff. One of his lessons in creative tension concerns the interplay of *kavanah* and *keva*—of inspiration and duty—in our daily lives as Jews. Being allowed to edit this collection has satisfied both impulses. It has been a personal satisfaction to be able to revisit favorite themes and visit new ones—to be able to conjure up his presence merely by turning a page. It has also been the fulfillment of *mitzvah*—to study with a great teacher and to make it possible for others to do the same.

In *Exodus* we read that when Moses asked to see God's face, he was refused but, instead, was placed in a cleft in the rocks and allowed to see God's goodness pass by. We may infer from this *Agada* that first impressions might be misleading or even dangerous and that we can only know a person's worth after the fact—after we have seen or shared their goodness. I began my relationship with Sam Karff's voice. Over the two decades since and in a wide variety of circumstances, I have come to know the man—our rabbi, our mentor, our friend.

Ira J. Black

SECTION I

Creative
Tension

CHAPTER 1

𝔄 𝔍ew at 𝔥arvard

I feel honored to stand here. Anyone would. How awesome to celebrate the 350th anniversary of our alma mater. But then all claims to venerability are relative.

The congregation I serve was founded in 1854, only nine years after Texas became a state of the Union. When I first heard that, I was very impressed. I still am, but ever since I addressed the Jewish congregation in Savannah, which received its permanent charter in 1790, my Texas bravado has dimmed substantially. Harvard at 350, that seems positively primeval and, for an American institution, it is. But I stand here not only as an alumnus of the Class of '53; I am a rabbi, a teacher of a tradition of 3500 years.

This morning I want to relate 350 to 3500. I shall speak of the relation between Harvard, prime gateway to the treasures and privileges of a secular American culture and Judaism, the millennial heritage which shaped me and others like me long before I first came to this campus thirty-seven years ago. I do so in the hope that whatever your own religious tradition you will find my words relevant to an appreciation of the precious milestone we share this week.

Address at The Memorial Church, on the occasion of Harvard University's 350th Anniversary

An American Jew's encounter with Harvard is, in some respects, the retelling of an old Jewish story. It is the story of our tradition's encounter with a threatening, challenging and seductive world. Threatening, because each such encounter could weaken our pristine loyalties. So the Israelites were warned against adopting the sophisticated ways of the Canaanites. They needed to hold their heritage in protective custody. At some point we too must say no to the allures of the outside world in order to preserve the sacred rhythms, symbols and values of our heritage.

In coming to Cambridge I didn't have to decide, *à la* Sandy Koufax, whether to pitch in the Harvard/Yale game on Yom Kippur. That remained fantasy. I did have to decide whether I would attend an important class on the holiest day of the Jewish year, whether I would eat the pork served in the Eliot House dining hall, whether I would get so involved on campus that I would totally ignore the Jewish Sabbath.

The larger world (in our paradigm, the Harvard world) was quite challenging. Here we encountered science and philosophy, the classics of eastern and western civilization. Harvard stood for all that was rational, intellectual, liberating, and empowering. That made this place all the more seductive. For some, perhaps many, Harvard was a place to keep a low Jewish profile. Here only one's humanness and intellectual prowess mattered. Indeed some thirty years ago Harvard was a place to keep a low religious profile regardless of your particular heritage. Beyond the Divinity School, religious narratives were regarded at best sentimentally and religious symbols were appreciated aesthetically, but neither religious story nor symbol was to be taken too seriously by one who revered the rigorous life of the mind.

So here at Harvard many American Jews sealed their assimilation into a privileged secular mainstream. Here they thought as little of their Jewishness and Judaism as the environment would allow and many thought very little indeed; though sometimes that environment reminded us that being Jewish was still a barrier to total acceptance, even here.

There were years when Jewish enrollment was carefully restricted at the highest administrative levels. There were years when a tenured Jewish faculty member was a conspicuous rarity. There were private clubs where Jewish students and other minorities were explicitly excluded. And for many years the course offerings of the college, including surveys of western civilization, signaled by their silence that no noteworthy Jewish thought had taken place since the dawn of the Christian Era.

And yet I stand here today as proud alumnus who wholeheartedly and gratefully celebrates this 350th anniversary. It is important to understand why.

Through the centuries my people learned to interact with the larger world of thought and culture, to learn from that world and be enriched by it without losing our Jewish integrity. Even thirty-seven years ago, and I suspect long before, it was possible to enter this heady world of intellectual splendor, and be immeasurably enlightened without weakening the precious fidelities within our souls. That was surely my experience in this place.

And that brings me to this morning's scriptural lesson. It so happens that those words from *Deuteronomy* are being read in synagogues all over the world this week. I chose them for that reason and because they relate so personally to my theme. Let us see how. The children of Israel are instructed, *"tzedek, tzedek, tirdof*—Justice, justice shall you pursue." Specifically the judges in Israel were commanded to imitate God. God is just. God judges persons according to their merit. Indeed God's covenant with Israel is a rational, conditional, contractual agreement. Israel remains chosen only as long as it observes the terms of the covenant. God is a fair judge. But elsewhere in the Torah, God is not a dispassionate judge, giving each his due. God is an emotionally involved, loving, caring parent. Israel is God's child, bound to the Holy One by unconditional love.

And why does this twofold image of the covenant seem so apt to my theme? More than thirty years ago in Emerson Hall, not far from where we stand, I took a class with Talcott Parsons, a great professor of sociology. He taught me to appreciate the distinction between a social relationship that is impersonal, rational, contractual, (which Parsons called "instrumental adaptive" and a relationship grounded in kinship, inherited privilege and love (which Parson's called "expressive"). I never forgot that conceptual tool. In fact a few years later at rabbinic seminary that tool helped me understand the narratives of Bible and Talmud. Talcott Parsons helped me explore the sustained tension between the conditional and unconditional dimension in the covenant which bound God and Israel, the tension between God as contractual partner and God as loving parent, the tension between justice and steadfast love.

Much of my approach to rabbinic theology, much of my preaching and writing over the years, including my doctoral dissertation, was based on the application of a Harvard professor's conceptual scheme to the study of ancient Jewish texts.

I use my experience as metaphor. Over the years Harvard did not mandate our assimilation, our loss of heritage. Many of us found in this highly-charged world an exciting opportunity to enrich our minds without compromising our cherished fidelities. Here we received priceless new tools for a re-encounter with our deepest selves.

To be sure, in my day one still needed to resist subtle pressure to diminish particular loyalties unless you happened to be white, Anglo-Saxon, Protestant. What makes this occasion even more sanguine is that during the past thirty years the Harvard world has continued to mellow and ripen. Today, to an unprecedented degree Harvard celebrates religious and cultural diversity.

Nothing signaled the change in climate more poignantly than a procession some years ago across Harvard Yard. Henry Rosovsky, then Dean of Arts and Sciences and a committed Jew, held a Torah Scroll in his arms and participated in a procession of students and faculty and alumni across the Yard to a new, more centrally located, vibrantly active Jewish Student Center. In my time that procession would never have taken place.

Today Harvard college has a new Center for Jewish Studies and Harvard Divinity School has a professorship in Jewish Religious Thought. Today as well, Harvard reflects our culture's greater openness to the sacred. There is even talk of intellectuals, Harvard intellectuals, some of them Jewish, who are recovering the religious dimension in their lives.

So an academy with Puritan roots that once taught Hebrew because it was the language of Christianity's Old Testament heritage, now proclaims unambiguously that there are many paths to religious truth. In that context Harvard has given an additional meaning to an ancient imperative: "Justice, justice shall you pursue."

This University strives to do justice to us all. It neither imposes nor actively favors a particular religious view. It provides a rich and open arena where each of us can learn from the other as we cultivate the life of the mind and the spirit. That is no small gift.

Therefore, whatever our particular religious story we gather here proudly, gratefully and prayerfully. May the One who has called us to this place sustain and prosper it. May we who cherish this academy and have been enriched by it proclaim the words spoken by my people whenever a significant milestone has been reached:

> *"Baruch ata Adonai Eloheinu melech ha'olam*
> *shehecheyanu vekiyemanu vehigianu*
> *laze'man ha'zeh.*
> *Praised be Thou, O Lord our God,*
> *Ruling Spirit of the Universe, who has kept us*
> *in life, sustained us and permitted us to reach*
> *this day."*

CHAPTER 2

Jacob's Fear and Distress

This morning, we read again of Abraham's great time of trial. Would God really require the sacrifice of his precious Isaac? God did not require it. It was only a test, a trial. Each of the patriarchs had his hours of trial.

Isaac had two sons, Jacob and Esau. Esau felt Jacob had deprived him of his birthright and vowed revenge. Jacob fled from his brother. Then came one of Jacob's major hours of trial. He heard that his estranged brother Esau was coming to greet him heavily armed. As Jacob was about to encounter Esau the Torah says: "Jacob feared greatly and was distressed." Why, asked the rabbis, did the Torah say Jacob "feared greatly and was distressed?" How redundant! If he "feared greatly" obviously he "was distressed." No, say the rabbis: the text uses two expressions to describe two distinct feelings. Jacob feared he would be killed by Esau and he was distressed that he might kill Esau.

That ancient rabbinic commentary is the most profound summary of the drama unfolding in Israel today. We and many of our kin in Israel share Jacob's double agenda. We fear those

Sermon—Rosh Hashanah Morning—5749, September 12, 1988

who threaten our people's right to live and we are distressed that, in the course of securing our survival, we may violate the personhood of others and betray the purpose of our being.

Actually a Prime Minister of Israel, Golda Meier, once rephrased Jacob's fear and distress. She said: "It is hard to forgive our Arab neighbors for killing our children. It is harder still to forgive them for causing us to kill their children." This double concern has, of course, been highlighted by the events of the past ten months in Israel. Many Israelis see the *Intafada*, the Arab uprising and its demand for PLO control of the West Bank and Gaza, as a threat to their security. Many also see the prolonged Israeli occupation and suppression of Arab resistance as a threat to the kind of nation Israel wants to be.

It is not a pretty picture, or a simple one. How can one observe a High Holy Day season (a season when we confront who we are and who we are intended to become) without speaking of such things? What should we say? There are a number of things I feel impelled to say on this day of reckoning and soul searching and my text is Jacob's fear and distress upon encountering Esau.

NO TIME TO DISTANCE OURSELVES

First of all, I am concerned that in this hour of Israel's trial some of us may be subtly or not so subtly distancing ourselves from our kin and forgetting the magnitude of our stake in Israel's well being.

Sure it was much easier to be "Israel proud" in the era of Paul Newman's portrayal of Ari ben Canaan in the movie *Exodus*, when we were viscerally aware that Arab armies had ganged up to destroy Israel and the few overcame the many. It was easier to be proud of Israel when we noted the transformation of the desert, the in-gathering of Jewish refugees and the pioneering work in medical technology shared with Arab and Jew alike.

It is more difficult to proclaim our commitment to an Israel mobilizing armed soldiers against people who do not want to be ruled by Israeli occupiers.

Yet it is precisely at this time when the depth of our commitment may be tested. It is precisely at this time we may need to be reminded what some of us may have begun to forget.

Israel's rebirth forty years ago enabled many of us and our children to come out of the Jewish closet and face a Jewish future with confidence and self-respect. After the Holocaust it was important, so important, that there was one tiny corner of the world where Jews could experience the joys and burdens of sovereignty; that there was one place where any Jew who needed a refuge could find one; that there was one little country unconditionally willing and able to defend Jews against would-be destroyers.

We who live here and are at home in America may permit ourselves to repress the stake we really have in Israel's well being, but that stake remains. Must it take a fear of imminent destruction to reclaim it?

I recall 1967, during the Six Day War, when for a few grim days it seemed that Israel was in mortal danger. At that time, I was in Chicago, but I am sure the same thing happened in Houston. Some of the most assimilated, uninvolved, marginal Jews I know came forth frantically, surprising themselves, pledging resources far above their means, as a gesture, a way of signaling "This must not happen, I must do all I can to see that it does not happen. Israel must live."

Each time I have taken some of you on a first trip to Israel there have been those who came as tourists (interested observers, very much as you would visit Australia or Greece for the first time). But something happens while at the Western Wall, or while waking in the depths of the night, or on the bus to Galilee: the defenses collapse and you realize for the first time, as a Jew, that the well-being of Israel is terribly important to you. You did not know it!

How comforting (even as an American Jew) that for the first time in two thousand years there is an empowered, sovereign

State of Israel and the fate of the Jews is no longer subject to
the whims of the Kurt Waldheims or the Yasir Arafats of this
world.

Yes, the exercise of power imposes special responsibilities
and there is no absolutely clean way to wield power. Power
means the loss of innocence. But after the cumulative experience of powerlessness, of being forced to wander from land to
land, of being subjected to the whims of the anti-Semite and the
genocidal schemes of the Nazis, we know that powerlessness
destroys. Better the moral ambiguity of struggling to use power
responsibly than the moral innocence of powerlessness. And so,
therefore, there is not a self-respecting Jew in the world who, in
his heart of hearts, is not deeply invested in the well-being of
that tiny, troubled country called Israel.

ISRAEL'S SECURITY REMAINS AN ISSUE

But some say the first of Jacob's fears, the concern for physical security and survival, is no longer a real issue. It is an
anachronism. Israel is exceedingly strong. Israel is now the
Goliath and the Palestinians are like David with his slingshot and
that is the issue in the Middle East today.

Such comments lack a sense of history and perspective. We
have not yet outlived Jacob's first agenda. Israel's physical security may not be taken for granted, though one would never know
it from a recent resolution of the Texas Conference of Churches.
That resolution includes the words: "Whereas, through a series
of wars from 1949 to the present, the Israeli nation has expanded its boundaries and through the War of 1967 militarily took
control of the occupied territories in East Jerusalem, the West
Bank and the Golan Heights ..."

Wow! What a gross distortion of history. Where is the recognition that in 1948 the Jews of Israel agreed to the U. N. parti-
tion plan dividing the land into a Jewish and Arab state? It was
five Arab states and their armies who launched an attack
designed to drive the Jewish settlers to the sea. During every

subsequent war, including 1967, the stated Arab intention was to destroy Israel.

Where in the Texas Conference of Churches Resolution is the recognition that the Golan Heights (before Israel wrested it from the Syrians) was used to launch relentless artillery barrages against the helpless Israeli *kibbutzim* in the settlements below? And today it is estimated that in the thirty miles between the Golan Heights and Damascus, Syria has deployed four thousand two hundred modern tanks. At Hitler's peak, he had three thousand two hundred tanks on a two thousand mile front with Russia.

For forty years Israel has not challenged the right of its Arab neighbors to live. Those nations (with the exception of Egypt) to this day have not recognized Israel's right to be. And should Israel feel secure when nations like Iraq, with fifty divisions under arms and modern missiles and a willingness to use chemical warfare, are also pledged to Israel's destruction?

And the PLO, which vies to establish control over a West Bank (at some points only miles from Tel Aviv), has never renounced the charter which commits it to Israel's destruction. When someone in Arafat's camp makes soundings to the contrary, other PLO factions quickly attack him as a traitor.

No, Israel has still to consider the first part of Jacob's agenda. The Middle East remains a dangerous place. And leaders have yet to emerge in the Arab world willing and able to undo the politics of hate, terror and destruction that has prevailed for four decades.

THE OTHER SIDE OF THE STORY

To be sure, there is more to the story. There are those in Israel, some in high leadership, who believe it is Israel's destiny to permanently control the Palestinian population in what is called Judea and Samaria. That position endangers Israel's soul. It does not address Jacob's distress. Remember Jacob was distressed that he might violate the personhood of Esau. Israel should respect the yearnings of the Palestinian Arabs to be free of Israeli occupation and to be ruled by their own.

And yes, in the interim, Israel must maintain order firmly. But it should strive to do the least possible harm to the life and personhood of those under Israel's occupation.

In the early stages of the Arab uprising, when news got out that beatings were to be used by Israel in putting down the uprising, many of us, like Jacob, were deeply distressed. Talk of beatings conjured up images of the times our people were mercilessly beaten in pogroms; and now, were Jewish soldiers to be cast as beaters?

Oh, there were explanations that beatings were less lethal than shooting as a form of riot control. But our misgivings remained. The declared policy itself of forced beatings seemed to encourage brutality against those Arabs who were already under Israel's custody. There has been ample evidence these ten months that yes, Israeli soldiers under stress can succumb to acts that are demeaning and cruel. Some of us have felt impelled to speak out.

Were we right when we publicly protested those media-exposed episodes of Israeli brutality? After all, look at the provocation. Judged by the repressive standards of Syria, Jordan, Iran and Iraq, doesn't Israel come off quite well? And, by our public criticism, weren't we merely giving encouragement to Israel's enemies?

I felt then, and I feel now, we were right and we are right to raise our voices. We as Jews cannot claim to be concerned with human rights everywhere in the world except in Israel. And I think our clamor, added to that of the Israeli citizens living in the only democracy in the Middle East has led to reclarification of the policy and greater restraint.

Here is the bottom line: we Jews are heirs to Jacob's double agenda. Yes, we must defend ourselves against those who would harm us, whether they come bearing rocks or missiles or fire bombs, but we must be no less distressed at the harm we may cause Esau.

OVERCOMING THE STALEMATE

How can the present ugly stalemate be overcome and movement made toward peaceful co-existence? Obviously, I have no ready-made answer to that awesome question. But there are certain pre-conditions if Israel and its Arab neighbors are to move toward peace. Last night, I said we do not live in the messianic era.

In a messianic world, Palestinian Arabs and Israelis might expect to achieve all that their hearts and minds envision and find that their total agenda can be accommodated to the total agenda of those on the other side. But in this world, to settle for nothing less than the whole thing can be destructive.

The Czech writer Milan Kundera uses the Bohemian word *litost*. *Litost* is a fanatical, spiteful, insistence on all or nothing. *Litost* is a rejection of all compromise. Kundera says: "A man obsessed by *litost* realizes himself by destroying himself."

If a path to Arab-Jewish reconciliation in the Middle East is to be found, this much is certain: it will be because leaders on both sides have discovered the need for compromise.

In this difficult period, we should not expect the Messiah, but we cherish messianic moments. Such a moment occurred in the West Bank village of Beta when some local Arabs acted to protect Israeli schoolchildren from a stone-throwing mob. Another such moment occurred when, after the Israeli Army misguidedly destroyed groves of olive trees in that Arab village, a group of Israeli Jews returned to Beta and replanted that grove with new olive trees.

If the Messiah were here, Jacob's twofold agenda would be obsolete. There would be no real enemies to fear and no struggle for survival where we might hurt others. In this world, Jacob's double agenda remains very real. And so we American Jews and our Israeli kin must promote a strong, powerful Israel and we must continue to be deeply and vocally anguished by policies and action which violate the personhood of Palestinian Arabs.

Living with these two agendas is not easy for us. It is, of course, infinitely more difficult for our Israeli kin. Their lives are on the line. There will be no quick fix for this tragic conflict, but we must dare to hope for openings toward peaceful coexistence.

Those openings, too, will be messianic moments. Those openings will be God's gifts to Arab and Jewish leaders who curb the impulse toward fanaticism in themselves and their people, who respect the need for compromise, and who are guided by Jacob's double agenda.

"And Jacob was very afraid and he was distressed," afraid for his own security and distressed that he might violate the personhood of Esau. So may it be. Soon—in our time.

CHAPTER 3

Contemporary Challenges to an Eternal People

The story is told of an affluent man swamped with leisure who eagerly collected exotic hobbies to fill his vacant hours. His latest hobby was scuba diving. In its pursuit he purchased all the conceivable gear. Armed with flippers, goggles, oxygen mask and tank, even a pad and pen that could be used underwater, he descended to the depths and cavalierly observed the subterranean scene.

Suddenly his eye glimpsed a strange, moving object. It was not an exotic fish or a sea monster but another man, totally unequipped for an underwater adventure, swimming towards him. Jolted by the surprise, the well-dressed sea-diver took his pad and pen and wrote indignantly: "What are you doing here?" The other man hurriedly took the pen and responded, "It's very simple. I'm drowning."

Now which of these two men would you cast as the historic Jew? We have never had to look for diverting hobbies. The struggle for our survival has been a full-time job.

But there have been interludes when many of us have tried

Banquet Address at 49th UAHC Biennial Convention,
Montreal, Canada, November 15, 1967

to act the part of the well-dressed, casual sea-diver. To their credit, the leaders of our movement have persistently reminded us of the urgent challenges of this place and this hour. Maurice Eisendrath has not permitted an affluent generation to forget its prophetic roots. Nelson Glueck has summoned his generation of rabbis to its unparalleled burdens.

The Union of American Hebrew Congregations and the College-Institute were born as 19th century responses to the challenges of an eternal people. These challenges were most dramatically presented on July 29, 1806, when a distinguished delegation of Jewish businessmen, financiers, rabbis and scholars arrived in Paris. They were received in the Hotel de Ville by an honor guard beating a drum tattoo. These Jews were summoned by Napoleon to answer a series of twelve questions. Among them: Does Judaism permit divorce? In the eyes of the Jews, are the French brothers or strangers? What behavior does Jewish law prescribe toward French Christians? Do Jews, born in France, consider France their country? Are they willing to defend it and obey its laws?

These questions were to ascertain whether or not the 19th century Jew was truly prepared to leave the ghetto and enter the modern world. All movements in contemporary Jewish life remain direct or indirect reactions to Napoleon's ploy. Our Reform elders were among the pioneer respondents.

We are over a century older than those Jewish notables. From our vantage point, Napoleon's questions may appear both insulting and irrelevant. We are veterans of the modern world. In incredible measure we have tasted both its sting and its honey. We know of Auschwitz and final solutions, of Israel reborn and the unparalleled American-Jewish success story, of space travel and the eclipse of God. As we chart a covenant course for this place and time, what can we learn from the past century and a half? How may that experience shape or define our present goals and strategy?

Napoleon's twelve questions are reducible to three. These three constitute the hidden agenda of that historic encounter.

Let us re-examine those unspoken questions with the benefit of hindsight and a willingness to learn from our past. Napoleon's first underlying question: Can a son of Abraham be fully a man or does his Jewish tribalism prevent him from truly acknowledging his obligations to the human community?

One answer to that question had already been given by a brilliant hunchbacked philosopher who, in the 18th century, left the ghetto of Dessau for the salons of Berlin. His name, Moses Mendelssohn. Throughout his life Moses Mendelssohn remained a proud, self-respecting Jew. Yet in one of his letters to a Christian minister and friend, Mendelssohn made this revealing comment: "Moses, the (*mensch*—human being) is writing to Herder, the *mensch*, and not the Jew to the Christian preacher."

Note well—Mendelssohn consciously distinguished and neatly separated out his Jewishness and his manhood. Indeed his biographer reminds us that although "he despised apostasy as abominable, Mendelssohn would gladly have joined his Christian friend ... in a society where there were neither Jews nor Christians." Mendelssohn envisioned a community of individuals surrendering their particularism to inherit their full birthright of humanity.

All of us have wrestled with Mendelssohn's dream. But whereas he dreamed of such a world, some of his modern descendants imagined they could bring it about. The experiment has taken many forms. In each case the Jew eagerly de-escalated his Jewishness only to discover that he received in return, not admission to a universal community, but marginal membership in another particularism.

Exhibit A, Mendelssohn's son and grandson. To claim his human birthright, Abraham Mendelssohn felt impelled to abandon his Jewishness. This he gladly did under the Cross of the Lutheran Church, and his son, Felix Mendelssohn-Bartoldy was raised, not as his grandfather had dreamed, simply a *mensch*, but simply a Christian.

And what of the Jewish vanguard in the Russian Revolution? Religion, they devoutly believed, was an opiate of the masses; anti-Semitism a relic of bourgeois culture; the Jewish People—an anachronism. As one writer put it, "Their fatherland was the revolution which had no frontiers, their country was mankind or the proletariat." One thinks of the Jew, Ilya Ehrenburg. He somehow managed to survive Stalin's anti-Jewish purges. He admitted he was a Jew only because he was not permitted to forget it. Ehrenburg was Russia's best-selling author but somehow, despite his vocal anti-Zionism, Ehrenburg, the Marxist and reluctant Jew, did not endorse Russia's stand in the recent Mid-East war, and when he died a few months ago, no Russian dignitaries attended his funeral.

In their own way, our Reform forebears also separated their personhood and their Jewishness. They did so by surrendering the Jew of the flesh and embracing only the Jew of the Spirit— by proclaiming that they were "Germans of the Mosaic persuasion." Abraham Geiger once said: "The people Israel is no longer ... it is resurrected as a congregation of faith and only what touches it has any indisputable right to our concern."

The charred crucible of the 20th century has since taught us that the Jew of the flesh and the Jew of the spirit are indivisible. Any invitation to greet the universal Messiah which demands that we surrender either, is neither truly universal nor truly Messianic.

Those days in June, 1967, were a crucial watershed in the annals of Jewish self-understanding. We, the chastened veterans of the modern world, affirmed that *Am Yisroel Chai*, The people Israel Lives, and a Jew who denies the claim of his people denies his faith and his manhood.

Can a Jew be a man? A Jew who rejects his peoplehood betrays his manhood, but *a Jew who forgets that he is a mensch is also not fully a Jew*. The covenant of Abraham was intended as a gateway to the covenant of man. At its best the Torah is the means whereby a man-born Jew cultivates his humanity.

Here was Reform's greatest and most enduring mandate to the emancipated Jew. The architects of our prayerbook accentuated the universal dimensions of Jewish piety—reminding the worshipper that "The Redeemer of Israel" is the Redeemer of all men, and the Jew who actively labors for the welfare of the total society is hastening the advent of the Messiah.

The crucial question before us: Can the synagogue of tomorrow nurture a *"Yisroel Mensch,"* a Jewish person? Can we, under conditions of unprecedented freedom, rear Jews who will both embrace their people and acknowledge their vital kinship with all the children of men?

A Jewish *mensch* will, as a matter of honor, forthrightly oppose a tide of black anti-Semitism, but he will also remember and heed the words of Isaiah when he asked the affluent of his time, "Do you want rest?" And answered, "(Then) give rest to the weary."

The soul of a Jewish *mensch* will be singularly seared by the lingering stench of Auschwitz. But emerging from that foul haze, he will empathize with the agony of the Vietnamese peasant, and seek to resist all the dehumanizing forces of our time.

A Jewish *mensch* will not flinch from condemnation of his own people but he will do so, not with remote disdain, nor only with the harsh accents of judgement, but with the pain of offended personal pride. He will seek not to escape from our ranks but to reform them.

A Jewish *mensch* will unequivocally defend his Israeli kinsmen's right to live, even as he will attempt to assist the Arab refugee.

A Jewish *mensch* will love America or Canada in one way, Israel in another, and submit all nations to the judgement of God.

Here surely is the way we must answer Napoleon's first question. *Can a Jew be a man? He must be fully both or he is neither and the particular covenant of Abraham remains his only authentic gateway to the universal covenant of man.*

■ ■ ■

When Napoleon confronted those Jewish notables, he asked

a second question: Are you Jews captives of the past or can you truly inherit the future? Does an antiquarian tradition enfold your life or are you free to hear and embrace the revelations of a new age?

Reform amply demonstrated by word and deed that we were not captives of our past. We quickly exorcised the skeletons in our closet and radically pruned the hedge which the sages had built around the Torah. We were anxious to be "hip"—at times, a bit too anxious! Samuel Holdheim, one of the most daring of the early Reformers, stated the matter thus: "The Talmud speaks with the ideology of its own time and for that time it was right. I speak for the higher ideology of my time and for this age, I am right." What was the ideology, the *zeitgeist* of the 19th century? A belief that history is automatically progressive. The wise man, indeed the good man, will both cheer and cooperate with history's inexorable thrust. The prophets of this age heralded history's latest offspring, the modern nation, and particularly the German state as an incarnation of man's noblest dream. Wishing to be "modern" many spokesmen of our people uncritically exclaimed, "Hallelujah, Hail the march of history! The new European state is the embodiment of our people's Messianic dream."

It is easy to be a Monday morning quarterback, but the events of the 20th century should have rendered us more critical of the New Revelations—even when dressed in the garb of the Messiah. If we are truly chastened veterans of the modern world, then we shall never again permit ourselves to be too easily mesmerized by the ideology of an age—and now is our time of testing.

What is the prevailing ideology of our age? We meet in the glittering city of "Expo 67." Here, during the past few months, fifty million people have been treated to an awesome, stunning display of human creativity and power. Expo 67 featured Man. Man, the creator, the explorer, the producer, the provider. Man has presumably come of age. Not history, but technology is our Messiah. The difficult we overcome today, the impossible—

tomorrow. We no longer need you, O Lord, our powers are now adequate to our needs!

According to the heritage of our fathers, man is God's vital partner. According to the emerging *zeitgeist* of the secular age, man is God's cosmic successor. Will we uncritically succumb to this *zeitgeist* or will we dare to engage in a bold dialogue with our past, this time neither defending its skeletons nor spurning its treasures?

Biologists tell us that we may soon have the power to manipulate the genetic structure of man. Does this signal the death of God the Creator, or the radical extension of that "dominion" promised Adam in the opening pages of *Genesis*? Perhaps the real meaning of this biogenetic age is found in the words of a medieval mystic who said: "Be ready at all times for the gifts of God and always for new ones."

What kind of man shall we breed? Who shall be trusted with the choice? What is to prevent the breeding of a race of imbeciles who would gladly minister to an intellectual elite? And if this is possible, is it wrong?

According to the *zeitgeist* of our time, man and not God is the ultimate source of good and evil. Suppose our elite sanctions such exploitation of genetic imbeciles. Is it still wrong? Why? Because such conduct violates the intended order of existence? Man alone asks such "boundary questions," and when man chooses and stands accountable for the quality of his life, he leaves the realm of technology for the precincts of Torah. He asks not *how* but *whether*; not only what *can* but what *ought* to be. Nor may all such value judgements be postponed to the distant future.

When is the sexual act good or evil? Technology has removed the fear of pregnancy and disease but is the glib jargon of "mutual consent" or the momentary affirmation of "love, love, love" an adequate norm? The Torah reveals a canny awareness of both the sanctifying and the dehumanizing potential of our sexual drives. Do the norms of our fathers deserve an earnest hearing?

On this issue as on others, a responsible Reform Jew will neither permit the past to enthrall the present nor the present to ignore its past. If all Torah was not revealed at Sinai, neither is it fully embodied in the latest issue of *Playboy*.

Every rabbi has a few encounters a year which persistently haunt him. Some months ago a woman in my congregation left the hospital bedside of her husband and, with a tormenting sigh of world weariness, asked me an unforgettable question. "Rabbi, what's it all about—is it worth it?" The *zeitgeist* of our age discredits such a question. If it persists perhaps you need a pill or an analyst. But in truth technology neither stifles the question nor provides an answer. The question does persist and surely by our acts if not our words most of us answer "yes."

We do not live as if life is absurd. We act as if there is transcendent value in what we do or decline to do, as if our finite days are more than a whiff of insignificance, as if, despite our persistent failures, we are not without worth, and despite life's traumas we are not without hope. Is this akin to the trust of our fathers? Do we need a new language in which to express such trust? Is this the major task of contemporary theology?

I envision a Reform Jew committed to the primary and enduring legacy of Sinai, sensitive to the seers of our own time and engaging in a true dialogue between them. Such a Jew will not say *Kaddish* for God. *He will emerge with a contemporary idiom for the faith that our expanding but finite powers, our soul-searing moral accountability, our indestructible trust in the worth of existence witness to Him whom neither our words nor our life can fully deny.*

■ ■ ■

There was one more question implied by Napoleon's confrontation with those Jewish notables. His first question, can a Jew be a man, and his second, is the Jew a captive of his past, led inevitably to the third. At this juncture of history, why be a Jew at all?

The early Reformers displayed an eloquent expertise in

answering this question: "Only when the *Shema* has lost its point of admonition and the *Alenu*, the Adoration prayer becomes an anachronism, will the Jew *qua* Jew feel free to unload his cosmic burden."

I do not depreciate this claim. To deny the mission of Israel would have been then, and remains now, a betrayal of the life and death of countless generations. Had our people lost its faith in its divine vocation, the Torah, like Hammurabi's Code, would long since have become an archeological relic to be exhumed by the diggers of the 20th century, and the Jewish people long since vanished from the earth.

But the mission of Israel is not enough to sustain us. It never was. Consider the analogy of marriage. Marriage exists to provide responsible parenthood. But what would we think of two persons who described their marriage exclusively or even primarily as a means of perpetuating the race? What would we think of a couple who felt no perceptible joy or meaning in their sustained intimacy with each other?

Traditionally, Israel's covenant with God served both divine ends and human needs. Our forebears did not just stand ready to advance God's kingdom on earth. They observed and were sustained by a Jewish style of being. They did not go around asking "Why should I remain a Jew?" They kept their Sabbaths and holidays; they quenched their human thirst for understanding in the study of Torah. They found in the *mitzvot* of the Covenant a glorious language in which to celebrate and to mourn, to praise and to argue with God; and in its disciplines, a way to temper their fear of death and renew their confidence in life.

But alas, *since the time of Napoleon, we have been far more eloquent in defining the mission of Israel than in evoking the richness and splendor of a Jewish style of life.*

What will many of our children remember of their Jewish existence? If asked what Judaism stands for, they may rehearse that catchy slogan, "The Fatherhood of God and the Brotherhood of Man," but what will they remember of a "Jewish way of life?" Perhaps a self-conscious rendition of a very abbreviated Passover *Haggadah*, an annual pilgrimage to the synagogue, a funeral after grandma's death. But what were those *mitzvot* which mother and dad performed more regularly and with more finesse?

They may remember parents attending dinners to raise money for our defense agencies or pledging generously, if conspicuously, at UJA rallies. They will remember Papa and even Mama shooting below par at the Jewish country club. In short they will remember the *minyan* of Jewish sociability far more vividly than the *minyan* of worship. They will recall the pursuit of the anti-Semite far more than the pursuit of Torah. They will know more of our defensive response to a lingering Gentile exclusivism than of our genuine delight in the mandates of a positive Jewish existence. They have seen Judaism more as a fate to endure than a faith to live by.

No, we cannot go home again. This is the key to our Reform posture. We cannot, simply by an act of will or submission, return to the world of Sholom Alechem and the *Shulchan Aruch*, but can we develop authentic styles of Jewish life? We shall not become "*Yeshiva Buchars*," unselectively pouring over the tomes of Torah, but why must our thirst for learning be totally quenched in the pursuit of professional passports, or in the secular study of God's world? Perhaps the cybernetic age of greater leisure will compel all men, including the Jew, to seek a *deeper* understanding of his place in this world.

We must rear a generation who will discover that the most crucial questions of Torah are the most crucial questions of life; a generation of Jews who, not in innocent faith but in the excitement of personal discovery, feel moved to declare: "A good teaching has been given unto us—we shall not forsake it."

The same may be said of the experience of worship. A return to the traditional *Siddur* will not make us "*davveners*." The Union Prayerbook has not made us worshippers, nor is there a guarantee that a new liturgy will do so. The question remains: Can we develop liturgies which will be unmistakably Jewish and more spiritually compelling? We must rear a generation who will find in the act of worship a vital form of covenant renewal, a deeper level of self-understanding, a vibrant way of wrestling with their doubts, of celebrating God's gifts, of sharing their anguish and hopes, of answering a call to judgement and personal renewal.

The Jewish calendar and the Jewish life cycle have also lost their pivotal place in our adult life. The Sabbath, the "Queen of Days," is virtually banished, her throne usurped by that King for a Day, the *Bar Mitzvah* boy. Sukkot, Chanukah, Passover, Shavuot, are almost totally for the children. In our generation, birth is just nominally a time to sanctify the gift of life, and the rites of death only an act of filial piety rather than a way of reaffirming the meaning of life.

Again: *We cannot simply re-appropriate the accepted disciplines of the past, but we must rear a generation who will rediscover the meaning of living by Jewish time. Our task is to fashion a covenant consciousness which is both a divine mission and a significant style of life.*

Dear friends, over a century and a half has passed since the western Jew received a conditional promise of emancipation. How may we, the descendants of those notables, answer Napoleon's questions this day? *Can a Jew be a Man? He is Yisroel Mensch. He may best be a man by remaining a self-affirming Jew who finds in the covenant of Abraham his primary window to the world.*

If this be our answer, then the synagogue of today and tomorrow will quiver with the creative tension between what we are and what we must seek to be. The synagogue must build far sturdier bridges—bridges of the flesh and spirit—between what we are and what we must seek to be. The synagogue must build far sturdier bridges—bridges of the flesh and spirit—between American Jewry and our brethren all over the world. It will forge ways the more vitally and boldly to register our concern with the fate of Jews in Russia, of black Americans in our inner-cities, of all men and women in Vietnam.

Are Jews captives of the past? We affirm the enduring claim of our covenant—submitting neither to the tyranny of the past nor the idolatry of the present.

If this be our answer, we must find imaginative ways of extending the time and the quality of our children's dialogue with Torah. We must be prepared to spend as much on the education of ourselves as we do on the education of our children. We must spend as much on the Jewish education of adult Jews as we seem prepared to spend on the education of adult Christians. With all the merit of interfaith dialogues, and I do not deprecate them, the most crucial confrontation of our time is not the conversation with our Christian neighbor, but the conversation with our Jewish past. We must spare no effort and no cost to recruit and sustain a rabbinate and lay leadership equal to this crucial dialogue.

Why be a Jew at all? The day to which we bear witness has not yet come, but the covenant remains not only Israel's divine vocation—it is the sacred scenario through which I, a Jew, may best affirm and sanctify my life as a man. If this be our answer, the synagogue must both enkindle support for the affirmations of covenant faith and foster styles of life through which we and our children may savor the sacred depth of a Jewish experience.

Fellow Jews, here are the outlines of our task: To seek in the past, to live in the present, to build for the future.

As they look upon our time of testing, may our grandchildren have cause to judge us kindly. May the One who has given us a particular burden and treasure, have cause to bless our efforts.

CHAPTER 4

Rethinking Our Liberal Faith

To deliver the Jonah B. Wise Lecture is a signal honor. I never met Jonah Wise personally, though I did spend a delightful evening in the company of his twin sister, Jean May, many years ago, and his son David was kind enough to send me a biography of his father from which I learned much.

During my student days at HUC in Cincinnati, I would listen to "The Message of Israel" and hear that distinguished, gravelly, sometimes grave voice. Rabbi Wise pioneered an airwaves outreach program across America. He embodied the great strengths of what has come to be known as classical Reform Judaism.

I have great respect for our Reform elders. Nothing I say tonight is intended to erode that appreciation. Yet we pay the greatest tribute to those pioneers when we ask for our time the question which Jonah Wise and his peers asked in theirs: How can we best fulfill our covenant with God under the conditions of our time and place? So let us this evening reconsider three core concerns of our classic liberal faith. Remember, reconsider

The Jonah B. Wise Lecture, Central Synagogue,
New York City, New York, February 5, 1988

may mean revise or reaffirm. I intend to do some of each this evening.

First, I turn to classical Reform Judaism's moral passion. The highest touchstone of religion, said our elders, is the sense of being commanded by God to lead an ethical life. There is nothing more religious than obeying a divinely grounded moral imperative. This classic Reform teaching is more critically needed in our American culture today than ever. It ought to be reaffirmed and for reasons our elders may not have anticipated.

Last summer a book appeared called *The Closing of the American Mind*. It is by Professor Allan Bloom of the University of Chicago. There was a time, says Professor Bloom, when we were taught that certain fundamental truths ought to shape and guide our lives. These truths reflected the cumulative wisdom of the generations or the revelation of a religious tradition. The purpose of education was to search out, master, and apply these truths.

Now, says Professor Bloom, moral truth is no longer something you find in a sacred book, something you discover, appropriate, and try to live by. Now truth depends substantially on how you feel about things. Does something make you feel good? Does it meet your needs?

We speak these days of "value clarification." A teacher discovers how different students feel about things. That's fine, but all too often value clarification is reduced to this: You think and feel differently from me about abortion or padding an expense account, or sex without love and commitment. And who's to say one of us is more right than the other? It is all a matter of lifestyle. Different strokes for different folks.

How serious is this loss of a sense of basic truth independent of me and my feelings? Very serious. Professor Bloom asked his students: Why is it wrong to harm another person? The most profound answer he would hear again and again from these sophisticated collegians was: "It's wrong because it's not good for me. If I did it to him, he could do it to me."

If the only reason for not harming him is that he could

harm me, it is not very far to the conclusion; but he is in no position to harm me, yet I can harm him. I can get away with it. I gain the advantage by doing so. I can, I may, I will.

Prudence and enlightened self-interest are okay, but, as the ultimate ground for one's values, they are shallow, dangerous, and very un-Jewish. The attitude toward values out there, the subjectivism and relativism of the world out there, is very different from the world we acknowledge this night in this room.

Why is it wrong to harm another person? "Thou shalt not place a stumbling block before the blind. I am the Lord." That person, like you, is of infinite dignity. That person is created in the image of God.

Some years ago I was walking in the old city of Safed in Israel's Galilee region. I was on my way to visit a cousin at the Herziliyah Hotel and was terribly lost. I confronted a group of boys about ten years old and I asked them in Hebrew: "Which way to the Herziliyah Hotel?" They hesitated for a moment and then each, in turn, smiled mischievously and pointed in a different direction. "There," one said. "No, there," said another. They were so amused. I was not.

With mock sternness I said to the ten year olds: "How can you act that way to a stranger? It is a *mitzvah* in the Torah not to harm a stranger. It is a *mitzvah* to help a stranger find his way." I had pushed the magic button, muttered the magic word—*mitzvah*. They suddenly grew very contrite, very serious. They asked me to follow them and led me right to my cousin's hotel!

For those schooled in the Jewish value system there is a *mitzvah*, an ethical command, God's intention for my life. Oh, it is not always so simple to determine what the particular *mitzvah* is. Our elders had to struggle for truth in those sacred texts. They used their minds, they debated, they disagreed with one another.

But none said it was a matter of convenience, or prudence, or depended upon how you felt about such matters. They believed there is a moral imperative and God is the ultimate Source of that imperative. "Thou shalt, thou shalt not."

Ask most of our people or our children, "What's a *mitzvah*?" They will answer: "A *mitzvah* is a good deed." That's not sharp enough. A *mitzvah* is an ethical deed I feel commanded to do or to refrain from doing because I am a Jew. Thou shalt, thou shalt not.

But is even this an adequate view of *mitzvah*? Which brings us to the second core teaching of our Reform elders. They taught that Judaism is ethical *mitzvah*, but once we get beyond the ethical commandment, we may get in trouble. Many of our classical elders had difficulty with the sense of ritual commandments. Some traditionalists, they feared, had reduced Judaism to a punctilious regimen of ritual acts. By being so preoccupied with the niceties of what makes a piece of meat kosher, or what you can do and not do on the Sabbath, those traditionalists lost sight of the big picture. They lost the forest for the trees.

So Reform insisted: Judaism is not ritual commandment. Judaism is ethical commandment and Judaism is message. There is a "message of Israel." Judaism is a view of God and of man. Judaism proclaims hope for a better world and our role as God's partner in bringing that world about. That's the essence of Judaism. That's what we need to focus on.

Those classical Reformers had a point, but they oversold. Their teachings have been used by a subsequent generation in ways not even they intended. So that if you ask many of us today what it means to be a Reform Jew, we will quickly respond, "Oh, we don't do this, we don't do that. We don't have to do this, we are Reform."

Actually, at least unconsciously, even the minimalists among us believe there are some symbolic ritual acts we should observe: naming a child in the synagogue, being in Temple on Yom Kippur, saying *Kaddish* when a loved one has died. But we are wary of referring to even these acts as commandment. "Custom and ceremonies," yes, but not *mitzvot*, not something I ought to do because I am a Jew.

I propose that if Reform is to be a vitalizing, renewing, force in our time, then certain symbolic ritual acts must regain the force of *mitzvah*, of conscious imperatives in our lives.

Oh, you ask, how can that be done without sacrificing the autonomy and freedom and diversity which is our Reform birthright in matters of ritual? Now some of us fast on Yom Kippur and others do not. Where will this rethinking lead?

I make a distinction between a category *mitzvah* and the specific acts which fall within the category and which may or may not become *mitzvah* for me. For example: as rabbi I believe I should urge my people to accept the *mitzvah* of living by Jewish time. It is a *mitzvah* for Jews to mark the sacred times of our heritage—to observe Rosh Hashanah, Yom Kippur, Sukkot, Chanukah, Purim, Passover, and Shabbat in a Jewishly identifiable way. "Thou shalt live by Jewish time" is a category *mitzvah*. There are others.

Beyond that I have responsibility to help define the underlying meaning and intent of the category *mitzvah*. For example: in Shabbat we celebrate the gift of life and our people's special covenant with the God of life by stepping aside from the burdens, competitiveness, aggressive self-assertion of the work-a-day in order to be—and not only to do.

Then as teacher, mine is the task to help my people explore those specific deeds which may become part of the Shabbat *mitzvah* for them: lighting candles, Torah study, public worship, refraining from unnecessary business, etc.

Now what combination of these specific deeds a Reform Jew feels commanded to perform will differ from person to person. Some will observe all. All will observe some. Some who take Shabbat seriously in my congregation may find the Saturday morning Torah study session and worship service an anchor point of their Shabbat *mitzvah*. Another person who retreats to a country house each weekend with the family may see that Shabbat is ushered in with a special meal replete with blessing the children, lighting the candles, *kiddush* and discussion of something in the Torah portion of that week. No two of us may have the same pattern of observance and that's okay. You choose your particular pattern (that's the Reform option) but we should all feel bound by the category *mitzvah*: "Thou shalt observe Shabbat."

How then do the specific acts which we choose under a category function as *mitzvah*? Isn't there an inherent contradiction between commandment and choice? Consider an analogy from the world of physical fitness. In this world the category *mitzvah* is: you shall exercise. But we choose the specific form of exercise, whether it be jogging or walking or aerobics or biking or swimming.

Once we make that choice, if we take the matter seriously, then (for example) jogging becomes part of our exercise *mitzvah*. We do it "religiously." I may wake up some morning and don't feel like jogging but I know I ought to. And if I miss a day or two I feel I betrayed an order of my being. I have violated the category *mitzvah* "thou shalt exercise" and what has become for me a specific *mitzvah* "thou shalt jog."

Translation obvious. If lighting Sabbath candles and reciting the *Kiddush* is part of our way of observing the Shabbat *mitzvah*, if we choose these acts for ourselves and our family, then we will do them religiously not erratically, not only when the spirit moves us, not only when it is convenient. And you and I will reach a point when we feel we have not kept faith with our covenant if we fail to light those lights, or be present for that Torah study session, or if we fail to observe Shabbat rest.

Why is the recovery of the ritual *mitzvah* so important? Because if we are to be Jews rather than simply members of the universal covenant of Noah, ethical *mitzvot* alone are not sufficient. After all, our Christian neighbors are also taught to lead the good life. And proclaiming the message of Israel can become so vacuous if we do not live the message.

Distinctive Jewish acts must have as much a place in the disciplined rhythms of our life as our ritual of jogging or walking. If we want Judaism to really shape our lives, if we want Judaism to matter to us and our children we need Sabbath blessings, Sukkot, Seders and Chanukah lights; not just noble words about the fatherhood of God and the brotherhood of man.

There is a hunger of the spirit among us. Many of us and our children yearn to be more religious, to find God. We are no longer mesmerized by technology. And we have discovered that we cannot live by bread alone. How is religious consciousness shaped? Clifford Geertz, the renowned anthropologist, has studied cultures all over the world. He concludes: "It is primarily out of the context of concrete acts of religious observance that religious conviction emerges on the human plane."

Generations ago the message of Israel needed to be liberated from the encrustation of ritualism. Today the message is that faith can best be affirmed by those who have recovered a life of the ethical and ritual *mitzvah*.

Now let us turn to a third core theme. Classical Reform opposed Jewish insularity or ghetto-mindedness. The Judaism we practice, said our elders, must not keep us from being full partners in the larger society. It should empower us to live in, influence, embrace and be embraced by that society.

What a noble vision. And to a magnificent degree that vision of classical Reform has been fulfilled. The evidence is all around us. Forty years ago there was much less mixed marriage in America. And when mixed marriage did take place it usually involved a Jew actively rejecting himself and seeking a secure shelter in the gentile world. Max Lerner has honestly confessed that what fueled his passion for non-Jewish spouses was his yearning to assimilate, to leave Jewish Brooklyn behind.

Today there is much more mixed marriage, but it is less a function of Jewish self-hate, or escapism, or compulsive assimilation. It is a natural price of living in and being so very much a part of an open society where Christian and Jew are more likely to feel free to fall in love with each other.

Obviously, for those concerned with safeguarding the Jewish future there is a new challenge today. We speak of outreach; the newest frontier of Reform is inreach, or a deepening of our Jewish self.

Our one-day-a-week religious schools, or two-afternoons-a-week Hebrew schools are functioning as best they can. But even at best, they impart a limited educational experience in a few fragmented hours a week, especially when those hours take children away from weekend play time. Afternoon Jewish schools inevitably signal that secular education is what really counts. It is the real thing. Jewish education is secondary.

In a society that is so open and pluralistic, we need a core of our youth to be exposed more deeply to the Jewish well-spring. We need some Reform children who view their Jewish education as an integral part of their human education—and not something added on to "regular school" when you are fatigued.

The most promising response to the challenge of an open society (next to our summer camp program) is the birth of the Reform day school. I know the instinctive resistance many of us have felt toward day schools. I used to be opposed to Reform day schools. I no longer am. Thank God we have rethought our stand. Our day schools signal most eloquently that Reform Judaism need not be the least-informed Judaism. We now have a depth track.

Our congregation has a fine religious school and Hebrew school, but our day school option offers a weightiness, a rich texture, an intellectual excitement, a spiritual resonance which is beyond the perimeter of an afternoon Hebrew school or Sunday school. How exciting to watch children study math and English literature and then, very naturally, proceed to the chapel for a worship service in which they are as comfortable with reading Hebrew as English, and then return to their classrooms to discuss the Torah portion of the week—all part of a seamless web.

And our day school is Reform. Children learn that all Jews need not observe the same way to be good Jews. They learn respect for other Jewish movements and for the religion of their Christian neighbors. They engage in *tzedakah* projects not only for Jewish causes but for the total community.

Nothing more eloquently speaks to the creative rethinking of Reform than the birth of the Reform Day School. Oh, our Sunday schools and weekday afternoon schools will remain the majority option. And those who spend the primary years in our day school will then move on to other public or private systems.

But oh what enrichment for those who experience this model during their formative years!

An earlier generation of American Jews needed to ask: "How can we, though Jews, share fully in American society?" We must ask: "How can we who so fully share in the larger society do so as knowledgeable and committed Jews?"

I have enormous respect for the legacy of classical Reform. Our task is to stand on their shoulders. The operative question remains what it was in the days of Jonah Wise: How can we best fulfill our covenant under the conditions of this time and place.

Reform has so much to contribute to the American Jewish future. Our elders responded eloquently to the challenge of their time. May we do no less for ours.

CHAPTER 5

Science and the Believing Jew

The year was 1633, an astronomer and physicist named Galileo claimed that the earth revolves around the sun. The Church condemned Galileo for heresy because Scripture teaches that the earth is at the center of the universe and immovably fixed on its foundation, and therefore the sun must revolve around the earth.

Galileo considered himself a believing Christian. He defended his scientific claims by saying that Scripture cannot err but it can be misunderstood. Scripture requires proper interpretation so it doesn't conflict with clear and certain reasoning.

Church authorities were not impressed. Galileo was condemned for heresy. He was placed on trial, forced on his knees to recant those scientific findings, to describe them as cursed and detested. Had he refused to recant, Galileo would have been burned at the stake. As it was, because he was an old man, Galileo was just sentenced to house arrest rather than put in a dungeon. Legend has it that as Galileo rose from kneeling before his inquisitors, he murmured: "Even so it does move."

This past October, 360 years later, the Pope and the Vatican

Sermon, April 16, 1993

acknowledged that Galileo was right; that the Church authorities of his day had been wrong. This episode triggers a number of thoughts. First, how fortunate for all that religious authorities today, at least in our part of the world, no longer have the power to impose or coerce belief or behavior and the state is not enlisted as an agent of religious coercion. Actually the cause of religious institutions and faith is best served—I would go even further—the cause of God is best served when we mortals have the freedom to say "no" as well as "yes" to those who claim to speak in God's name.

Galileo was right in another sense. One can be a scientist and a religious believer. Galileo claimed to be both. Last year a book was published: *Cosmos, Bios, Theos*. It contained the religious views of sixty world-class scientists including twenty-four Nobel Prize winners. The co-editor is a Yale physicist named Henry Morgenau. He believes "there is only one convincing answer" for the intricate laws that exist in nature and that is their creation by an omnipotent omniscient God.

Rabbi Zvi Hirsch Lederberg was an Orthodox rabbi who died about thirty years ago in Jerusalem. He happened to have been a cousin of mine on my mother's side. Rabbi Lederberg had two sons. Both became men of science. One of them, Joshua Lederberg won a Nobel Prize for his work in genetics. While Rabbi Lederberg had spoken of "the image of God within us," Joshua the son was intrigued by the bio-chemical determinants of our nature.

After he received the Nobel Prize, Dr. Lederberg wrote an article of tribute to his father. He said that as a believing Jew he felt very comfortable in the world of scientific research. He added: "The one God of the Jewish tradition is inseparable from the universe ruled by law."

In other words, as God's partners we are invited to discover God's laws and use them to improve the quality of existence. Genetics at its best extends what the Bible calls "our dominion over nature." The fact is that science and religion are really dealing with different, not necessarily conflicting questions.

The goal of science is to discover the order of things in the universe and to express that order in the simplest and most inclusive way. The goal of religion is to discover the purpose and meaning of our world and our place in it. That brings us to the fundamental relation between the two. Many, many centuries before Einstein and before Lederberg, an ancient rabbi read the first chapter in the Torah and told this story. When God created Adam and showed him the Garden of Eden, God said to Adam: "Adam, see all that I have created is a blessing for you, but beware lest you spoil my world for if you spoil my world there is no one to repair it after you."

Thus did an ancient rabbi recognize that with our dominion over nature comes awesome responsibility. God not only gave us a world and the power to understand it through science, God also gave us a Torah to guide us in this world. Who among us living in the 20th century needs to be reminded that scientific knowledge without Torah may be destructive.

This very weekend we commemorate *Yom Ha'Shoah*. In Hitler's Germany there were distinguished men of science who performed experiments on human beings the very thought of which should cause us to shudder. Why was it wrong to perform those experiments? Why was it wrong to use the latest scientific technology to efficiently destroy millions of persons because they were Jews?

The answer to those questions is not found in the realm of science but in the realm of religion. It is wrong because we learn in the Torah that we are created in the image of God. There is a sacredness, a sanctity to the human being which must not be violated. In Yiddish, *m'turnisht*—you must not. To do so is a sin, and to respect the sanctity of the human creature is a *mitzvah*.

Science can empower us to do something; religion asks: May we, should we? Will doing it enhance or endanger human life on earth? Will doing it be in sync with God's intention for our lives and our world? One of the greatest scientific minds of our time understood well the need for partnership between science and religion. Albert Einstein said, "Religion without science is lame. Science without religion is blind."

Einstein's own life story poignantly illustrates the difference between a scientific and a religious/ethical question. When Albert was in his late teens he had a love affair with a twenty-one year old woman named Dollie. Both were young science students. Dollie was also doing studies in advanced mathematics. Albert's parents disapproved of their relationship. She was an older woman with a different religion and presumed lower social class. Albert was torn apart by the conflict between his loyalty to his parents and his love for Dollie. He continued to love her. Dollie became pregnant. Neither Albert nor Dollie could afford to get married or to rear a child until graduation. What should they do? Should Dollie get an abortion? Neither Albert or Dollie considered abortion as an acceptable option. Einstein decided to quit school, to find a job immediately, any job no matter how modest and marry Dollie so that "no one can cast a stone upon your dear head."

Dollie would not allow Albert to interrupt his studies. "You shouldn't take a really bad position. That would make me feel terrible and I couldn't live with it." Dollie sacrificed her studies. She left school at great cost to her career and secretly bore the daughter they called Lieserl. They decided after much anguish that it would be best to give up the child for adoption.

Einstein was able to complete his education and after graduation he landed the kind of a job which enabled him to pursue his theoretical work. He then married Dollie. They had two sons. And three years after their marriage, at age twenty-six, Einstein produced three scientific papers that changed the course of history.

In his own personal life, Albert Einstein discovered the difference between two kinds of truth—scientific truth and ethical/religious truth. The questions raised in this story were not about quantum theories, or laws of motion, or the theory of relativity; the question was about accepting personal responsibility and about love and sacrifice and about doing what is right and about the kind of person we are and want to be. Those questions are not addressed by science.

Two great paradoxes arise in our time. First, the more advanced we have become scientifically, the more we are drawn to the conclusion that reason and science alone cannot bring us a total understanding of ultimate reality. Paul Davies a mathematical physicist writes: "A rational explanation for the world in the sense of a closed and complete system of logical truths is almost certainly impossible." One might add: total spiritual understanding of the universe also eludes us. There are elements of impenetrable mystery for the scientist and for the religious believer.

The other paradox is that the more technological advances we make, the greater the religious and ethical dilemmas we must confront, for which science as science can give us no answer. Every Bio-Ethics Committee at our various wonderful hospitals in this city understands this as its members probe the question: under what circumstances should we do what we are technically empowered to do, and under what circumstances should we refrain?

There is another reason why science will never substitute for religion or religious faith. A man came to my office and said in effect: Rabbi, my wife is very ill. We have been told that statistically 70% of the persons who have this type of cancer do not live beyond five years. Rabbi, when you are given those kinds of statistics how do you hope?

By that one query the person in my study was really raising a number of different questions. Science has diagnosed and is treating the disease and is searching for its cure, but on what basis does that woman dare to affirm, "I'm going to be among those who live, I'm going to be among those who beat the statistical odds?" How does she affirm the power to carry on with dignity and courage during those uncertain days or years ahead? On what basis may she declare, "even if I should die, my life will have been meaningful!"

In what context may she ask, "If I die, am I more than the

chemicals in my body? Do I have a spirit, a soul, which binds me to God, not only in this life, but for eternity? Will the God who created me and cared for me be with me during the days ahead?"

These are questions beyond the realm of science. At the heart of Judaism today, as in ancient days, is a faith that science can neither prove nor disprove. Science is NA—non-applicable. This faith proclaims that the world is God's creation, that in, through and beyond the processes which science discovers stands the purpose and love of God.

Religion proclaims the faith that we have been placed on this earth and given special powers and gifts to help God redeem and heal the brokenness of God's world; that our deepest and noblest strivings during our earthly life are conserved, not lost even by death, that our finite efforts are somehow complemented and fulfilled by the God of the universe. That is what Judaism means by the assertion that our life has transcendant meaning.

Anthropologist Loren Eisley understood the turf of religion and the turf of science when he wrote these magnificent words:

> It is not sufficient to listen at the end of a wire to the rustling of galaxies. It is not enough even to examine the great coil of DNA which is encoded in the very alphabet of life. These have extended our perceptions, but beyond lies the great darkness of the Ultimate Dreamer who dreamed the light and the galaxies. . . .
> Let us remember the man who came across an ice age to look into the mirrors and magic of science . . . did not come to see himself or his wild visage only; he came because he was at heart a listener and a searcher for some transcendent realm beyond himself. This he has worshipped by many names, even in the dismal caves of his beginning.

Thousands of years ago our ancestors opened themselves to some transcendent world beyond themselves and proclaimed: "*Sh'ma Yisrael.*" Today in an age of science we continue to yearn for and open ourselves to that transcendent realm beyond ourselves as we say: "*Sh'ma Yisrael, Adonai Elohenu. Adonai Echad.*"

CHAPTER 6

The Children of Isaac and the Children of Ishmael

Shalom, welcome to Beth Israel. During my thirteen years in Texas I've developed a warm spot for the Texas Conference of Churches. With persons like Monsignor Bob Rehkemper and Reverend Frank Dietz, that's not hard to do. I am mindful that this is the first time you have held a session in a synagogue. We feel privileged that you have chosen us for the occasion.

We have come a long way. When I grew up in Philadelphia in a mixed Jewish/Catholic neighborhood, I never set foot in the Holy Name Cathedral, nor did my Catholic football player comrades think of crossing the threshold of my synagogue. Part of the greatness of America is that we have gone beyond even entering each other's houses of worship with some level of comfort. We've gone beyond bland niceties exchanged from time to time. We can, in a spirit of friendship and some trust, speak to each other of the joy and pain in our heart and of our yearning in this world that has yet to be made whole.

During the past several months you and I have been hearing so much of events in the Middle East. Jerusalem, the city of

Address to The Texas Conference of Churches Assembly,
Houston, Texas, February 22, 1988

peace, has not been very peaceful. We have seen ugly, violent encounters between young Arabs and young Jews.

I speak tonight as a believing Jew to believing Christians. I speak as one anguished by my brethren's role as controllers of a people who do not wish to be controlled. I am all too mindful of the biblical dictum: "You know the heart of the stranger, for you were strangers in the land of Egypt. " I dare speak as one troubled by some of the responses to these events in the Jewish and secular press.

I speak as a lover of Zion with an enormous personal, psychic, spiritual stake in the survival and security of Israel and a deep concern about the kind of state Israel becomes. I want to sort out some of my thoughts and feelings. The highest compliment I can pay you is to honestly share those thoughts and feelings with you. Needless to say I do not speak for all Jews or all rabbis. I speak for myself. But I dare to believe that in some way I reflect the feeling of many of my kin, and that words spoken from the heart will enter the heart.

This is a religious Christian fellowship. Let me then begin by insisting that for me and for many Jews—even those not theologically articulate or "religious"—Israel's rebirth as a Jewish commonwealth has been an event of the deepest religious significance. By this I mean more than the relatively obvious. Yes, our Torah roots our people in the land of promise. Our age-old prayers have yearned for return to the land. The messianic hope has been couched in images of "out of Zion shall go forth the Torah and the word of God from Jerusalem." Jeremiah's eschatological hope speaks of the voices of groom and bride heard again in the cities of Judah and the streets of Jerusalem.

But I speak as a Jew who has no intention of living in Israel, who feels very much at home in America, and who does not believe that the restoration of a Jewish State heralds the imminent coming of the Messiah. What then is at the heart of Israel's religious significance for me and for others?

Some months ago, while driving to the airport, I turned on the radio and caught a talk show. A caller asked: "What do you do to a wandering Jew?" The host replied: "You wipe 'em out, zap 'em with XLM solution. That will take care of them." Momentarily my adrenalin flowed furiously. Then I realized, this was a garden show and the host was talking about the creeping plant called "Wandering Jew."

When I got home, not knowing much of plants, I looked it up in the dictionary. Sure enough, it is one of several plants which obviously have a way of wandering. But the primary definition of Wandering Jew, given in that same dictionary, went like this: "A Jew held in medieval legend to be condemned to wander the earth until the second coming of Christ for having mocked Him on the day of the crucifixion."

The Wandering Jew legend and the wandering Jew plant remind us of a painful part of our history. Oh, we had the privilege of bearing witness to our covenant with God in different lands, and our ancestors contributed much to the culture of each land to which we wandered, but at what a price: vulnerable to the vagaries of the particular ruler, subject to persecution when a society needed a visible scapegoat. In our time, being a vulnerable minority almost totally destroyed us. I speak, of course, of the age of Hitler and the Holocaust.

The Holocaust numbed the surviving remnant of our people and could have precipitated a monumental crisis of faith. How does one believe in a gracious God's covenant with Israel in a post-Holocaust world? There were a few rabbis who spoke of it as a judgement for not being observant enough of the covenant. In the light of one million children exterminated by the Nazis and considering that many of the victims were among the most pious of our people, this response to the Holocaust is obscene.

Others sought to understand those terrible days by invoking the image of Isaiah's "suffering servant." The covenant to which we bear witness was anathema to Hitler and his hordes. Those Jews suffered for God in an unredeemed world. They died for the sanctification of God's name. This response found more resonance among us.

But you know, there is a limit to how long a people can be sustained as suffering servant. Everyone, every people, need victories, moments of grace. The Church proclaimed the passion of Christ and called on Christians to bear the cross of suffering. But Christian morale was sustained by the Church's established power and majority status in the kingdoms of Europe for many, many centuries.

After the Holocaust the Jewish people desperately needed a sign of grace. Israel's rebirth, phoenix-like out of the ashes, has served as such a sign. That is the religious significance of Israel's rebirth and reality in our time.

That is why Israel captivates the heart of virtually every Jewish pilgrim. Israel the State offers a post-Holocaust Jewish community an end to the Wandering Jew syndrome. Robert Frost said: "Home is where, if you have to go there, they have to let you in." For the first time in 2000 years our people has an unconditional refuge; a refuge which was not available even in these United States when it was desperately needed in the 1930's. Israel offers the Jew one tiny corner of the world where we as a people can experience the joys and burdens of being a majority. Israel offers the place where a society lives by Jewish sacred time. (For all the glories of America, and for all the separation of church and state, this country is still more Christian than neutral.) If Israel does no more than this, it is exceedingly precious to a remnant of our Holocaust-scarred people.

But we want more. We want Israel to embody the values of our heritage: justice and compassion. Israel has given us much cause for pride during these forty years. We are proud that it has been a refuge to Holocaust survivors and to hundreds of thousands of Jews from Arab countries. We are proud of Israel's reclamation of barren land, transforming wilderness into green meadow. We are proud of its technological achievements in medicine shared with Arab and Jew alike. We are proud that it is the only real democracy in the Middle East. The very self-criticism so rampant in Israel today is an eloquent expression of that democratic spirit.

But when we see Israeli soldiers forcefully subduing rock-throwing Arab youth, we are anguished. When we see an "iron fist policy" resulting in brutality inflicted upon those already in the custody of the authorities, we are horrified. We do not want to see Jews cast in the role of Pharaoh. There is a Palestinian Arab community, a people, who do not want to be ruled by a Jewish State, and who also have a claim to that same small land.

We need to struggle for a way to respect their claim without endangering the very existence of Israel as a Jewish democratic state. That is the terribly difficult and demanding challenge of this hour. It is painful to see some Jewish leaders who refuse to acknowledge that there is a conflict here between two just claims.

It is painful to see outsiders—critics of Israel, who fail to place this tragic conflict in perspective, who see it as a simple morality play in which the more powerful Israel wears the black hat. You may have seen that cartoon depicting Israeli soldiers, grinning demonically out of a greeting card which bears the caption: "Happy Holocaust to Arabs on the West Bank and Gaza." I wonder if that cartoonist realizes how far he exceeded the boundaries of decent political criticism. Imagine comparing a country which even under siege, does not permit capital punishment even for terrorists convicted of murdering innocent men, women and children to a regime which murdered millions of innocent men, women and children only because they were Jews.

It is painful when the world forgets that in 1947 the United Nations acknowledged the two claims to the land and partitioned it. The Jewish settlers accepted the plan. The Arab States joined in a war against Israel which was resumed in 1956 and 1967 and 1973. In each war, if Israel had lost, there would be no Israel today. Because of the 1967 war, Israel now occupies the West Bank and Gaza and is responsible for administering those territories until a negotiated settlement is reached.

It is painful to note Arab countries permitting refugees to languish in their misery and resisting, during these forty years, any attempt to alleviate the plight of those refugees by Israel lest that be a first step toward annexation. Those same countries have consistently refused to grant any refuge to their kin. It is hard for us to imagine 500,000 Jews trapped in misery without our doing all within our power to alleviate the pain of their conditions rather than permitting them to become a political pawn.

It is painful to note that since 1948 only one Arab leader, Anwar Sadat, came forward and said unequivocally, "we accept your right to be here as an empowered Jewish State. All we ask is some recognition of Palestinian claims to independence in this land. Let's sit down and negotiate that."

Over these two months there has been great grief in many of your Jewish neighbors' hearts. We are sickened by the sight of Jewish soldiers beating and shooting Arab youth and we are appalled that those young soldiers are daily confronted by life—threatening situations which require forceful, sometimes lethal, response to save themselves from the angry mob.

We want Israel to be in a position to vacate most of those territories but how can an area as close as ten miles away from Tel Aviv be left in the hands of those who shout slogans that call for Israel's destruction? Israel's occupation is a threat to Israel's soul, but under present circumstances, withdrawal from the territories could endanger Israel's life. It seems that Israel is between a rock and a hard place. We want Israel to be righteous. We need Israel to live. We know that power may corrupt, but we also know only too well that powerlessness destroys. And in a post-Holocaust world we are not longer willing to permit the fate of our people to be left to the whims of the Yasir Arafats or Kurt Waldheims of this world. That is why there is a bottom line commitment to Israel's survival within the Jewish community.

What would we ask of our American Christian neighbors in these perilous times? Not acceptance of all that a given Israel government stands for. We don't make that demand on ourselves. Not that you disavow your concern for the plight and yearning of Palestinian Arabs. Many of us share that concern.

We would ask you to be aware of our people's past and of the history and context of the Middle East conflict. We would ask that you try to understand why your Jewish neighbors are so intensely concerned about Israel's survival and security. We would ask you to understand that only a strong Israel, an Israel that America helps keep strong, can take the risk of relinquishing some territory in the hope of peace when it is surrounded by 100,000,000 Arabs, most of whose governments have, over these forty years, failed to recognize Israel's right to exist.

We would ask you to understand that peace is possible if Israeli leadership is willing to take seriously the national consciousness of Palestinian Arabs and if credible Arab leaders emerge who are committed to coexistence with a Jewish State—not its destruction. If Palestinian Arabs persist in the "uprising" without leadership that demonstrates comparable political courage and political wisdom, Israel will be compelled as a matter of self-preservation to forcefully suppress the uprising. That cycle of violence and response would be tragic for both peoples.

In this little land the destinies of the children of Isaac and the children of Ishmael are inextricably intertwined. I believe that each cannot save himself without helping to affirm the right and dignity of the other.

We communities of faith—schooled in the ambiguities of life, aware of life's tragic dimension—nevertheless cling to hope: a hope rooted in our faith that the One who summoned us to this world is present to redeem us from despair, to open new possibilities, and establish the work of our hands. May the God of *Shalom*—of wholeness and peace—the God who first gave us a vision of peace in those Judean hills, bring to that place the sounds of joy, of love, of justice and peace and let us say. Amen.

CHAPTER 7

My Faith
and Yours

It is good to address this Society. Over the years I have been enriched by the presentations of others. That benefit imposes some obligations, especially when one comes, as I do, from a tradition that speaks about works as much as grace. I hasten to remind you that both Judaism and Christianity do believe in grace—that is receiving more kindness than we deserve—and I shall surely depend on your exhibiting such grace this evening.

The topic assigned to me by your president is one with which I have wrestled over the years. I am committed to the truth claims of a particular heritage, Judaism. I believe the God who is the Creator of the world singled out the people Israel for a unique covenant, and by remaining faithful to that covenant and transmitting it to my children I fulfill God's intention for me and participate in God's redemptive plan for the world.

My Christian colleagues believe that God's purposes and power were uniquely and decisively revealed through the life, death and resurrection of Jesus Christ. And that a believing Christian is faithful to God by affirming the unique role of

Address to the Houston Philosophical Society,
Houston, Texas, October 17, 1985

Christ, by transmitting the faith to his children, and by seeking to bring the Gospel to those who have not heard or received the good news.

Moreover, each of us, Christian and Jew, lives our faith not in isolation from the claims of the other. If I choose to, I can expose myself to the Christian Gospel by turning my radio dial or flicking the TV switch to any number of channels on a Sunday morning. Christians can, and apparently some do, tune in my Jewish message on Sunday morning. My students at Rice, some of whom grew up in a strong particular religious tradition, may take a course on religious ethics jointly taught by John Sellers, a Christian ethicist and by me.

How do we respond to the presence of faith systems other than our own which we cannot forcefully deny public expression (even if we wanted to) and which make different and at certain points conflicting claims about the way in which God's power and purposes are manifest in the world?

One possible response is to assert the exclusive and absolute truth of my faith, ascribe at best partial validity to all others, and seek wherever possible to proselytize—i.e., to persuade the uninitiated to accept my faith.

Another possibility is to deny the absolute claim of any particular faith, including my own; to assert the one we call God is not fully encompassed by any of our theologies, and to live one's own faith while engaging in constructive dialogue with others. Through that dialogue I may not only correct some misconceptions I have of the other faith but I may learn from it.

David Tracy, a Catholic theologian at the University of Chicago Divinity School contends that a classic religious text like the New Testament or the Talmud can impart insight to those who do not live within the particular religious traditions to which the text primarily belongs.

Such leading Christian theologians of the 20th century as Paul Tillich and Reinhold Niebuhr publicly acknowledged the positive impact of Judaism on their thought. Niebuhr felt that the Hebrew prophets in a unique way judged a society by the manner in which it addressed the issues of social injustice, especially the plight of the powerless.

Paul Tillich once said that the holy, the sacred appears to us in two guises: giving presence and commanding presence. Christianity, as he understood it, was heavier on the giving or sacramental type of religious experience. The incarnation, God's gift of the divine self through Jesus to save humanity from sin and death is an example thereof. Whereas Judaism was heavier on the commanding or ethical presence as evidenced by the events at Sinai which yield Torah—commandments through which God's children are called to sanctify the world. Tillich thought of Judaism as a permanent "ethical corrective of sacramental Christianity."

What about Jewish theologians acknowledging the corrective aspect of Christianity on Judaism? Before addressing that question directly, let me point out it is easier for a believing Christian to come into my synagogue and participate fully in the service and even acknowledge the faith claims of our liturgy than it is for me to do so in a church. Why? The Christian views Judaism as his roots of which Jesus is the flowering tree. For the Jew, the acceptance of the Christian claim is a negation of Judaism, for we believe that the Messiah has not yet come.

Still, informally, Christianity does serve as a corrective to thoughtful Jews. Let me give two personal instances. Classic Judaism has kept in strong tension the relationship between justice and love—between what we need to do for God and what God can do for us. Judaism holds in tension the conditional dimension of the covenant (our accountability to God for the quality of our life) and the unconditional dimension (God's acceptance of us in our brokenness.). Judaism affirms both and keeps them in creative tension so that I could tell my congregation during the High Holy Day season that "forgiveness is not a totally free gift. It must in part be earned." Sometimes we tend to lose the tension and overemphasize judgement and accountability, and underestimate unconditional love and grace. The strength of Christianity is its demonstration of the power of a prior unconditional forgiveness to free the sinful individual from the burden of guilt and empower that individual to drastically change the nature of his or her life. I find this Christian Gospel a helpful corrective to my Judaism.

Let me give a second example of the learning I have received from my immersion in Christianity. Judaism has been so wary of lifting a human figure to divine status (Moses was buried in an unmarked grave) that the Passover liturgy speaks only of God rather than also of Moses in the Passover story. Moses is not mentioned lest he be worshipped in place of God. I resonate to this teaching, yet for me the New Testament conveys sublimely the power of a person as model to transform by his life the lives of others. Jesus' impact on his disciples is the paradigm. Some notion of the power of personal witness is certainly present in biblical and Talmudic and post-Talmudic literature but nowhere is it expressed as poignantly or as powerfully as in the New Testament account of Jesus as model. In this way too, Christianity has functioned as a corrective in the way I formulate my Jewish theology.

Beyond such learning from each other we come to a basic issue: what truth, what validity can I assign to the other tradition and its basic claims? For a Jew the question may become "What do Jews think about Jesus?"

From the very beginning of the Jewish-Christian encounter Jewish thinkers have denied that Jesus is the Messiah. In the pre-modern age there was no place for admiring Jesus the man, or the teacher, or the exemplar (the man for others) much less Jesus as Christ. In modern times Jewish thinkers have found it possible to acknowledge the grandeur of the human profile of Jesus and to remind ourselves and others that many of Jesus' teachings are Jewish. What Jesus regarded as the two greatest commandments are, of course, taken directly from Hebrew scripture "You shall love the Lord your God with all your heart, soul and might and you shall love your neighbor as yourself." It is Jesus as Christ we cannot affirm.

In the early Christian period Judaism was a proselytizing

faith until the Roman Empire forbade Jews to seek converts. But the basic Jewish stance has been that Christians need not become Jewish to be saved. The *Tosefta*, an early rabbinic work, declares "The righteous among all peoples have a place in the world to come." The Jew advances the coming of God's kingdom not by insisting that others formally embrace Judaism but by remaining a faithful witness to the covenant of Israel until such time as "The Lord shall be one and His name shall be One." By my survival as a Jew I advance the kingdom of God, whether or not I actively seek converts in the world-at-large.

In that context it was possible for some Jewish thinkers since the Middle Ages, (like Maimonides) to assert that through Christianity and Islam, monotheism was brought to those who did not know the one God. In that sense a Jew could say that Christianity and Islam serve a transcendent purpose in the divine economy.

In the 20th century the Jewish theologian Franz Rosenzweig found precisely this way of reconciling the salvation claims of the two faiths. He posits two valid covenants: God's covenant with Israel and God's covenant with the Church and Islam. He begins with the Christian claim: "No one may come to the Father except through the Son." But says Franz Rosenzweig, "Israel is already with the Father while the other peoples are on the road. They may indeed come to the Father through Christ, but we have always been with the Father. Our goal is to live in faithfulness and wait for others to acknowledge the One God of Israel."

Karl Barth, Cardinal Bea of the Second Vatican Council, and Hans Kung would say no. It is a sign of God's grace that Jews still live and are accepted as Jews and that God's covenant with Israel stands, but Jews as witnesses to Judaism have no positive transcendent theological role once Jesus has appeared.

Other Christian thinkers like Coert Rylsaarsdam and Father John Pawlikowski have found a way of acknowledging the continuing role of both Judaism and Christianity in salvation history. For Rylsaarsdam the Jewish and Christian messages complement each other. Judaism continues primarily to teach the kingdom of God as a reality of this world (the central story of Judaism is that God redeems slaves from Egyptian bondage and brought them to a land of promise) while Christianity locates God's salvation primarily within the human soul and in the world beyond (through victory over sin and death). The different emphasis of the two covenants enables them to complement each other.

Let me now briefly outline my own position in these matters. One: there are similarities and differences in the respective truth claims of Judaism and Chrisitanity. The differences remain real and not reconcilable by us. In a sense if I believe the Christian claim, I should stop being a Jew. Surely, from the Jewish perspective the position of "Jews for Jesus" is a nonstarter.

Two: I believe in faith, that Judaism's vision of God's covenant with the Creator is truer than the one espoused by my Christian neighbors; not just truer for me, but truer. I fully expect my Christian colleague to make the same claim for Christianity.

Three: I believe there is genuine validity to each tradition. Judaism and Christianity each has a role in God's plan though I am not able to accept Christianity's faith claims or fully understand its role.

Four: My belief in the truth of Judaism is in tension with my awareness of the incompleteness of all human attempts to envisage the infinite. God is larger than all our images and theologies. Things are yet to be made clear in the end of days. So I live in tension between embracing the truth of Judaism and acknowledging the inadequacy of all theology. I stake my life on Judaism's truth but acknowledge God's covenant with other people and their role in God's salvation history. I wait for God to bring ultimate clarity to our vision and to arbitrate our conflicting claims.

Five: In the interim, mine is the task to affirm the common humanity of all God's children. The greatest touchstone of my religious authenticity is my power to live within my own heritage while respecting and responding in love to those whose vision of sacred reality differs from my own.

One closing comment. A question was raised in an interview with George Rupp which appeared in the Harvard Divinity School Bulletin before Dr. Rupp's departure from Cambridge to become President of Rice University. The questioner asked essentially: Once you enter into dialogue with other traditions and critically confront your own and acknowledge there is some validity in those other religious perspectives, don't you thereby weaken your own faith? Are not fundamentalists inherently more passionately committed to their tradition than religious liberals? Dr. Rupp responded that the Harvard Divinity School had forty different denominations, confessions or religious traditions represented therein. The goal is to encourage students who will become ministers to open themselves to a critical appraisal of their own tradition and of others.

Dr. Rupp acknowledged that in the short run such critical openness may temper religious fervor but he felt the mission of the school is to make students aware "that our understanding has been limited, that there are resources of which we have been unaware, that affirmations we take seriously have to be subject to criticism ... We make the resources of our traditions our own in a new way."

I too would suggest we need to build a world where we can be loyal to our respective traditions without losing a sense of our common humanity. If the danger of religious liberalism is that it may diminish our fervor, the greater danger of militant religious fundamentalism is that it may threaten the sense of our common humanity.

Perhaps the last word should belong to a rabbinic jester friend of mine who quipped: "In the end of days the Messiah will come. The Jew will say 'Welcome;' the Christian will say 'Welcome back.' The Jew will say 'So you have finally come'; and the Christian will say, 'You have returned.' And the Messiah will look at both lovingly and say, 'No comment.'"

CHAPTER 8

The Perception of Christians in Jewish Liturgy: Then and Now

In moments of worship a religious community defines itself.[1] Through its liturgy a people asks, as do Jews near the end of the Yom Kippur service, in this traditional translation of an equally traditional prayer:

> What are we? What is our life? What is our goodness? What is our virtue...What can we say to Thee, Lord our God and God of our ancestors...Yet from the first, Thou didst single out mortals and consider them worthy to stand in Thy presence...Thou, Lord our God, didst graciously grant us this day of atonement ending in the complete forgiveness of all our iniquities.[2]

Through the inspired flow of a liturgist's pen the members of a community proclaim a double paradox: I, a finite creature, have been granted the dignity of a covenant with the infinite God; the infinite God of all creation is uniquely bonded to the people of Israel. Through that bond I, a Jew, find my primary path to forgiveness and renewal of life even in the midst of my brokenness.

From The Changing Face of Jewish and Christian Worship in North America, *edited by Paul F. Bradshaw and Lawrence A. Hoffman, © 1991 by University of Notre Dame Press. Used by permission of the publisher.*

Although the early rabbis focused primarily on God's relationship to Israel, they viewed the Jewish covenant within the matrix of God's relation to all humanity. The covenant with Adam and Noah preceded the covenant with Abraham. Nor does the covenant with Abraham invalidate those earlier covenants.

Rabbinic literature reflects an abiding awareness of God's relation to every human creature through the use of such terms as *adam* or *enosh* (human being) or *beriyot* (humankind). Thus we read: "If one sees the sages of the peoples of the world one should say: 'Praised be Thou who has given of His glory to humanity' (literally: 'His creatures,' *beriyotav*)."[3]

To be sure, the acknowledgement of the universal is almost always enmeshed in an affirmation of the particular. Thus, in the prayer cited earlier, the infinite God's relation to *enosh*, all finite creatures, is followed by the assertion that Yom Kippur's reconciling power is God's special gift to his people Israel. Note, there is nothing here to suggest that other people have no access to Divine forgiveness; only that this particular medium of reconciliation reflects the special bond between God and Israel.

When one lays claim to a special covenant with the Eternal, one may at times speak as a child who, in the intimacy of parental embrace (and in the physical absence of siblings), acts as if his or her bond with father or mother is not only different from, but more precious than, the others. Let us press the metaphor. If the relation between siblings is sorely strained, that moment of intimacy with a parent may also be a time for hostility against the others and an appeal to the parent for deliverance from them; perhaps even a time to challenge their claim to equal consideration by the parent.

Given the painful, bruising quality of much of the Jewish-Christian encounter in history, we should expect some liturgical traces of anti-sibling, i.e., anti-Christian sentiment. Let us briefly examine the record.

THE LITURGY OF PREMODERNITY

We begin with the more subtle polemics. The *Mishnah* informs us of a time when the daily recitation of the *Shema* ("Hear O Israel, the Lord our God, the Lord is One") was preceded by the recitation of the Decalogue. Why was the Decalogue subsequently omitted from the service? The Talmud explains: "So that the *minim* (sectarians) might not charge that these commandments alone were given to Moses at Sinai."[4] According to some scholars this reference to *minim* could well refer to Christians who no longer felt the binding character of the biblical ritual commandments or the oral Torah of the rabbis.[5] The rabbis therefore replaced the Decalogue with a prayer that declares that God so loved Israel, God gave Israel the Torah. "Incline our hearts to perceive, learn, and teach, to observe, do, and fulfill gladly, all the teachings of your Torah."[6]

Liturgical polemics were frequently much more confrontational and invidious. Consider, for example, the poetic insertions (*piyyutim*) that probably originated in Palestine during the fifth and sixth centuries. During that period of Byzantine hegemony, Christianity flourished. Even as Justinian (reigned from 527 to 565) built great churches in the Holy Land, he severely constricted the Jewish community. Some Jews were forcibly converted. Synagogues were transformed into churches. The study of the oral Torah was banned. In this grim environment the polemical *piyyut* was born. In measured cadences these liturgical poems expressed immeasurable pain and hostility. Yannai (fl. sixth century), one of the most prolific of the early poets, wrote *piyyutim* that directly challenged the faith claims of the Church. In one poem Yannai denies that God gave birth to a son and asserts that Christians revered a dead man rather than the living God.[7]

The most anti-Christian *piyyut* came to be incorporated in the Yom Kippur liturgy. It was entitled "Who Does Not Fear You Who Are the King of the *Goyim* [the non-Jews]?" In this poem Jesus is described as the son of a wanton woman. Even when included in the liturgy, however, such expressions were printed ambiguously with letters or words omitted, and in any event, all such *piyyutim* have long since disappeared from the Jewish prayerbook; but they offer historical traces of Jewish anguish and anger seeking a liturgical catharsis. They bear witness to the grimmest periods in the encounter of synagogue and church.[8]

The twelfth benediction of the *Tefillah*, part of the very core of the daily liturgy, has also been shaped by the Jewish-Christian encounter. In its present form this benediction reads: "May the slanderers have no hope; may all wickedness perish instantly; may all Thy enemies be soon cut down. Do Thou speedily uproot and crush the arrogant.... Blessed art Thou, O Lord, who breakest the enemies and humblest the arrogant."[9]

Known as *Birkat minim* (the benediction concerning sectarians), this prayer dates back in one form or another at least to the end of the first century. Scholars theorize that the word *malshinim* (slanderers) may well have been directed at Jews who converted to Christianity and who then proceeded to malign the texts and teachings of their abandoned heritage. In place of *malshinim* (slanderers), an earlier version of the prayer contained the word *meshumadim* (apostates)—that is, those who were baptized. Several texts of this benediction taken from the Cairo Genezah go further still, identifying the subject of hostility not only as *minim* (sectarians) but as *notzrim* (literally, Nazarenes, or Christians).[10] Whether, as some claim, the prayer was originally directed against Jewish sectarians or, as others insist, against Judeo-Christians,[11] there is no reason to doubt that over the centuries this prayer was directed against enemies of the people of Israel, among whom Christians were often to be reckoned.

The *Alenu* prayer, too, has a polemical dimension. Rooted in antiquity, this prayer has been used since the fourteenth century to conclude the worship service. The *Alenu* begins by praising God for having singled out the people Israel for a special covenant and witness ("Who has not made us like the nations of the world") and concludes with the hope that some day "the world shall be perfected under the reign of the Almighty" and all will "accept the yoke of Thy dominion."[12]

Originally the prayer included an invidious distinction between Israel and those who "prostrate themselves to vanity and emptiness and pray to a God who cannot save them" (based on *Isaiah 30:7* and *Isaiah 45:20*). Jewish apologists over the centuries have claimed that this paragraph was directed against pagan idol worshipers of antiquity alone, but there is some evidence that in post-Crusades Europe this paragraph expressed both anti-Christian and anti-Moslem animus. A commentary from the period notes:

> I have heard that one should say "vanity and emptiness" because the arithmetic sum represented by the Hebrew letters that constitute these words is the same as the sum of the Hebrew letters that make up "Jesus and Mohammed." Therefore, all who believe in the two of them "prostrate themselves to vanity and emptiness.[13]

Either in self-protection or in response to the demands of government censors, this paragraph of the *Alenu* was dropped from the liturgy of Ashkenazic Jews. Yet we can actually find it restored in several contemporary Orthodox prayer books.[14]

For the final entry in this cursory survey of anti-Christian polemics we turn to the Passover home prayer book (the *Haggadah*). At one moment in the seder ritual, the door is opened so that Elijah, the harbinger of the Messiah, may be welcomed into our homes. As the doors open, participants recite:

> Pour out Your wrath on the nations who know You not and upon the kingdoms that call not upon Your name (*Psalm 79:6-7*).
> For they have devoured Jacob and laid waste to his habitation.
> Pour out Your indignation and let the fierceness of Your anger overtake them (*Psalm 69:25*).
> You will pursue them in anger and destroy them from under the heavens of the Eternal (*Lamentations 3:66*).[15]

This declaration on Seder night probably dates from

Machzor Vitry (eleventh–twelfth century) and may well have been fully integrated into the Passover liturgy after the depredations of the Crusaders.[16] Those Biblical verses, originally directed at Israel's enemies in antiquity, seemed painfully resonant to medieval Jewry. The underlying sentiment may be paraphrased: "Why, O Lord, do You seemingly direct your wrath at us who bear the price of serving You in this unredeemed world? Pour Your wrath upon those who by their actions express contempt for Your purposes."

NINETEENTH- AND TWENTIETH-CENTURY LITURGICAL REFORM

Such liturgical hostility toward "the other" remained unchallenged as long as it mirrored the world of the Jewish worshiper. It became problematic only when new social and political developments spurred some western-European Jews to view the world through different eyes. Particularly, as the liturgy was translated, its editors felt the need to respond to the afterglow of the Jewish Emancipation from the ghetto, the promise of citizenship, and the aura of Enlightenment—with its declaration of a human sphere that transcended all religious particularism. Some Jews now felt the need for a new prayer book, with Israel no longer imaged as "a people who dwell apart" and the world no longer perceived as the enemy camp.

In particular, Reform Jews of nineteenth-century Germany perceived themselves, and wished to be perceived by others, as a religious fellowship (not a nation) proclaiming the universal message of ethical monotheism in a spirit of reconciliation with the enlightened sectors of the non-Jewish world. The liturgical implications of this new self-image were obvious to rabbis like Abraham Geiger (1810–1874), a leading advocate of reform and rabbi in Breslau, Frankfort, and Berlin, who declared: "The separation between Israel and the other peoples which existed at one time has no right to be expressed in prayer. Rather ought there to be an expression of joy that such barriers are increasingly falling."[17] If indeed the prayers of the synagogue were to be recited increasingly in the language of the land—the language we and our neighbors understood—and if under the new climate our neighbors would more likely venture into our synagogues from time to time, it was all the more essential that our liturgy not even appear to alienate us from them.

The new liturgical spirit came to be embodied most eloquently in the prayer books of the American Reform movement. Indeed, with one exception, the remainder of this essay will focus on American Reform liturgy, which has been at the cutting edge in articulating a post-Emancipation theology of "the other."

The classical liturgical statement of American Reform Judaism is to be found in its *Union Prayer Book* (UPB) of 1894–1895. Though revised twice since then (in 1924 and again in 1940), it remained in essence Reform Judaism's book of worship here until the 1970s, when the *Gates* series supplanted it. Conspicuously missing from all editions of the *Union Prayer Book* are the poems that lament our degradation at the hands of others. Gone completely is the twelfth benediction of the *Tefillah* which invokes God's wrath against the slanderers of our people. Deleted from the *Union Haggadah: Home Service for Passover* (1923) are the words, "Pour out Thy wrath upon the nations who know Thee not." Added however, is a prayer for "grace to fulfill [our] mission with zeal tempered by wisdom and guided by regard for other men's [and women's] faith."[18]

Gone also is the phrase in the *Alenu* prayer that praises God for having not "made us like the nations of the lands." Featured instead is the part of the prayer that proclaims that the God we worship is the Creator of all. Elsewhere, in place of the phrase, "Grant peace to us and all Israel your people," the Hebrew is changed to read: "Grant peace . . . to us and all who revere Your name."[19]

The Reform liturgical consensus that prevailed during the first half of the twentieth century accentuated and made explicit the universalism implicit in classic Judaism. This liturgical model was reappraised and found wanting after World War II, when the Reform prayer book's balmy spirit of meliorism and its tilt toward universalism seemed strikingly incongruous to a Jewish community that had emerged from the Holocaust. Real enemies remained in our world. A Jew who prayed history could not liturgically ignore the Holocaust or the traumatic rebirth of a Jewish state called Israel. The Messianic Age was not virtually within human grasp, as Reform liturgy had suggested.

And yes, the accent on universalism had rendered Reform too porous a vessel for a millennial heritage. Was not Judaism's staying power a function if its sinewy particularism? If our covenant was too bland, too undifferentiated, how could it engage and nourish us? A re-balancing was necessary to mirror a post-Holocaust world and to respond to American society's new respect for pluralism and diversity. Our liturgists were now challenged to be at once unapologetically particularistic and patently respectful of "the other." So the *UPB* gave way to the *Gates of Prayer* and *Gates of Repentance*.

These new Reform prayer books restored to the *Alenu* the words claiming that God has indeed "set us apart from the other families of the earth, given us a destiny unique among the nations," even as they retain the universal hope for the time when "all will acclaim You as their God and, forsaking evil, turn to You alone."[21] After considerable debate the new Reform *Haggadah* continued to omit the words, "Pour out Your wrath upon the nations who know You not," even though the artist, Leonard Baskin, commissioned to provide art for the work, had included a full-page illustration to accompany the phrase in question (Baskin's rendering was omitted as well). By way of illustrative contrast, we note that the Conservative movement's new *Haggadah* retained the formula but only with this clarifying meditation:

> Why does the impassioned invocation of Divine wrath belong in our celebration of freedom? Because by opting conveniently for chronic amnesia, the world compels us to remember freedom's foes. So we remember the Hadrianic persecutions, the Crusades, the ritual murder accusations, the Inquisition, the

pogroms, the Holocaust ... and we remember God-fearing men and women of all nations who risked their lives for us in so many valleys of the shadow of death.[22]

One can virtually hear the studied effort to balance a remembrance of Israel's particular pain with an embrace of those who risked all for the sake of a shared vision of the sacred. Here, too, is an open particularism.

CONCLUSIONS: PARTICULARISM, NOT ETHNOCENTRISM

Surely the last liturgical word has not been written, nor the final edition of our liturgy been published. In every generation, implicitly or explicitly the liturgy proclaims a theology of "the other." What guidelines emerge from the tradition and from the efforts of contemporary liturgical poets?

1. Liturgy is intrinsically particularistic. The worship service is a time for the community to evoke its inner history—its own singular experience of the living God. So, for example, after duly celebrating God's creation of the world, classic Jewish liturgy praises God for redeeming our ancestors from Egypt and giving us the Torah. The Yom Kippur liturgy proclaims the paradox of an infinite God's relation to all human creatures, but then the service acknowledges the special gift of Yom Kippur to the people Israel. The moment of worship is Israel's private time with the Divine Parent. It is the hour to confirm our special bond with the One who has become known to our ancestors and to us. That evocation of Israel's covenant with *Adonai* gives Jews a sense of the particular claims that the covenant makes upon us and upon God. Thus in the midst of confessing our sins and seeking forgiveness on Yom Kippur, we hear the cantor and choir recite the medieval poem:

> We are your people; You are our king.
> We are your children; You are our parent.
> We are your possession; You are our portion ...
> We are your beloved, You are our friend.[23]

2. The liturgical moment is also a time for a mission statement—a time to affirm the transcendent significance of
Israel's particular witness to God in the world, a time to
confirm that God's world needs Israel's testimony. So we
say, " It is our duty to give thanks to Thee, to praise and
glorify Thee, to bless and hallow Thy name. How good
is our destiny, how pleasant our lot, how beautiful our
heritage."[24] As a part of its mission statement the liturgy
also confirms that the meaning of my life derives from
being faithful to Israel's task.

3. But responsible liturgy does not permit a moment of
intimacy to become a moment of theological ethnocentrism. Our prayers must allow that the One we call
Adonai is in some sense known by those outside our
covenant and is involved redemptively in their lives too.
After all, the biblical heritage proclaims that the one
who redeemed Israel from Egypt also freed the
Philistines from Caphtor (*Amos 9:7*). And the One
who became known to Moses was also heard by the
non-Israelite prophet Balaam (*Numbers 22:9-12, 23:26,
24:1-2*).

Thus, after duly affirming God's redemption of Israel
from Egyptian bondage, *Gates of Prayer* translates the
Hebrew phrase, "who answers His people," as "who is
the answer to all who cry out to Him." And elsewhere:
"We give thanks for our sages and teachers of all peoples
and faith who have brought many to a deeper understanding of You and Your will."[25]

Be it granted that, on occasion, our classic literature
and liturgy did proclaim an exclusive paternal-filial
bond of love between God and Israel. Today's liturgist

should help us preserve the mystery of Israel's election without implying a greater Divine love for Israel than for others and without even appearing to denigrate the integrity of God's other covenants. There is a subtle, but real, difference in tone between praising God "for not having made me a non-Jew," as does the traditional liturgy, and praising God for "having made me a member of the household of Israel"—as does our new Reform liturgy.

Is it really necessary during my people's private time with God to explicitly affirm *Adonai*'s relation to those outside my covenant? Given centuries of liturgical ethnocentrism, it is time for some "affirmative action." If there are others who still make me pay a price for being Jewish in an unredeemed world, I have even more reason to acknowledge that some of God's noblest servants are also others.

4. These preliminary guidelines for contemporary liturgy do not encompass a special dimension of the Jewish-Christian encounter today. Christians visiting a synagogue may be inclined to join in the English responses. Such visitors report feeling at home with the general spirit, if not with all the specific claims, of the Jewish liturgy. After all, was not Jesus a son of the synagogue? In opening themselves to the experience of Jewish worship, are not Christians reclaiming their Judaic roots?

This phenomenon is asymmetrical. Christians feel more comfortable in a synagogue (especially where there is substantial English in the liturgy) than do Jews in a church. For Christians, the Jewish liturgical experience is a pilgrimage to their roots. For Jews, the Christ-centered liturgy of the church marks the gospel we cannot profess.[26]

The Christian's empathetic response to Jewish worship creates no theological problems for Judaism. Non-

Jews were welcome to pray—even to bring offerings to God—in the ancient Temple. Christian responsiveness to Jewish worship may be considered an intimation of Messianic times.

However, the Christian's role in Jewish worship does become more problematic when one moves from reading or hearing prayers in a pew to a visible role on the *bima* (pulpit). Consider the case of a mixed marriage. Suppose the children are being raised as Jews and the time has come for the child's *bar-* or *bat-mitzvah* ceremony. Both parents will be on the *bima*. In many Reform synagogues the mother of the child recites the blessings over the kindling of the Sabbath lights. There may also be a symbolic transmission of the Torah Scroll from grandparents to parents to child—signaling the child's acceptance of the privileges and obligations of his or her heritage.

If the child's mother is Christian, shall she be invited to kindle the lights and lead the congregation in the blessing? The Responsa Committee of the Central Conference of American Rabbis concludes: "It would be appropriate to have that parent participate in some way in that service, but not in the same way as the Jewish parents."[27] The traditional blessing praises God "who has sanctified us by His commandments and commanded us to kindle the lights of the Sabbath." The Christian does not feel accountable for such ritual commandments. For that reason Jews traditionally regard Christians as members of the Noachide covenant: they feel bound by the moral laws applicable to all God's creatures and have rejected idolatry. Hence, strictly speaking, the Christian mother of the child does not live under the commandment to kindle those Sabbath lights. The non-Jewish mother may be asked to recite another text or that part of the kindling liturgy that does not declare the unique covenantal obligations of a Jew.

Our synagogue's Torah transmission ceremony makes the same distinction. The non-Jewish parent helps dress and undress the Torah Scroll and stands with the child when he or she reads from it, but the Jewish parent alone affirms some variant of the words, "This is our Torah which I now hand to you."

Such attention to boundaries is ultimately more respectful of each tradition. Christians who profess a love for their Jewish neighbor or spouse or child and who feel a bond to the synagogue are, from a Jewish perspective, the equivalent of *Yirei Adonai*, God-fearing gentiles. While they may feel part of Israel, and the church regards itself as the "new Israel," they cannot be so regarded by the synagogue. The new spirit of mutual respect that is so precious a part of our inter-religious scene and the realities of mixed marriage summon us to love each other without denying our otherness.

5. Nor does civility and openness compromise the Jewish liturgical claim to transcendent truth. Our liturgy proclaims that we are charter witnesses to a truth not yet acknowledged or fully lived by us or the world. By being Jews we acknowledge that truth. When we live our covenant, we do the most we can to further the coming of God's dominion. The new Reform prayer includes: "You have chosen us and set us apart from all the peoples, and in love and favor have given us the Sabbath day as a sacred inheritance."[28]

Our liturgy (including the *Alenu* prayer) presumes that Israel's vision of God is in some sense fuller and truer than alternative visions and that others will, in time, acknowledge ours. I expect a corresponding claim from my Christian neighbor. We leave it to God to bring ultimate clarity to our separate visions and to arbitrate our conflicting claims. In the interim our task is to be faithful to the truth entrusted to us and to respond with respect to those whose noble vision differs from our own.

Buber wisely observed:

> The mystery of another lies deeply within him [or her] and it
> cannot be observed from without. No man [or woman] outside
> of Israel knows the mystery of Israel and no man [or woman]
> outside Christianity knows Christianity. But in their ignorance
> they can acknowledge each other in the mystery.[29]

To be sure, this capacity to "acknowledge each other in the
mystery," to be stirringly particular without violating the integrity of the other, is ultimately a function of the social climate in
which the liturgy and the liturgical people live. In periods of
enforced isolation and persecution, ethnocentrism rears it head.
Our current liturgical spirit is a tribute to the openness and freedom of America. May its benign ambiance continue to inspire
the liturgies of tomorrow.

NOTES

1. I am grateful to Lawrence A. Hoffman for directing me
to some of the relevant sources consulted in the first part of this
paper.

2. Philip Birnbaum, ed. And trans., *Machzor Hashalem
Lerosh Hashanah Veyom Kippur: High Holiday Prayer Book* (New
York, 1951) pp. 1004-6.

3. Ber. 58a.

4. Ber. 12a, P. T. Ber. 3c

5. See G. F. Moore, *Judaism in the First Centuries of the
Christian Era* (Cambridge, 1927), vol. 3, pp. 95-96, n. 64.

6. See Philip Birnbaum, ed. And trans., *Hasiddur Hashalem:
The Daily Prayer Book* (New York, 1949), pp. 76.

7. See Tzvi Rabinowitz, *Machzor Piyyutei Rabbi Yannai
Latorah Velano'adim* (Jerusalem, 1985), pp. 45-60.

8. See E. D. Goldschmidt, *Machzor Layamim Nora'im*
(Jerusalem, 1970), pp. 186-87. Cf. The discussion by Goldschmidt in his *Hashlamah Lamachzor Leyom Hakippurim, Kiryat*

Sefer 31 (1964): pp. 146-51; and the brief listing by Israel Davidson, *Otsar Hashirah Vehapiyyut*, reprinted. (New York, 1970), vol. 2, pp. 181.

9. Birnbaum, *Hasiddur*, pp. 88.

10. Cf. Jacob Mann, "Genizah Fragments of the Palestinian Order of Service," reprinted in Jakob J. Petuchowski, ed., *Contributions to the Scientific Study of Jewish Liturgy* (New York, 1970), pp. 416.

11. See Reuven Kimelman, "*Birkat Haminim* and the Lack of Evidence for an Anti-Christian Jewish Prayer in Late Antiquity," in E. P. Sanders, ed., *Jewish and Christian Self-Definition*, vol. 2: Aspects of Judaism in the Greco-Roman Period (Philadelphia, 1981), pp. 226-44, notes on pp. 391-403; and Lawrence H. Schiffman, *Who Was A Jew?* (Hoboken, N. J., 1985), pp. 53-61, notes on pp. 94-97.

12. Birnbaum, *Hasiddur*, pp. 138.

13. See E. A. Urbach, ed., *Arugat Habosem* (Jerusalem, 1939), vol. 3, pp.468-69.

14. Cf. The standard Israeli prayer book, *Siddur Rinat Yisrael*, pp. 193; and in America, *ArtScroll Siddur* (New York, 1969), pp. 84. Even E. D. Goldschmidt restores the line to his scientifically "accurate" test of the daily service, both for the standard Ashkenazic rite of northern Europe, and for Hasidic congregations who altered that rite in accordance with what they believed to have been the practice of Isaac Luria (sixteenth century). Cf. E. D. Goldschmidt, *Siddur Tefillat Yisra'el lefi Nusach Ha'Ashkenazim Ba'arets Uvachuts La'arets* (Israel, 1969), pp. 71; and *Siddur Tefillat Yisra'el el lefi Minhag Hachasidim Lerabot Chasidei Chabad* (Israel, n.d. [1969?]), pp. 88. Both works are compiled "along with additions that were deleted by censors" (see title pages).

15. Cf. Menachem M. Kasher, ed., *The Passover Haggadah* (New York, 1962), pp. 197; Phillip Birnbaum, ed., *The Birnbaum Haggadah* (New York, 1976), pp. 114-15.

16. See discussion E. D. Goldschmidt, *Haggadah Shel Pesach Vetoldoteha* (Jerusalem, 1970), pp. 62-64.

17. Quoted in Jakob J. Petuchowiski, *Prayerbook Reform in Europe* (New York, 1968), pp. 299.

18. *Union Prayer Book* (1940 ed.), pp. 34 (thereafter UPB).

19. Ibid., pp. 141. For earlier attempts by Reform editors to expunge *Alenu's* particularistic message, see Petuchowski, *Prayer Book Reform*, pp. 298-306. For Reform Judaism's attempt to recapture its particularistic message, without, however, blunting its universalism, particularly in its *Gates* liturgy in use today—and for a survey of the tension between universalism and particularism in American Reform liturgies preceding the UPB—see Lawrence A. Hoffman, "The Language of Survival in American Reform Liturgy," *CCAR Journal* 24/3 (1977), pp. 87-106.

20. For details, see Hoffman, "Language of Survival."

21. *Gates of Prayer* (New York, 1975), pp. 615 (hereafter GOP).

22. Rachel Ann Rabinowicz, ed., *Passover Haggadah: The Feast of Freedom* (New York, 1982), pp. 101.

23. Cf. Traditional text in Birnbaum, ed., *Machzor*, pp. 545-48; and Reform version in *Gates of Repentance* (New York, 1978), pp. 279.

24. Birnbaum, *Hasiddur*, pp. 26.

25. *GOP*, pp. 304, 322.

26. On the phenomenon of a liturgical gathering containing both Jewish and Christian worshipers, cf. Lawrence A. Hoffman, "Worship in Common," *Cross-Currents: Religion and Intellectual Life* 40/1 (Spring, 1990), pp.5-17; and the responses that follow, pp. 18-46.

27. Walter Jacob, ed., *American Reform Responsa* (New York, 1983), pp. 23. Cf. Lawrence A. Hoffman, "Non-Jews and Jewish Life Cycle Liturgy," *Journal of Reform Judaism* 37/3 (Summer, 1990), pp. 1-16; and the response thereto by Gunther Plaut, pp. 17-20.

28. *GOP*, pp. 719.

29. Martin Buber, quoted in *The Jewish-Christian Argument* (*Die Stunde und die Erkenntnis*, pp. 155) (New York, 1963), pp. 167.

SECTION II

Ani Ma'amin—
I Believe

CHAPTER 9

Faith for Our Time

Some time ago a woman in our congregation spoke to me about her neighbors. "They really believe," she said. "They have faith. They take it seriously. I wish I did, or could. I really envy them."

We don't speak much openly about our faith in God. It is a private matter. We may wrestle with our faith in one way or another. We may all yearn for faith but we don't talk about it. The Hebrew word for faith is *emunah*. *Emunah* means trust. *Emunah* is commitment to One who cannot be formally demonstrated or directly experienced. Faith is not conventional knowledge based on proof. Faith is an inner knowledge, a knowledge of the soul.

What is the difference between knowledge based on demonstration and faith? Suppose at this moment we said: "*Adonai*, if You are real, if You are present in our lives, then let a clap of thunder be heard?" And, lo and behold we heard a clap of thunder. If this kind of predictable experiment or demonstration were possible again, and again, and again, we would have a knowledge of God based on demonstration rather than

Sermon, January 2, 1981

faith. But such a God would be more like a cosmic puppet under our control than the God revealed in the Hebrew Bible. Even when *Adonai* does appear in Biblical story, God remains an "elusive presence" who cannot be seen or conjured by man. Moses asked for a full understanding, a full definition and was told only: "I am as I am." Elijah heard God not in a thunderclap but in the "sound of silence." The prophets proclaimed their faith in the triumph of a kingdom of justice and of love. Job trusted in God even after he experienced undeserved suffering in God's world. Faith, *emunah*, is trust in the presence of mystery.

In religious matters, in matters of ultimate concern, final, decisive demonstrations are not possible. We travel always on the edge of the unknown. That is the essence of *emunah*, of religious faith. It is "hanging in there," affirming something or someone who may not be seen directly or fully proved.

The word *emunah*, faith, is related to another Hebrew word. We may not have thought about it, but it is the word *amen*. Have you ever wondered why we say *amen* all the time? We say it at the end of any benediction or prayer. "Praised be Thou, O Lord, who gives the Torah. *Amen*." "Heal us and we shall be healed. Save us and we shall be saved. *Amen*." "May the Lord bless you and keep you. *Amen*." Why? *Amen* is usually translated "so be it" but, considering its relation to the word *emunah*, it can also be rendered "we trust it will be so." Notice that no prayer is complete until the congregation declares "*amen*," until we respond: "We trust it will be so." It is to suggest, as it were, that our very trust, our belief is a necessary part of God's effective presence in our lives. Our trust, our faith in God affects God's power to enter our lives.

This notion of the power of faith itself applies not only to faith in God. Some years ago the anthropologist Ralph Linton reported a strange case of a man who entered a New York hospital and claimed that he had been hexed by a witch doctor and that unless the hex were removed he would die at noon the next day. Linton suggested to the physicians that, with the cooperation of the man, they at least try to locate the person he believed hexed him. But they simply examined him, found nothing wrong medically, and put him to bed in isolation and quiet. The next day at noon he died. An autopsy revealed nothing medically wrong, and Linton's point is that the man's belief in the power of that spell killed him.

When Norman Cousins appeared at our "Coping with Health" symposium, he spoke of the power of the witch doctor; but then he went on to talk about the power of the modern physician. In the presence of a distinguished panel of physicians who agreed with him, Cousins said that the patient's trust in the physician and in the medication given him by the physician is itself an important factor in healing. Psychoanalysts understand that only after the patient's "resistance" has been removed can the therapeutic process work. The patient must trust the analyst and the process. Analysis can work in an atmosphere of trust, of faith.

The power of faith in something or someone is related to our *amen*, our affirmation, our trust in that something or someone.

The word for faith in God, *emunah* is not only related to the word *amen*, it is also related to the Hebrew word *aman*, which means craftsman, workman, artist. We help release the power of faith not only by our attitude of trust, but by our actions.

Will Barrett, professor of philosophy at Columbia, put it thus: "I establish my faith, my conviction, in the only way I can, by multiplying the occasions in my life when I put it into practice." What did he mean?

Doubt doesn't build synagogues or discover new lands or launch businesses. Faith-inspired action does. Columbus had faith that the world was round. He acted on that faith. He attempted to travel around the world. Medical researchers who are struggling to find a cure for cancer are prompted by the faith that the cure is possible. It has not been proved that a cure is possible but it is that faith-inspired action which enables them to persist in experiments and theorizing, to confront puzzlement and dead ends, and still go on. The action inspired by faith will make a cure possible.

The same is true of the most comprehensive faith of all: faith in God. *Emunah*, faith in God is an attitude of trust, followed by a leap of action—by living as if there is a God. That's the problem with the agnostic. The agnostic says: "I can't prove it and I can't refute it, so I am going to take the reasonable position. I don't know, so I will suspend judgment. I will be a theological fence-sitter."

The problem is that the possibilities of faith in God can only be discovered by trusting in the presence of mystery and by acting faithfully. A *hasid* was asked: "Where is God?" He replied: "Where we let God enter our lives." The agnostic says: "Prove to me that there is a God and then I will pray to Him." But God can only enter our lives if we pray and act faithfully.

So far we have ignored one of the most important questions of all. Granted that faith is power, and that our attitude and our action based on faith is significant and decisive, does that mean it matters not what we believe in as long as we believe? If faith's power was real for a man who believed he was hexed by a witch doctor and acted on the basis of it; if faith's power was real for those who believed in the Reverend Jones and acted on it by following him to Guyana, how do we sort out the true from the false, the constructive from the destructive in the realm of the spirit? That is a very important question.

Such sorting out is the function of our minds. Our reason, properly deployed, helps sort out what is consistent with the best we know in other realms of experience. Our reason helps us distill the wisdom, the experience of past generations. Our reason helps us distinguish between serving God and serving an idol. That is the function of reason. And one of the strengths of Judaism is that our heritage has always encouraged the maximum use of our mind in defining and establishing the boundaries of faith.

But reason alone cannot establish a relationship to God. Religion at its best requires an interplay of faith and reason. To paraphrase Einstein: faith without reason is blind, reason without faith is deaf.

Modern researchers of the human brain apparently have discovered two hemispheres with different functions. The right hemisphere controls intuition, creativity, imagination. That part of the brain enables us to create and respond to music, to art, to poetry. It may also embody our capacity for faith.

The left hemisphere controls our reasoning capacity. It is analytical. It makes benefit-cost analyses. It weeds out contradictions and inconsistencies. It is calculating. This left hemisphere might help us define the appropriate form of faith.

The right hemisphere may express our capacity for faith. The left hemisphere defines the appropriate form of faith. There appear to be different dimensions to our being. There is a *rational* dimension and, for want of a better word, a *spiritual* dimension. It is the *rational* part of us which, after the Holocaust (after six million innocent men, women and children died in gas chambers) led many of us to conclude that God must not be in control of everything that happens in the world. Some things may happen that God does not want to happen. God may, in some way, be limited by the world He has created. It is the *faith-nurturing* part of us which enabled survivors of the Holocaust to go to South America and establish a congregation named *Lamrot Hakel*, which means "in spite of everything." In spite of everything we continue to trust in God and will remain faithful witnesses to His covenant.

When we have been told that we have a particular kind of cancer, the left hemisphere of the brain might help us assess our statistical chances of survival and help us program a plan of action; the right hemisphere of the brain—the faith-nurturing part of us—enables us to pray to God for healing and to declare, as someone in the hospital declared to me just the other day, "as long as there is life, there is hope."

With *reason* we analyze what commandments in the Torah can be meaningful in our life today. With faith we are overwhelmed by emotion and moved to tears as we witness or share in the passing of the Torah Scroll across the generations.

The act of prayer is primarily a right-hemisphere phenomenon, like art and music and poetry. And the faith we affirm in our prayer tonight and at every service is at once simple and very deep. We affirm by attitude and by action that our life is not simply the product of random swirling atoms but a precious gift of *Adonai*—as we pray "Praised be Thou, O Lord, Source of Life." We affirm that our life has a value, a purpose, that there is an intended direction for our life—as we pray: "Praised be Thou, O Lord, Giver of Torah."

We affirm that an ancient ancestor entered into a covenant with *Adonai* and that we are commissioned to enter into that covenant and to transmit it to the next generation—as we pray: "For You have singled us out for a special witness among the nations." We affirm that our small, stumbling, fumbling efforts to pursue life's goal are not simply futile gestures in a vast void, but that our little life has some abiding significance and "our little deeds find their permanence as part of God's eternity"—as we pray: "The Lord shall reign forever and ever."

These prayers express our *emunah*, our faith. They cannot be formally demonstrated or proved, but can only be tested by our attitude—by our trust in *Adonai*, by our actions, by our faithfulness to the One we affirm. One of the best statements I have heard on faith came not from a theologian, but from a novelist. Lillian Smith said: "To believe in something not yet proved and to underwrite it with our lives is the only way we can leave the future open. To accept uncertainty quietly, even an incomplete knowledge of God, that's what man's journey is about...."

CHAPTER 10

The Passover Story and the Ḧolocaust

This past week we observed Passover. We commemorated the Exodus and proclaimed God's redemptive power in history. Next Wednesday evening our community will assemble in this place for a radically different commemoration. If Passover affirms God's redemptive power, the Holocaust would seem to proclaim God's awful silence in history.

The question we all must ask at one time or another is why? Why does a God active in history, a God of power and goodness, the God of the Exodus, permit this to happen to our people, to any people? The question may of course also be raised even if a single child dies in this country from some disease or if a single child died in the Holocaust. As we know more than one million Jewish children died in the ovens and gas chambers of Hitler.

But the question is ultimately the same, whether it is one or a million or six million. Whether we respond to the events as people to whom the child belongs or whether we are that child's mother or father; whether the child is Jewish or not, the question is the same: why?

Tonight let us explore the question from the perspective of

Sermon, April 24, 1992

a particular people, our people. Judaism has stressed the story of the people Israel, covenanted to God. This people has borne witness to God and affirms that God brought us out of the land of Egypt, out of the house of bondage. This people proclaimed that God is a saving presence in history. When bad times befell our people, we have struggled to understand and to carry on.

When the Assyrians exiled the northern tribes, or the Babylonians destroyed the first Temple and took our people into exile, when the second Temple was destroyed by the Romans, when our ancestors were oppressed and then forced to convert or leave Spain in 1492, and again in the time of Hitler, the same questions were raised: Why, O God? Where is the God of history? Where is the Redeemer of Israel who brought us out of the land of Egypt?

Many answers have been given. Let it be said at the outset that no answer comes even close to being adequate. Still, answers have been given. One answer: Because of our sins, God is chastening us. The prophet Jeremiah explained the Babylonian exile as punishment for idolatry and social injustice. Some rabbis explained the destruction of the second Temple by Rome as a consequence of the groundless hatred of Jew for Jew within that community.

When pogroms broke out in Spain in the 14th century, Solomon Alami explained: "We and our iniquities caused this." He blamed affluent Jews who forgot their poor kin. He blamed Jews who had become lax in their Sabbath observance. In our time a few rabbis have said the Holocaust came upon our people because so many Jews in Germany totally assimilated and neglected their heritage.

Times of evil trigger individual or communal self-scrutiny and judgment. There is a place for self-judgment at such a time but from Biblical days to our own, from the *Book of Job* to Elie Wiesel, radically different voices have said: it is obscene to blame the victims for such catastrophes and assume one has given an adequate answer.

One such voice belonged to a prophet whom we know as

II Isaiah. He said that a people may suffer not because of what they do wrong; they may also suffer for doing right. Israel, said Isaiah, was God's "suffering servant," paying the price for bearing witness to God in a world not yet ready to receive the message.

After the destruction of the Temple by the Romans one rabbi quoted *Psalm 44*: "For Thy sake, O God, are we killed all the day and counted as sheep for the slaughter." We suffer, O God, because we are your people, *because* we are your servants, the people Israel! We suffer because by our very existence we bear witness to Your message in a world not yet ready to receive it. To re-phrase the matter in a contemporary way: When will all anti-Semitism cease completely? Only on that day when the God to whom we bear charter witness in history is truly acknowledged as the God of the universe. When "the Lord shall be One and God's name One."

Another powerful attempt to understand suffering in our world was given by the Kabbalists who gathered in the Holy Land after the expulsion from Spain in 1492. One of those Jewish mystics, Isaac Luria, taught that evil in God's world is a consequence of creation itself. Before the creation of the world, God was all and all was God. To create a world, to make space for the world, God contracted the Divine Self. But that process of God stepping back to make room for the world and then infusing that separated world with divine radiance resulted in a cracking, "a breaking of the vessels" and a flawed creation.

The consequence of creating a world separate from God is its brokenness, and the price of creating a human creature in that world with free will is the possibility, even the probability of much evil. Creation made possible not only a Moses, a Jeremiah, an Albert Schweitzer and a Mother Teresa, but also a Pharaoh, a Torquemada, a Stalin and a Hitler.

Isaac Luria concluded that we, God's creatures, are God's partners. We must help redeem God's world. We must help redeem God. As God's partners, we must engage in *tikkun*, repair. How? By our *mitzvot*, by living the faithful covenant life, by our prayers and by our deeds in the world.

This metaphor of God paying the price of creation and suffering the travails of creation is echoed by novelist André Schwarzbart in his Holocaust-inspired novel, *The Last of the Just*. A Jewish doctor in that novel who is a prisoner in a concentration camp is asked, "If God is real, why is Auschwitz possible?" The doctor replied, "When I was a gentleman one of my friends used to tease me by asking if God in His omnipotence could create a stone so heavy that He couldn't lift it, which is my position, I believe in God and I believe in the stone."

More difficult still than trying to explain God's silence, is to live through it and to keep the covenant going. And this too, our people has done. We have wrestled with God, we have argued, we have expressed both anger and yearning, and many of us have continued to believe. We have discovered it is still more impossible to live in a world without God than to struggle with a God who is both hidden and revealed.

In his autobiographical novel *Gates of the Forest*, Elie Wiesel describes how after he watched his father die in the camps, he couldn't bring himself to recite *Kaddish*. He had been taught as a devout Jewish boy that when your father dies you recite *Kaddish*, but he couldn't do it! Later, when he did recite the *Kaddish* he described it as "that solemn affirmation filled with grandeur and serenity by which man returns to God His crown and His scepter."

We need God more than ever when we are assaulted by despair. That was the meaning of his *Kaddish*. We need God more than ever when we are a generation that has experienced a Holocaust. For if there is no God by what ultimate standard can we explain that what Hitler did to us and to others was absolutely wrong? Only if there is some moral law imprinted in the universe can we ground that absolute command: Thou shalt not deny the image of God in another. "Thou shalt not murder . . ."

We must ask another question. Once we have confronted the mystery of God's apparent silence, do we still also experience the God who took us out of Egypt? Do we now still experience God's redemptive power in history?

I believe we do and nowhere more awesomely than in our very survival as a people to this day. An ancient Egyptian inscription, found by archeologists, records a ruler declaring that "Israel is destroyed, it is no more" and presumably will not be heard from again! That obituary proved premature.

How poignant it was for a group of us, just seven weeks ago, to return to Spain from which King Ferdinand and Queen Isabella expelled us "in perpetuity" in 1492. Now 500 years later, on the Sabbath before we visited Granada to see the tombs of Ferdinand and Isabella, we worshipped in a Madrid synagogue with Sephardic Jews who had returned to Spain and were singing again the prayers of our people and bearing witness to the covenant of Abraham and Sarah in the Iberian Peninsula.

For a believing Jew, our very survival as a people to this day is a recurring sign of God's redemptive power in history.

In his new book Eugene Borowitz raises the question of God's redemptive presence in our time. He writes: "I have experienced some great historic moments when the hand of God's redemptive power was manifest. The Civil Rights struggle of the early 1960s, the salvation of Israel's Six Day War, the liberation of communist Europe in 1990—(moments) that I knew to be shaped as much by God as by human agency. God redeems."

Yes, we are a people who bear charter witness to a God who redeemed slaves from Egypt, and over the centuries we have known and continue to know the exultation of redemption and the anguish of God's silence. If we are blessed, we remain able to cherish the redemptive moments and to endure with faith, the times of silence.

In every age, including our own, there have been Jews who experienced the worst of our history without forsaking that faith. In a cellar in Cologne during the Nazi period, a Jew in hiding scrawled these words on the wall: "I believe in the sun even when it is not shining. I believe in love even when not feeling it. I believe in God even when He is silent."

The other day I visited a member of our congregation who is a Holocaust survivor. He described how he and his mother were the only survivors in his family. He described being in the camp. Not unmindful of God's awful silence in those days, he was able nonetheless to thank God for the deliverance in his life and in the life of our people. He was still able to smile and to hope. I stand in respectful awe of those who have known the darker side of history and still believe.

When all has been said, there are no adequate explanations for the mystery of God's hiddenness. Ultimately, we must choose our take on life. We all know moments when God seems absent, and hopefully we all know many redemptive moments.

As we move this coming week from the celebration of our redemption from Egypt to a solemn remembrance of the dark years of the Nazi Holocaust we should remember the rabbinic story that the Red Sea did not part until the children of Israel moved forward and did all they could to be God's partner in redemption. We should remember the words of Rabbi Luria: God needs us for *tikkun olam*, for the repair of the brokenness of creation.

And we need God. So we pray: "Redeem us, O God, and we shall be redeemed. Establish Thou the work of our hands, yea, the work of our hands, establish Thou it."

CHAPTER 11

Suffering
and Faith

All of us have the will to believe in God, the source of being in whom there is abundant power and love; the God who is giver of Torah and a caring, healing presence in the world.

What makes this faith so difficult for us at one time or another in our lives? Surely, the reality of human suffering. The tragic dimension of existence can choke the flame of faith.

In the Biblical creation story we read "and God saw everything that He had made and behold it was very good." Yet almost from the very beginning the negativities of life assault us. Cain murders Abel. God obviously disapproves but does not intervene. We suffer in many ways from the evil humans do to each other. This is called moral evil.

But even more perplexing and faith-shattering can be the evil we encounter in nature. Today I want to focus on natural evil as an obstacle to faith. In Camus' novel *The Plague* a doctor, once a believer, stands helplessly by as children die a torturous death from disease. The priest says to the doctor: "Love what you do not understand." The doctor responds: "Until my dying day

---

Sermon, December 31, 1993

I shall refuse to love a scheme of things in which children are put to torture."

Last summer when the Mississippi River's wild rampage became a vivid metaphor for nature run amok, the lead story in *The New York Times* began: "No one alive has seen the father of rivers yawn this high or this wide ... The unimaginable has happened. Across the Midwestern corn belt it has rained in Biblical proportions for forty-nine straight days, often in torrents ... forcing 36,000 people from their homes."

If God is Lord of life and nature then why, why? And can one speak of such a world and say "It is very good" and can we believe in, trust, draw close to the Creator of such a world?

What are some ways of addressing this question? The Bible often links natural evil to moral evil. The flood at the time of Noah was regarded as a divine response to pervasive corruption on earth. Humankind deserved it. Some attempt has been made to place the Mississippi flood disaster in a rational, moral context. We human beings imprisoned the mighty Mississippi within narrow walls of dirt and concrete levies. The price of such ecological wantonness was a sudden and catastrophic flooding when excess rainwater, forced into a narrow channel by the levies, ran out of places to go and could not drain naturally. So the human choice to exploit rather than live in harmony with nature brought a day of judgment.

This is a bit like saying there is a statistically significant correlation between lung cancer and heavy smoking. Some of the evil and attendant suffering in God's world has to do with our violation of the laws of our body and the natural world around us.

This understanding of the ravages of flood and disease has some validity, but only some. We know that one can play by the rules and still be assaulted by natural disasters and disease! The author of the *Book of Job* makes clear that we don't necessarily deserve our suffering. Job didn't. Job's friends may have thought he deserved his misfortune but God didn't think so.

Some would say the answer lies elsewhere: God has created

us as partners and much of the evil and suffering we experience is only a sign that the world is not yet fully what God intends it to be. We are God's partners in helping to make it so.

God's spirit empowers us to comfort the afflicted and to support research in the laboratories of the world to find a cure for their afflictions. When we feed the hungry we are God's partners and when we vastly increase the productivity of the soil we are helping to repair the brokenness of God's world. We can and do win significant victories: polio, a dreaded disease when I was growing up, is now under control. New medication has helped relieve depression.

And here is the paradox. The very incompleteness and brokenness of God's world, and God's need of us to help repair it, is the ground of our life's meaning. Behold all God's creation is very good, including the incompleteness, the brokenness thereof—for that very brokenness, that suffering, defines our sacred vocation in this world.

There is validity in this response too but also some danger for it may lead us to believe that most of life's suffering results simply from our having not yet fulfilled the potential of our partnership. We've not yet harnessed technology to fully master God's world. If and when we do there will be no more suffering and pain!

This view seems to suggest that someday we won't have to worry about body-crippling diseases; someday we won't have to worry about floods and other natural disasters. We will control the climate. In 1953, scientist Edward Teller actually proposed to President Eisenhower the possible use of atomic devices for changing the weather by changing the dust content of the air.

We worry about the Mississippi River run amok! We may need to worry more about human beings, especially scientists who feel that natural evil and suffering only signify that we have not yet attained ultimate technological mastery over the world.

Why stop with conquering floods and hurricanes? Why not conquer death? Some decades ago a professor at Columbia University contended that as long as we humans live with an expectation of death, we can't be happy. The professor envisaged the transformation of the human creature through computer technology into "conscious machines" that would defy death.

Alas, in our time the wisdom of Torah seems more compelling than ever. Remember, Adam and Eve eat from the Tree of Knowledge but they are not permitted to eat from the Tree of Life that will make them like God, ie., death-less beings. Indeed the very advances in our technology are already compelling us to acknowledge that death remains the price of life. Mortality and self-consciousness are the price of our humanity. Our failure to acknowledge death as part of life may only increase suffering, pain, and evil in our world.

In this age of artificial respirators—we are coming to appreciate that prolonging life by all means can mean we are only prolonging dying. Death comes not as an enemy but as friend, and the height of human wisdom is to come to terms with death as an inescapable part of human life.

Now we come closer to the most significant understanding of the problem of natural evil in God's world: suffering is simply the price of creation. An author whose name escapes me has written that "the very conditions that make human life possible and even pleasant make suffering inevitable . . . we are doomed to live in bodies that must eventually fail us and to love what we must inevitably lose." Part of the difficulty of believing in God is our inability to accept a world in which the very things we cherish must cause us pain as well as joy and happiness.

Some suffering is the price we pay for the cherished privilege of being human. In his book *Man's Best Hope*, Rabbi Roland Gittelsohn tells of a visit with some friends, Caroline and Alexander Magoon. He visited with them in the snow-covered hills of southern New Hampshire. The couple was grieving over the recent death of their thirty year old son.

Rabbi Gittelsohn writes: "Our second afternoon with Caroline and Alexander we had come in from an invigorating walk in the snow and were sitting around a blazing fire. We listened to uplifting music while Alexander read us paragraphs from the eulogy he had written for his son's funeral service. We shed tears as we listened, all of us without inhibition or shame. We tasted the full tragedy and beauty of life together. We were drawn closer than ever to each other and to God by the bonds of ineffable love."

Rabbi Gittelsohn adds: "I almost forgot, there was a fifth member of our circle, Caroline's cat was on her lap. The cat played with a piece of string all the while we were there. It shed no tears, suffered no pain and was aware of no evil, but it was also the only one of us which heard no music and was uplifted by no inspiration and felt no love."

The meditation we recite before the *Kaddish* (Mourner's Prayer) expresses a similar truth. "We could not have our sensitivity without fragility. Mortality is the tax we pay for the privilege of love, thought, creative work—the toll on the bridge of being ... just because we are human we are prisoners of the years."

That suffering we call grief is the price we pay for our love and all that we mean when we say: I love him, I love her, or she loves me. All that we mean by such love is tied to our being human and to be human is to be mortal.

What does it mean to accept God's judgment of creation as very good? It is to accept a God who wills the good for us but who creates a world in which there is necessarily both good and evil, joy and suffering. It is to believe that life is a package deal with good and evil inextricably intertwined. It is to believe that this package called life is worth its price.

Our religion not only affirms this faith but arms us in our quest to attain it. Sometime ago I met with a man in our congregation for whom I have the highest respect. He is a proud self-respecting Jew but, by his admission, his conscious relation to God has been under-developed. Chalk it up to a home that was not religious. But there is more. When he was a young man he experienced a tragic accident and the loss of a childhood sweetheart. Later, chronic emotional illness rendered his first wife no longer capable of relating to him or to others.

It seemed rationally impossible under such circumstances to believe in a God of power and love and so he tuned God out of his life. His life has been very satisfying in many ways, but he now feels he may be missing much by not opening himself to the religious dimension. What would I suggest? he asked.

Actually I suggested, among other things, that he take home a prayerbook and, as part of his early morning routine, that he recite a series of prayers which are full of praise and gratitude for God's gifts.

In those benedictions we praise and thank God for this day of restoring my soul and renewing my life. We thank God for the power to stand and walk and see and work and love and be loved.

The other day this man told me that he had been following my advice. He had been praying these prayers of praise and thanksgiving each morning before he went through his physical exercise routine and it felt good and he is just going to continue doing it. He is not sure where it will lead, but he feels embarked on an open-ended journey to deepen his spiritual life.

Why is it important to pause and count our blessings? Because of the human temptation to pray only prayers of asking for something at those times when we are aware of the pain and the unfulfilled yearnings in our life.

We can only move toward an acceptance of the words "and God saw all that He had made and behold it was very good"—we can only begin to accept the all of life and affirm that life is worth its price—if we lift to consciousness in a disciplined way all the good stuff in our lives.

The rabbis say a faithful Jew is obliged "to praise God for the evil as well as the good." I take that to mean an acceptance of the world and creation as a "package deal." But if we focus only on the pain and suffering and take for granted the good stuff unless it is gone, if we can only ask God for what we lack but cannot pause to thank God for what we have, we will be less able to affirm that life is worth its price or that life is very good.

Our tradition arms us for the faith journey in still another amazingly important way. We are called *Yisrael*—Israel for (like Jacob) we must wrestle and struggle for our faith. There will be times when we do not feel that life is worth its price. There are times when the words "Behold it is very good" stick in our craw.

The life of faith is a wrestling match, an engagement that will be punctuated with moments of anger, disappointment, and confusion. At times, we will feel God's distance or absence. Even then, we are bidden to hang in there, to live responsibly and do God's commandments even when we doubt the Giver; to pray even when we feel bitter thoughts, to hope for times when we will be able to re-affirm and experience God's nearness again— the God who is present in us through us and beyond us to relieve that suffering in creation which can be healed and lessened; the God who is present to help us cope with what we cannot change and to come to terms with suffering that is the price of creation.

Ultimately, we come to such moments not by solving cosmic mysteries or intellectualizing unanswerable questions but by wrestling with, living in the presence of and giving praise to the One who is the Source of being—so that we may be able to declare: "Life is a blessing. God's gift is worth its price. God's world is worth its price, *v'hinay tov me'od.*"

CHAPTER 12

The Three Dimensions
of a Spiritual Life

Jewish spirituality is rooted in faithfulness to an experience and a memory—the memory of a people who stood at Sinai and experienced the living presence of God. At Sinai the people Israel entered into a covenant with God. At Sinai Israel first heard the command: "Ye shall be holy." Let every sphere of your life bear witness to the reality of your covenant with God!

Spirituality is covenant-mindedness. It is a man acknowledging, in all his ways, a faith in the reality of his covenant with God. What are some of the dimensions of this covenant faith?

The covenant faith is, first of all, an attitude toward our own value as persons. It enables man to affirm: I am worth more than the chemicals in my body, more than my services or talents can command in the marketplace, more than the sum of my good deeds, more than the number of people who like me, more than the place or no place accorded me in man's social register. My worth measured by these standards is exceedingly ephemeral. Whenever any man, however ingenious his talents or weighty his relative accomplishments, contemplates his labors

Address given at the UAHC 48th Biennial,
San Francisco, California, November 1965

against the infinite backdrop of the universe on which he struts, these fruits of his hand and mind pale into paltry nothingness.

No wonder that even some of the greatest artists and statesmen have recorded in their diaries crises of self-evaluation, doubts concerning the significance of their acts and their labors. And when man, with all his flaunted and ever-increasing dominion over nature, ponders his prowess amid the span of the galaxies, what indeed is he? In the perspective of astronomy, Harlow Shapley reminds us, the destruction of our planet would be but "a local disturbance. Such an episode would leave the stars untouched and unconcerned."

Nor does man fare better when he is defined bio-chemically. In pre-Nazi Germany the following definition of man was popular: "The human being contains a sufficient amount of fat to make seven cakes of soap, enough iron to make a medium-sized nail, a sufficient amount of phosphorous to equip two thousand match-ends, enough sulfur to rid oneself of fleas."

We all know that a man's true sense of dignity is not always derivable from the posture with which he confronts the world. Some of modern man's most extravagant escapades in self-indulgence—whether in the conspicuous consumption of material goods, social status, sex, or alcohol—betray a pitiful compulsion to obscure or escape from a sense of worthlessness.

For the believing Jew self-respect is rooted in the covenant. There is a prayer in the daily liturgy which is also recited on the afternoon of Yom Kippur. It begins with the confession: "What are we, what is our life, what our righteousness, what our justice, what our virtue, what our power, what our heroism," and then the words, "from the beginning Thou hast distinguished man and hast recognized him so that he may stand before Thee." Hermann Cohen reminds us that this prayer is part of the *Amidah*, the standing prayer, and he concludes homiletically, "man has been appointed to stand before God."

Man is distinguished from other forms of creation, not uniquely by virtue of his intelligence but by virtue of his capacity to enter into a covenant with the Source of his being. Man feels at home in the universe only if his life bears witness to his kinship with his Creator.

We talk much of the *chutzpa* (brazenness) which the classic Jew displayed in relation to God: Abraham acknowledges that he is but dust and ashes, yet argues with his Creator on behalf of the people of Sodom. Jeremiah calls God a "deceiver" and Sholom Aleichem's Tevya prays in his hovel, "Blessed are they that dwell in Thy house" and then adds irreverently, "I take it, O Lord, Thy house is somewhat more spacious than mine."

The argument is significant. We argue with one whom we care for and have reason to believe cares or is capable of caring for us. The Jew's "lover's quarrel" with God was based on a faith in Him—a faith in God's covenant. The Jew's boldness in God's presence is Judaism's most fruitful symbol of man's dignity, a dignity rooted in the covenant faith that God is real and that God cares for me. The classic Jew's argument with God was far more spiritual than our polite invocation of Him.

This covenant-rooted sense of dignity has been the Jewish people's most formidable defense against the perils of history. One finds a secular hero of this faith in Saul Bellow's *Herzog*. The hero, hemmed in by dire circumstance, never completely surrenders his own sense of worth nor does he yield to the miasma of despair.

What is the source of this dignity? Of his family, Herzog says: "All the branches of the family have the cast madness of *yichus*. No life so barren and subordinate that it didn't have imaginary dignities, honors to come, freedom to advance." Herzog the Jew was rooted in a family (shall we say a people) that did not permit its sense of self-respect to be governed by the objective conditions of the moment. Even when the surrounding world disdainfully confined him to the ghetto, he dwelt there biding his time until the world would be ready to accept his precious treasures.

Herzog used the word *yichus*. The Yiddish meaning is "good stock." It comes from the Hebrew word for *relatedness*. What was the source of the historic Jew's indestructible dignity? It was his sense of "divine *yichus*"—his sense of living in relationship to God.

There is no adequate substitute for a self-image rooted in the faith that, as a rabbi put it, "I am a son of the King of the universe."

Is this sense of election an inexcusable arrogance? Only if one fails to add that so are all men. The sanctity of every human personality is rooted in a divine *yichus*. It stems from the faith that every man "has been appointed to stand before God."

■ ■ ■

A second dimension of Jewish spirituality defines an attitude toward time. Time is an awareness of our own mortality. Time is the sense of our "vanishing reality," or, as Dr. Langdon Gilkey put it, "the feeling that our existence is slipping ever more rapidly away from us into nothingness and we can do nothing about it."

Man's anxieties inspire the major themes for his laughter. So it is that we tire not of Jack Benny's classic jest. We laugh about our effort at age concealment because we regard the inexorable march of time as no laughing matter. The specter of time is especially ominous in our American culture. We place an ever-increasing premium on youth in our business executives, our presidents, and even our rabbis. But the sting of time is not peculiar to our day or age. Even in a society which respected its elders far more than we, the psalmist did still lament, "The days of our years are threescore years and ten, and if by reason of strength they be fourscore years, yet is their span labor and sorrow for it is soon cut off and we fly away."

Covenant faith does not enable us to elude the Angel of Death. It does offer a way to invest our fleeting days with abiding significance. We live our lives on different stages. The conditions which frame our existence are not the same for any of us. We may enjoy varying degrees of health and material wealth. We may be single or married or widowed. The events which intrude upon us are not the same nor are they often of our choosing. But though we cannot transcend time, we are able to answer for the time that is ours.

Martin Buber once wrote: "Each concrete hour (of time) allotted to the person is speech for the man who is attentive but the sounds of which the speech consists are the events of our personal, everyday lives. The words of our response are spoken in the speech of our doing and letting."

To whom do we answer? Ultimately to the God who created us. In all that we do with the time allotted to us we are answering for or against Him. Here then is the key to the significance of our lives. We cannot conquer time but we may sanctify it.

The classic introduction to Jewish prayer declares: *Baruch atah Adonai Elohenu Melech ha olam asher kidshanu*—"Praised be Thou, O Lord our God, ruling Spirit of the Universe, who hast sanctified us," who has rendered our lives significant *b'mitzvotav*—"by giving us commandments wherein we may respond to Thy will."

The reality of our covenant with our Creator, the reality of our power to serve Him or betray Him by our deeds, endows our mortal lives with their only significance. The most comprehensive term for a life which responds affirmatively to God's summons is *Kiddush Hashem*—the sanctification of God's name. It is the duty of a son and daughter of the covenant to sanctify God's name, to be loyal to Him in every sphere of life. This is our divine vocation.

At times this summons has required (as Akiba knew so well) the surrender of one's very life with the words of the *Shema* lingering on one's lips. But neither is death nor self-denial the only way of answering "yes" to the God of the covenant. As the rabbi says to the king in Judah Ha-Levi's classic: "Your contrition on fast days does not bring you nearer to God than your joy on the Sabbath and holidays if it be the outcome of a devout heart."

The range of responses by which a man-born Jew may be called upon to sanctify God's name is poignantly suggested in three words—words which sound alike and which stem from the same root: *Kadosh* (holy—sacred). I speak of the *Kaddish*, the *Kiddush*, and *Kiddushin*. A Jew reciting the *Kaddish* sanctifies God. He affirms trust in God's wisdom even in the presence of death. He affirms life's meaning in the presence of life's mysteries. He says "yes" to God even in his hour of grievous loss.

A Jew observing the Sabbath recites the *Kiddush*. He, too, sanctifies God. He bears witness that God is the Creator of the world and the Redeemer of the oppressed who desires that man pause to enjoy the fruit of his labors.

In the hour of their troth a bride and groom hear the rabbi proclaim: "Praised be Thou, O Lord, who sanctifies Thy people, Israel, through *Kiddushin* (the covenant of marriage). In their faithfulness to each other, bride and groom sanctify Him—say "yes" to Him by whose grace man and woman may become "beloved friends."

Of all the means by which a Jew is called upon to sanctify God, none is more crucial than his conduct toward his fellow-man. Commenting on the verse "thou shalt love the Lord, thy God," the rabbis explained, "May God's name be beloved because of you." As God's witnesses you have the power through acts of justice and love to reflect honor upon His name among those who do not acknowledge Him. By acts of injustice, you have the power to profane His Name. In our age of little faith this mandate is all the more compelling and significant.

Covenant faith is an attitude toward the time of our life. Either life degenerates into a futile race against time or our life pulsates with the saving truth: "Praised be Thou, O Lord, who hast made our fleeting life significant by enabling us to do something for Thee." Life's significance, said Leo Baeck, derives from "the consciousness of being able to give an answer every day, a personal answer to God."

■ ■ ■

The covenant faith not only affirms an attitude toward self and time, it affirms a vision of the world—the space—in which we spend or expend the time of our lives. The strident dissonance and radical disarray of our world has driven many a mortal to echo the sentiments of Dostoevski's Ivan: "I don't accept this world of God's although I know it exists. I don't accept it at all. It's not that I don't accept God, you must understand, it's the world created by Him I don't and cannot accept."

Yet it is of this world of ours, this world racked by racial and political conflict, this world imperiled by over-population and nuclear annihilation, this world in which innocent children are plagued by disease, and innocent men struck down by disaster— it is of this world that God said, "And behold it is good." This declaration embodies the third dimension of Jewish spirituality.

What can this faith mean? In the Biblical story God creates every beast of the field and every bird of the air, but it is man's task to name them, and "whatever man called every living creature that was its name." Harvey Cox of Harvard Divinity School reminds us that "the Hebrew naming did not mean simply attaching an arbitrary label. It meant conferring on something its meaning and significance." We are thrust into an unfinished world. We are summoned to answer God's call for covenant, for partnership. We are called upon truly to share in fulfilling the promise of creation.

But under what conditions do we labor? Are we like Sisyphus condemned to push a large boulder to the top of the hill only to have it roll down, so that in an eternal cycle we may begin again and again?

No, the world is not a tormenting trick. The cards are not stacked against man as in a Greek tragedy. The aces are in the deck. God is forever creating opportunities for man to share in forming order out of chaos, good out of evil, light out of darkness. Covenant faith proclaims: Man is able to answer the challenge of life and God's world is responsive to man's answer.

Even our folk humor betrays this world view. There is the story of a Catholic, a Protestant, and a Jew who have been apprised of an impending tidal wave. The Catholic and Protestant pray for God's miraculous intervention. The Jew concludes soberly, "We'll just have to learn to breathe under water."

This bit of humor reveals not so much a skepticism of God's redemptive power as a bold confidence in the essential congruity between man's basic needs and the world's possibilities.

Genesis promises man dominion over nature. If we use our God-given powers in a world created by Him, "we shall overcome."

For this reason, too, the believing Jew, contrary to the prevailing mood of our time, does not call the world "absurd." An echo of this spirit is again found in Saul Bellow's *Herzog*. At one point Herzog, who himself dangles perilously over the abyss of breakdown, chides a boyhood friend. The friend is a Jewish intellectual who in print and at cocktail parties persistently bemoans the dismal prospects of mankind. Herzog writes his friend a letter, saying, "I can't accept this foolish dreariness. We are talking about the whole life of mankind. The subject is too great, too deep for such weakness, cowardice. Too deep, Shapiro, you were too intelligent for this. You inherited rich blood. Your fathers peddled apples."

Herzog's fathers were nourished on the *Talmudic midrash* which compares man to a king's son who has strayed from home and is lost in an eerie forest. The king sends a messenger to remind the lad of a path leading out of the forest, to assure him that if he will but turn toward that path his father will meet him.

God has not set us in a world whose paths are all lurid labyrinths, say the rabbis. There is a path of promise. Man, who has been endowed with the power to unleash the atom, has been endowed with the power to control it. The God who grants man safe walks in outer space does not deny him the power to build cities where men of different colors may live together in justice and peace.

New challenges will ever beset us. We shall ever be called to move from where we are to where we ought to be. This is the meaning of the *mitzvah*, of the divine summons to man which is heard until the end of history. The world in which we live remains unredeemed but brimming with promise. By God's grace our challenges do not exceed our powers. The world is not absurd. If we move toward the path which God has set, we shall be met.

■ ■ ■

The Jewish view of the spiritual life is rooted in this

covenant faith. It is a threefold faith. (1) I am sacred because I have been "appointed to stand before God." This is the sanctification of self. (2) My fleeting days are significant by virtue of my power to do something for or against God. This is the sanctification of time. (3) God's world is brimming with promise if man will fulfill the conditions of his covenant with his Creator. This is the sanctification of space.

The reality of the covenant is a faith to live by, not a hypothesis which may be empirically validated. When the ancient Israelites threatened to worship Baal, the prophet Elijah asked for an unmistakable demonstration of Baal's impotence and God's supreme power. "Lord God of Abraham, Isaac, and Jacob, give proof this day that Thou art the Lord God . . . and art calling their hearts back to Thee."

According to the Biblical historian, Elijah's pleas were answered. The bulls brought to the altar by the prophets of Baal remained untouched, but a divine fire consumed Elijah's offering, and we are told: "the whole people fell face to earth and raised a cry, 'It is the Lord who is God, it is the Lord who is God.'"

Have the tests of God's being and the covenant's reality ever been that compelling? Hardly. Else most men would, out of prudence if not virtue, be faithful witnesses to God's majesty. Alas, we are fond of quoting a more subtle and ambiguous incident of divine self-revelation. It was of the selfsame Elijah that we read: ". . . And a great and strong wind rent the mountains and broke in pieces the rocks before the Lord, but the Lord was not in the wind: and after the wind an earthquake, but the Lord was not in the earthquake; and after the earthquake a fire, but the Lord was not in the fire; and after the fire, a voice of gentle silence . . ."

The vindication of our faith is more like a voice of gentle silence than a dramatic spectacle of fire. The covenant has hidden clauses. The life of sanctification is to be embraced or rejected in freedom. Each generation must struggle to hear the call: "Where art thou?" Each must choose to answer: "Here am I, send me."

SECTION III

A Good
Teaching

CHAPTER 13

The Land of
No Second Chances

Larry Fineman's room was filled with toys and books and games that any six year old boy would love. But Larry was only interested in his racing cars. He had them in all shapes and sizes and in every color of the rainbow. Larry loved to race them against each other, to compare their designs and to sort them into groups by color, size or speed.

One day, while Larry was sorting his race cars, he noticed that one was missing. It was one of his favorite cars, a bright red Ferrari that had a yellow racing stripe down the middle. He looked under his bed, behind a stack of blocks in his closet, and even in the pockets of his favorite pair of blue jeans. The red Ferrari was nowhere to be found.

Later that day, after Larry had turned the house upside down in search of his favorite car, the doorbell rang. Larry's best friend, Mark, was standing at the door with the missing car in his outstretched palm.

"Where'd you get that?" Larry asked Mark. "I borrowed it when we were playing yesterday," Mark answered nervously. He could tell that Larry was angry. "I just wanted to show it to my brother. It's so cool." "You stole it!" Larry shouted. "I never gave you permission to take that car!" "Well, I didn't think you'd mind. I guess I wasn't thinking," Mark said. Larry grabbed the car out of Mark's hand. "I'm never playing with you again. Ever! You're a big awful thief!"

"I wasn't going to keep it," Mark said. "Really. Please forgive me. I'm so sorry."

Larry glared at him. "No way! I don't forgive you!" And he slammed the door in Mark's face.

Larry returned the Ferrari to the box that held all the rest of the race cars. He started to play with them but he wasn't in the mood. He was angry and upset for the rest of the day.

At bedtime his mother tucked him in and gave him a kiss. "Can't you turn that frown upside down?" she asked. "You look miserable."

"I am miserable," Larry told her. "I have my red car back but my best friend is an awful, stealing, jerk!"

"Don't you think you could give Mark another chance?" asked Larry's mom.

"Never! No way! Why should I?" Larry said and he closed his eyes and tried to fall asleep and forget the whole bad day.

Suddenly, Larry was in a car with his mom driving down the freeway. His mother was trying to find the exit sign so she could get off. "Oh no," his mom said, "I guess I missed the exit."

"Don't worry mom. We'll just take the next exit and turn around and go back." But Larry and his mom kept driving and driving and there were no more exit signs. Then Larry saw a huge neon sign hanging over the freeway up ahead of them. As they got closer they could tell that the sign said: Welcome to the Land of No Second Chances: If you missed the exit . . . tough! Keep driving!

A few miles later there was an exit marked: Land of No Second Chances. "We better get off here," Larry's mother said, "or we might be on this freeway forever."

The next thing Larry knew, he was in an unfamiliar class-room. All the kids were sitting at their desks taking a test. He looked down at his desk and there was a copy of the test, but he didn't understand any of the questions.

Larry raised his hand, and the teacher walked over to his desk. "What's the problem, son?" she asked in a harsh whisper.

"What happens if I fail this test?" Larry asked. "You'll just repeat the first grade next year," she answered.

"Just for one test? I never even learned this stuff. Can't I take it again later?"

"No way. Never. Not here, young man. This is the Land of No Second Chances!" and the teacher hurried back to her desk.

Larry raised his hand again. This time the teacher signaled for Larry to come to her. "Now what, son?" she asked in an agitated voice. "I just wondered if I could have a pencil with an eraser so I could correct my mistakes."

The teacher stood up with a grin on her face and addressed the class. "Children, would you like to hear something funny? This new boy, Larry, wants a pencil with an eraser!"

The whole class started laughing, first little giggles and then huge loud chortles and guffaws. Larry felt the tears start to gather in the corners of his eyes. "What's so funny?" he asked.

"Our pencils have no erasers," said the teacher. "This is the Land of No Second Chances. You aren't supposed to make mistakes!"

"I'm getting out of here," Larry screamed as he ran out of the classroom as fast as his feet would go. He ran down the hall, turned the corner and kept on running until he came head-to-head with a little girl and they both fell to the floor.

"What's your problem?" the little girl shrieked at Larry. "Are you blind? I was right in front of you!"

"I'm sorry," Larry said. "I was in a hurry. I didn't mean to hurt you. Honest. Will you please forgive me?"

"Not a chance," said the girl as she readjusted her barrette and gathered her books and papers. "We don't forgive here! I'm never going to play with you and I'm going to tell everyone else not to play with you also! So there!"

Larry stood up and started running again. "I've got to find

the door ... I've got to get out of here. I need to get home," he thought.

Just then, Larry felt a light tap on his shoulder. "Shhh. Wake up Larry. I'm here. You must've had a bad dream." Larry opened his eyes and hugged his mother. "It was awful," he told her. "I was in the Land of No Second Chances and I couldn't leave."

"That was just a silly old nightmare," said his mom. "Now get up and get dressed. It's time to go to Temple. We don't want to be late for Yom Kippur services."

Larry jumped into his clothes and ran next door to Mark's house. When Mark answered the door, Larry handed him the red Ferrari.

"What's this for?" Mark asked. "I want you to borrow it. I'm sorry I got so mad. Please say you'll forgive me. I know you didn't mean to steal it. Can we please still be friends?"

"Sure," said Mark. "But why are you so upset?"

"I just don't ever want to go back to the Land of No Second Chances!" said Larry.

"The Land of what?" asked Mark.

"Never mind. I'll tell you all about it later. Let's go to Temple!"

———

I am grateful to my daughter, Rachel Karff Weissenstein, for adapting an oral story into a written text.

CHAPTER 14

Coming Home

Can it really be that another year has passed? Must be! The *shofar*, the raised pulpit, the double service; a New Year is upon us. And as I look out upon some of you this night, I know that the past year has been a *Shanah Tovah*, a good year. For others it has been a very difficult one. Whatever the prevailing mood we bring to this place at this time, we are here and our presence is a statement: I am a Jew. A Jew should be in the synagogue to hear the sound of the *shofar* on Rosh Hashanah.

What does it mean to be a Jew beyond feeling some tug to this place on this day? For one thing it means responding as an insider to such stories as this: Sadie goes to her travel agent and asks for a ticket to a remote corner of the world. The agent tries to discourage her: "Sadie, it is a twenty-four hour plane trip, a twelve hour train ride, a full day's journey in a cart up torturous mountain roads. You don't want to go there."

Sadie insists: "Get me my ticket." Twenty-four hours later she is in India, twelve hours later in the Himalayas; after a full day's journey by cart she reaches the remote village and is greeted by the leader, who asks the purpose in her coming.

Sermon, Rosh Hashanah Eve, September 7, 1983

Sadie explains: "I've come to see your guru." The leader responds: "Our guru doesn't see anyone without an appointment. Is he expecting you?"

"No."

"What's your name?"

"Sadie Schwartz."

"Well, I'll try but don't be disappointed if the answer is 'no.'"

An hour later the leader of the village returns and announces with some surprise: "The guru will see you but remember, in his presence, you may speak only three words, only three words, is that clear?"

"Yes." So Sadie is brought before the guru. She looks into his dark, penetrating eyes and she says: "Sheldon, come home."

To be a Jew is to respond to this story with a peculiarly poignant chuckle, or smile, or even a tear. For wherever we are coming from and wherever we are at (even if we come to this place but twice a year) we want our children and grandchildren to be Jews. Never mind our children or grandchildren, what about us? Oh, there is no danger of our abandoning our Jewishness. But for some, perhaps many of us, the covenant remains relatively at the margin of our lives. Don't most of us have some coming home to do? In this season of spiritual leverage, when we are more open, when we hold before us the model of a fuller, more authentic life, let us think less of Sheldon than of Sadie, less of our children than of us.

We begin with the word *mitzvah*. If I asked you "what is a *mitzvah*?" most of you would answer "it's a good deed." A *mitzvah* includes good deeds but its full meaning is much deeper. *A mitzvah is something you feel commanded to do, something you feel you ought to do because you are a Jew.* For most of us being here tonight is not a good deed, but it is a *mitzvah*. Most of us would feel uncomfortable if we did not appear in this place on Rosh Hashanah. Some of you may have been so tired after a full day's work today that a part of you did not want to get off that easy chair, turn off the TV, and come here, but you felt you ought to. You, a Jew, ought to be here at the turning of the year.

There can be no responsible, no authentic Judaism unless we feel some sense of ought, unless we feel the claim of some *mitzvah*. If we simply manipulate the Torah to suit our every whim or convenience, we are not taking our Judaism seriously. "You shall not go astray after your own eyes and heart. . . . You shall be holy." You are *commanded* to keep certain promises, to do certain deeds.

What should be a *mitzvah* for you and me? What claims should we acknowledge and respond to? Because we're Reform Jews that is not an easy question. I can offer you no detailed prescription. To be Reform means you're the quarterbacks, calling your own Jewish signals. I am, at best, the coach who provides you with the structure of plays, a guiding framework within which each of you must make your judgment. But aren't there limits on the freedom of any quarterback who would play the game responsibly? And aren't there limits on a Reform Jew who would live Judaism responsibly? So on this night when you are my captive congregation let me suggest some guidelines for coming home again. Let me share the standards by which I, a Reform Jew, judge the fullness of my own Judaism and yours.

THE ETHICAL MITZVOT

First, we must turn to our heritage for the ethical *mitzvot* of our life, for our answers to the question: what do I owe other persons in my life because I am a Jew?

An easy example: *tzedakah*. We live under that commandment. Most of us already acknowledge that it is a *mitzvah* to help those who are in need whether they be Jews or non-Jews. We may need to apply the *mitzvah* to a specific case or cause or project, but it wasn't difficult mobilizing generous support in this congregation for a program to feed the hungry in Houston. Most of you felt it was something you ought to do because you are a Jew. We are about to organize an effort to help those in our congregation who are victims of the recession and are in need of employment. Again, many of you will respond to the call as a *mitzvah*.

The imperative of *tzedakah* is self-evident. Acts of righteousness to help those in need are a part of our Jewish repertoire. But what about consciously turning to Torah for guidance in the other ethical judgments of our lives? What ought you do or not do and under what circumstances when you are considering an abortion? Or when you consider requesting that artificial life support systems be removed from a loved one's bed? Or when you are considering whether or not to transfer a parent to the Jewish Home for the Aged, or when you are considering selling flawed merchandise to a customer who is not fully aware of its problems? What ought I do or not do because I am a Jew? What is a *mitzvah*?

Judaism's judgments may not always be explicit and specifically applicable and they may not all be acceptable, but *it is a mitzvah to turn to my heritage for guidance, to search within it, to wrestle with it for the ethical directions of my life.*

Rabbi Harvey Fields tells of a Jewish professor who was speaking to a group in Toronto on a very controversial subject. He so exasperated one of the women in the audience that she interrupted him by saying, "Can you prove that statement?" The professor was so flustered, so angry that he responded by putting down the interrupter with a slashing verbal flourish. She cringed visibly. He continued with his talk for a few moments. Then he stopped suddenly, left the podium, placed his hand on the woman's shoulder and said: "The Torah teaches me that a person who insults another publicly must seek forgiveness, please forgive me." He returned to the podium. The audience was stunned by this gesture.

If we would come home to a fuller expression of Judaism, we need to feel the authority of Torah in our relation to other persons. We need to find more occasions when we can say, "The Torah teaches me ..."

LIVING BY JEWISH TIME
AND BEARING PUBLIC WITNESS

I said earlier that *mitzvah* is more than a good deed. It is also more than a good deed we feel commanded to do. It is a *mitzvah* to be here tonight. Why? Because it is a *mitzvah* to live by Jewish time. If we would come home again we should respect and observe the sacred times of the Jewish year, whether or not our children are at home. (That may be the most crucial test.) It is a *mitzvah* to sanctify the times of our personal lives in a Jewishly recognizable way: birth, coming of age, love and death.

Let's speak for a moment about responding to that moment of life called death. It is a *mitzvah* to mourn our dead. We Reform Jews rebelled against the elaborate prescriptions of the tradition for mourning. We found them too extensive, too rigid, too insensitive to our own particular needs and situations and temperament. As I have observed over the years I think many of us have strayed too far in the other direction. We have under-ritualized our response to death. We have been too cerebral, too philosophical. We have rushed back to our normal routine at times too quickly. We have cheated ourselves of an important support system. We have neglected to take seriously enough the healing *mitzvah* of mourning.

Again, as Reform Jews we will not necessarily feel impelled to do all that is prescribed as it is prescribed. We won't observe our Sabbaths or do our mourning in an identical manner; some less, some more. There is room for individualization or innovation without feeling guilty. *But it is a mitzvah to sanctify the times of the Jewish year and the times in our personal lives in a way that testifies: I am a Jew; that is what a Jew ought to do.*

Coming home again to a more full-bodied Judaism means also that we accept what I like to call the *mitzvah of public witness*. It is a *mitzvah* to publicly proclaim our membership in the Jewish people and to acknowledge the Jewish community's claim upon us. A strictly private Jew, a "cardiac Jew" (a Jew at heart) is a contradiction in terms.

I was annoyed recently by a Jewish man Joan and I encountered, who proudly told me that he's against organized religion, will have nothing to do with the synagogue; he doesn't believe in that stuff. Then, in the course of conversation, he admitted that he hoped his grandchildren would be Jews and he had respect for Jewish values. I think of a person who feels very Jewish until members of the Jewish community expect her to be a supporter of the United Jewish Campaign. Now granted, the only thing two Jews agree on is what the third should give to the campaign, still it is my obligation to be a visible, supportive member of the Jewish community. It is part of the *mitzvah* of bearing public witness.

THE OBLIGATION TO STUDY

There is just one other *mitzvah* that I would add to my guidelines. In the Talmud we are told that there are certain acts which, if you do them, you get a reward in this world and an even greater reward in the world-to-come. Now that's something! Those acts must signify something about the Jewish value system. It's a small list. What are the acts that are included? Honoring parents, practicing lovingkindness, hospitality to strangers, visiting the sick, being sure no bride is denied a dowry, that every person gets a decent burial, and being a peacemaker. But the very last phrase proclaims that "the study of Torah exceeds them all."

How can the study of Torah be greater than all these other wonderful acts? Because, say the rabbis, Torah study is more than an intellectual exercise. At its best it lifts to consciousness who we are and what we ought to do. And so ideally the study of Torah will lead to all the other acts. For Reform Jews the *mitzvah* of continuing study is even more crucial. Since we insist on our freedom to choose our style of Jewish life, since we insist on the priority of conscience, let our conscience be informed.

Those of us who want to come home again, to place Judaism more at the center of our lives, will resolve this year to accept the *mitzvah* of some Jewish study: by the books we read, or the Sabbath Torah Study hour, our new Center for Jewish Enrichment program, or any kind of program which opens us continually to our covenant and its meaning for us.

WHO COMMANDS US?

I've spoken of *mitzvah*, of what we ought to do because we are Jews; but whose *mitzvah*, whose commands do we seek to discover and live by? We read on this night: "O Lord, our God, when we lie down and when we rise up, we will meditate on Your Torah and *mitzvot* forever."

Why then have I spoken of *mitzvah* without even mentioning belief in God? That's very Jewish. We Jews start with deeds and end with theology. We don't box each other into a theological corner. We don't say: "Do you believe such and such about God? If not, you are not a good Jew."

The rabbis portrayed God as saying: "Would that My children forsook Me and observed My commandments, for by observing My commandments they will come to experience Me." By living under the covenant, by doing the ethical commandment, by observing our Sabbaths and Passovers and Rosh Hashanah, by doing our rejoicing and seeking our comfort in a Jewish way, by bearing public witness to our membership in the Jewish people, by studying Torah we will come to experience God's presence in our lives.

I believe that, but I also believe that too many of us have become complacent citizens of a so-called secular age. Let's admit it. We find it awkward to speak about God. We may talk about our covenant with fellow Jews, about Torah, about *mitzvah*, about helping Israel much more easily than we are likely to talk among ourselves or to our children about the role of God in our lives.

Many of the Sheldons and Shellies who have joined the cults have been asked at one time or another: Why? And so many of them have responded that while growing up Jewishly in Hebrew school in the synagogue they sensed a lack of spirituality. They felt they had to seek elsewhere for what seemed absent in their own homes or in the synagogue.

Well, it's not missing. It simply has not been adequately tapped. Oh, we modern Jews have our support systems, the self-help books, the fifty-minute therapy hour, the rational mind for problem-solving, the persons who really care for us when we hurt and who truly rejoice in our good fortune. At their best these support systems are part of God's good gifts, but they do not fully embody or satisfy our hunger for God's presence in our lives.

I believe there are at least moments in all of our lives when we have been overcome by a trembling wonder at the mystery of being (the fact that we are, that we exist); moments when we felt a throbbing gratitude for unearned gifts; moments when we felt commanded from a source deep within us and beyond us; moments when we felt our world collapsed under us and we cried out in despair (perhaps the truest form of prayer) and somehow found strength, a nurturing power, a "courage to be," and yes, moments when we walked totally alone through a valley of shadows and felt somehow that we were not alone.

These moments don't happen all the time; they may not happen frequently. They are not predictable. They can't be programmed experimentally but they are part of our human experience if we do not repress or ignore or dismiss them because we are afraid of playing the fool.

On this our first night together at the turning of the year, I pray that we may be less concerned with our children's life as Jews than with our own. Let this be a year when we come home again. (And who among us does not have some coming home to do?)

Let us recover and expand our sense of *mitzvah*, the awareness of the things we ought to do because we are Jews. And let us open ourselves to the source of *mitzvah*, the mysterious One who gives us life, who summons us to its tasks; the One who empowers us to face the uncertainties of the future with dignity, with hope, and with the assurance that beyond the mystery there is meaning.

CHAPTER 15

Toward a Life of Significance

Yom Kippur, the holiest day in the Jewish year. This day our religion pulls out all the stops. We spend long periods of time in this room. We listen to the *Kol Nidre* melody. We confess our sins. We hold a special service to reflect on those whose life has ended. Many of us fast. It is a heavy time if we take it seriously.

So what is supposed to happen? What are we to think about? Feel? Become? A visitor from another planet who observed what we say and do in this room would get a certain picture: These are Jews. They are part of a community in relationship with God. They call that relationship a covenant.

They believe that by following this covenant they serve God and fulfill their sacred vocation—their purpose in life. So they want to express regret for their failures, renew their commitment and become reconciled (be at one with God).

Community, covenant, commitment, sacred vocation. Thus speak the prayers. My distant ancestor, Rabbi Pinchas of Koretz, could stand before his congregation and take it for granted that they "dug those words." I cannot. We recite the prayers, but you and I are also part of a different world. We were born in the

---

Sermon, Yom Kippur Eve, September 26, 1985

West—after the 18th century. We live in America at the end of the 20th century.

We are accustomed to a different vocabulary. We start not with God and covenant and vocation and calling. We start with you and me in search of personal fulfillment. From the moment of birth to death our culture teaches us to be preoccupied with filling our needs.

We are individuals endowed by our Creator with inalienable rights and among these rights are life, liberty and the pursuit of happiness. We are, first of all, in covenant with ourselves. All other covenants, whether with God or humans, all other arrangements (including marriage) are justified by their fulfilling our needs. Entrepreneurs spend billions of dollars to tell us and sell us what we need to look well, to feel well, to be successful, to be happy.

We may enter therapy to get in touch with our feelings, and to learn to love ourselves and be more assertive of our needs. We will join organizations, including this synagogue, and remain members as long as it meets our needs.

Is this profile familiar? A new study of the American character by five leading sociologists, a study called "Habits of the Heart" says that's where the American middle and upper middle class is. We see ourselves as individuals committed to fulfilling our needs.

The authors note that we ourselves do have generous impulses. We do care for others and help others from time to time. But if we are asked why, "Why did you do that?" We respond: "I felt like it" or , "It makes me feel good" or , "I needed to." We use the language of self-fulfillment.

We do not say "I did it because that's what I am here for, it's part of my covenant. We are put on earth to be of use, to help others." Such a response would seem corny, pretentious, weird. The language of obligation, commitment, (the language of our prayerbook) is strange. It does not come easily to our lips.

So what is wrong with seeing everything—(even the kind acts we do) as a way of meeting our needs, making us feel good, making us happy? If we look around us we will find the casualties of this mindset.

One of the greatest casualties is that human relationship we call marriage. The divorce rate in our society is staggering. True, some marriages *should* end. And it is a blessing that they can be terminated these days without social stigma. True, those marriages that do work today have more of a sense of intimacy and communication of feelings than those of a generation ago.

But one of the reasons so many marriages don't work today is that there is no firm commitment to the other person and little commitment to the relationship as such. There's no sense that staying together has any purpose beyond the satisfaction of each person's individual needs. If you view a relationship only in terms of the ratio of personal cost to benefit, inevitably one or another partner will wake up someday and decide the marriage is not cost effective. "I'm giving more than I'm getting." Such a mindset is not conducive to the permanent binding of two individuals or the preservation of the family unit.

Mary Gordon, a gifted American writer has a new novel. She writes of Ann, a young married woman who finds herself driven in many directions, including an interest in a man other than her husband and a strong desire to be successful in her professional career. She struggles with her impulses, with all the possibilities and options. Ann attains sudden clarity when she realizes that she deeply cares for her husband, and that (here are the author's words) "the whole shape of her life must be constructed to make her children safe."

That seems so unmodern. We know that couples shouldn't stay together for the sake of the children! Some of our parents, we think, did that and it didn't work. But here's the point: virtually all marriages have rough spots and such rough spots can only be weathered if the marriage is more than simply an arrangement to meet our personal needs. Most marriages can only be sustained if we have a commitment to the other person, and a commitment to the family as family; if we see the marriage as more than just a vehicle for each party's self-realization.

Marriage is not the only casualty of our cultural mindset. Civic responsibility is also imperiled. We find it difficult to give of ourselves to a cause in steadfast commitment. Ours is usually a very limited, conditional investment. We support an organization only as long as it meets our needs, for sociability, or honor, or as long as it is fun to be part of. When anything arises that frustrates our needs we disengage from the cause. That cause may still need us and is intrinsically worthy, but that does not matter. What matters is that we no longer need the cause.

Another casualty of the self-fulfillment—meet-our-needs—mindset is the sense of community. Our investment in any community is very tentative and provisional. We can't permit ourselves to get too emotionally involved, with our neighborhood or our neighbors. We may not know who they are--we play it cool. We have to keep our options open for we may have to disengage. We may have to move on to meet our needs. No wonder Americans report an increasing feeling of isolation and loneliness.

The greatest thing wrong with the "meeting our needs" mindset is that it doesn't really meet our needs. Think of most of the truly fulfilled persons you and I have known; better yet—think of the most fulfilled moments in our own lives. They have not been moments when we were consciously preoccupied with meeting our needs, but times when we were gripped by a cause that took us out of ourselves. We felt needed by another person and we felt we were serving a purpose beyond the confines of our ego.

The truth is that we cannot be happy if we do not live for something higher than our own happiness. Some of the most bored and boring people I know have nothing or no one to give themselves to. They spend the day pursuing and consuming a variety of pleasures, but their souls remain very hungry.

In view of all we have experienced in recent years—the threat to the integrity of the family, the erosion of civic responsibility, the increase in loneliness and isolation, the fact that the most popular neurotic syndrome is no longer guilt but depression—in view of all this, it is time to question our culture's obsessive preoccupation with "meeting our needs" and self-ful-fillment and the calculated pursuit of happiness.

Dr. Larch, the hero of John Irving's novel, *The Cider House Rules*, runs an orphanage in Maine. Again and again he speaks of the importance of being of use. He has taught his protégé that more important than to be happy is to be of use. Why? Because happiness, viewed as intense, physical and emotional pleasure, is a very fleeting experience. The deeper, more abid-ing well-being comes from the sense that we are of use, that our life serves some purpose.

We say to our children: "All that I want for you is that you be happy. Find happiness!" I've come to question that formu-lation. That's not the way our tradition really looks at life. Happiness is not something to aim at, pursue and find. It is, at best, the by-product of a purposeful, meaningful life. The core commandment of our Torah is not "You shall be happy—but "You shall be holy"—You shall lead a life of significance.

When a newborn child is welcomed into our community at the *bris* or naming ceremony, we pray that the child will be initi-ated into the study of Torah, *chuppah* (marriage), and good deeds.

Those words always get to me. I am deeply touched and strangely exhilarated. Here the infant, sometimes only a week or so old, cradled in parent's arms, goo-gooing or spitting up, or struggling to focus the eyes, surrounded by admiring family and friends, totally dependent at this stage on parents for his/her own needs and we express the hope that in time this little bun-dle of life will grow into a person, a *mensch*, capable of under-standing and accepting the responsibility of life (Torah); that she will find a fitting helpmate with whom to build a home based on the values of our heritage (*chuppah*), and that in her lifetime this child will have ample opportunity to perform good deeds. Oh, what a strong message is conveyed at that moment, not to the infant but to the rest of us.

Judaism certainly speaks of our fundamental human needs. Our tradition is neither ascetic, other-worldly, or joyless but when it does address our earthly needs they are linked to the larger purpose of our life. Take physical health for example. Oh how we Jews value health. We say again and again, if you're got health, you've got everything. In greeting each other for the New Year, more than anything, we are likely to wish each other good health. The Jewish tradition itself places great emphasis on health.

But the traditional prayers for health often include the thought: "Make me well, O Lord, sustain me in health, O Lord, that I may be able to serve You." Living an additional week or month or year in good health is not an end in itself. Health is an opportunity to live well, to fulfill the purpose for which I was created. To be of use, to serve, to make a difference for good.

I am aware that some of you are much imbued with a sense of life as vocation. Indeed some of you need to be reminded that part of the vocation includes taking care of yourself—not giving more than you are able—and in counseling I have felt it my rabbinic duty to remind you of this. And I would like to think that there are at least moments when all of us have lived life as sacred vocation, moments when we serve an organization not because it is fashionable or chic but because it is worthy and needs us; moments when we visit a person confined to home or hospital, not in search of recognition or pleasure, but because we are needed; moments when we have reached out beyond the consumption of life's goodies to ease the pain or distress of another soul because we felt we ought to; moments in our marriages when we were tempted to act out urges but resisted, not because we feared we might get caught, but because we realized the act would hurt someone we love or destroy our marriage covenant or hurt our children.

At such times we have been closest to what life is really all about or intended to be. But on this night of truth let us admit that many of us and our children have been too mezmerized by the dominant credo of our culture. Meeting our needs, pursuit of happiness and self-fulfillment have been the operative slogans of our lives. When we survey the sterile landscape and count the casualties we have to question the adequacy of this vision. This is a night for such questioning and re-appraisal.

The hallmark of these twenty-four hours is a fast. Not to keep our weight under control but to place some restrictions on the impulse to immediate self-gratification; to reaffirm that we are here to serve a purpose beyond ourselves—that there is more to life than life itself!

The prayerbook uses a vocabulary different from the one to which we have grown accustomed. On this night of nights let us return to the words of our prayers and what they represent. If we must speak of fulfilling needs, let us take our cue from Martin Buber who reminds us: "You need God in order to be and God needs you for the very meaning of your life."

How do we become aware of and respond to God's needs? Through our awareness of being needed by other persons. Their need is the sign of God's need. Our response to their need is our answer to God's need.

We are here tonight to be reminded, "We need God in order to be and God needs us for the very meaning of our lives."

Baruch ata Adonai. Praised be Thou O Lord, *asher kidshanu*— Who has made our lives significant, *b'mitzvotov*—by giving us acts to do so that we may be of use in this world."

CHAPTER 16

Ꝛope

It is hard to realize that this is my 39th Rosh Hashanah morning sermon since ordination. For most of those years I have preached on the same story we read from the Torah today. I'd like to think no two of those sermons have been the same or, as one of you put it, "always the same but always different."

As we read the story this year I want to focus more on Sarah than Abraham and I want to speak about that precious thing we call hope. We cannot live without some hope. Earlier in the Torah we read of Abraham and Sarah going forth from Ur of the Chaldees to the land of Canaan. And the Torah says, "Now Sarah was barren, she had no child." Here we are dealing with hope in one of the primary contexts of life, the desire for a child. Human desire begins with a sense of absence. It begins with someone or something missing. Desire is the seed bed of hope. In our time we have a different understanding of the physical dynamics of fertility and infertility and we know that the hope for a child may also be fulfilled through adoption.

For Sarah, the hope of motherhood rested on conceiving, and by the time she was promised she would conceive she

---

Sermon, Rosh Hashanah Morning, September 25, 1995

greeted the promise with great skepticism and a self-mocking laughter. Sarah had given up hope. When she does conceive, the laughter of self-mockery is transformed into the laughter of hope restored. In fact Sarah will name her son *Yitzhak* which means laughter.

When we speak of hope we also speak of faith. Faith is trust that God remains actively and lovingly present in our lives despite appearances to the contrary. Hope is based on that trust. Interestingly enough the Hebrew word for hope is *tikvah* which literally means to wait expectantly. When we hope we pray for something that we know is beyond our power alone to bring about. That is why hope includes expectant waiting and prayer. But to live with hope is also to act and to do all that is in our power to help bring something about. When we hope we not only wait and pray, we act. If we have lost hope, we neither pray nor act.

The opposite of hope is despair. Hope is often a struggle against despair because life is a struggle. Life tests us, it challenges us, it demands that we leave the comfort of the known for the unknown. Life always denies us final victory. Life does not permit us to freeze precious moments, to hold on to what we now have and love and cherish.

HOPE AND EIGHTH GRADE FOOTBALL

Hope is a necessity and a struggle because in every life there is a sense of absence, something we want but do not have, or something we have but cannot hold on to.

My summer neighbor in northern Michigan is Tim Shields. In the winter, back home in Indiana, Tim coaches eighth grade football. Last season his son Kelly was on the team. Tim told me this story with much relish. It was the last game of the season and the winner would claim the championship. It was the last play of the game and the other team had the ball near the goal line. If Tim's team held them they would win the game and the championship. If not, they would lose.

What happened? Tim's son Kelly tackled the runner of the other team and kept him from scoring. The game was over. Tim and Kelly's team were champions. The winning teammates were ecstatic. They jumped up and down, they hugged each other, they high-fived each other. When Coach Tim ran out on the field he found son Kelly still poised on his knees, sadly pensive. "What's wrong son, you did great. Why aren't you celebrating with your buddies?" Kelly answered, "Dad, this is the last game. I'll never wear this uniform again." Tim turned to his son and said, "Kelly, we're always moving from one thing to another. There's life after eighth grade football, son. You've got to believe that. Go on, celebrate the moment with your buddies."

Kelly had seized upon an issue familiar to all of us. It's not only the absence of something that spurs desire and requires hope. Losing what we now have also requires us to hope. Hope gives us the courage to move on beyond eighth grade football, and, ultimately, the courage to move on from youth to each stage of life. When our grown children prepare to leave the security of home we parents hope we will find fulfillment despite the empty nest. And we hope our children will be able to handle that separation. And yes, when the boomerang generation returns to live at home, we hope the time will soon come when they will leave again and set up a home for themselves! We need hope when we anticipate moving from familiar surroundings to a new job in a new city. We need hope when we anticipate moving to that uncharted land called retirement.

Because it empowers us to face the uncertain future, hope also enables us to enjoy what we have and to savor the present moment even though we know it will not last. Whether it be eighth grade football or a wonderful vacation with only a few days left, or the knowledge that most of our life is behind us, or that this visit may be the last with the person we love—*hope is what empowers us to cherish and enjoy what we have while we have it even though we know we do not possess it forever.*

HOPE WHEN WE HAVE LOST OR ALMOST LOST

Hope is even more difficult and more essential when what was present and cherished has already become absent. We enter marriage with the expectation of a lifelong partner and now find ourselves divorced. Or we find ourselves grieving for a loved one suddenly cut off from the living by an accident or a fatal illness. There is a gnawing absence, a void, an emptiness. Many of us have been there or will be there. Hope is often shattered and must be recovered and it takes time. The recovery of the zest for life and perhaps of our will to love again is the surest sign of hope restored.

There is still another way hope may be lost and despair overtakes us, and that brings us back to Sarah. Remember Sarah desired and hoped for a son and when she had given up hope, her prayer was answered. Isaac came and brought laughter and joy to her life. He was so precious to her. And then, unbeknownst to Sarah, came that test on Mount Moriah. Abraham and Isaac are on their way to the mountain of sacrifice. Sarah was not consulted. In fact the rabbis suggest the reason Abraham and Isaac left so early was because they were afraid if Sarah was up and saw them she wouldn't let them go. Father and son went to Moriah but the sacrifice did not take place. It was only a test. What happened when Isaac returned home? The Torah does not say but, as you can imagine, the rabbis filled the gap.

In one rabbi's version, Isaac finally returned from the mountain and mother Sarah asked, "Where have you been, my son?" Isaac tells his mother the truth. He tells her of going up to the mountain with his father, of being bound on the altar, of Abraham taking the knife and, just in the nick of time, the angel appeared. Sarah gasped and asked, "Does that mean my son that were it not for that angel you would already be slaughtered?" Isaac says, "Yes." At that Sarah screamed and wailed like the *shevarim*, the shrill wails of the *shofar*. She had not finished her wailing when her soul flew away and she died. And that, says the rabbi, is why the very next section of the Torah announces Sarah's death. You see, Sarah was the real victim of the events on Mt. Moriah.

One of our greatest rabbinic commentators, a man called Rashi, carries this version forward and asks rhetorically, "Why did Sarah wail and die? After all, Isaac is standing before her, he survived. She didn't actually lose her son." The answer: *Sarah wails and dies from the unbearable awareness of the hair's breath that separates life from death.* After all Sarah had gone through in her life, living in a world where the threat of death and loss is always with us finally became unbearable. The revelation of what had *almost happened* to Isaac plunged her into total despair and her soul left her.

Many of us have had those close calls where we almost lost our lives or the life of someone precious to us. One of you came to see me a few weeks ago after your car was hit on the highway and rolled over. When you regained consciousness you were told your survival was amazing. You emerged from that ordeal with deep gratitude but also with a terrifying sense of the dangerousness and uncertainty of life. It shook you up very deeply. For Sarah, Isaac's account of what almost happened on Mt. Moriah was too much. After all her cumulative experience with the precariousness of life she had reached the breaking point. We can understand Sarah as we can understand others who have been overwhelmed by the cumulative difficulties of life.

HOPE ON THE OTHER SIDE OF THE ABYSS

Still, in Judaism, despair must never be permitted to speak the last word. There is another scenario, and it is offered to us by a Rabbi Isaac who said that we all have moments, even days when we come face to face with the anguish of living. Despair threatens to overcome us. And yet, paradoxically, many have discovered that by facing the depth of our anguish and fear, and hanging in there and moving through the storm we can emerge with an even deeper appreciation of the preciousness of life and living. *Yes, out of our very encounter with the abyss, out of having been on the very edge of death can come the profoundest kind of hope for life.*

That is the meaning of the *shofar* calls we are commanded

to hear as we usher in the New Year. We listen to the *shevarim*, the shrill dark broken notes reminiscent of Sarah's wail. But we don't end with those shrill wailing notes; we end with the *tekiah gedolah*, that sustained triumphal note which affirms the hope that in spite of our encounters with trial and trouble we may yet experience the fulfillment that makes life good.

In all the situations we have described this morning, where does such hope come from? Surely it comes from other persons we know who moved through the stages of life with hope, persons who have themselves faced the serious loss of loved ones and who have recovered their zest for living and their will to love again, persons who have known the thin line between life and death, who have even stood on that line, but who cherish life and each day of life all the more intensely. Such persons may inspire *us* to hope.

Ultimately however, their hope and ours comes from the deepest faith: faith in the One who calls us into life and who is with us even in those darkest moments when we cry out of the depths. This hope rooted in faith goes beyond reason alone. It cannot be proved or disproved in a laboratory. It's not based on statistical probability. It refuses to be dismissed as a form of denial. This "hope against hope" is rooted in the faith that the God who created us loves us, is with us, and as Master of the Universe ultimately preserves what is good from destruction.

So, we gather here and usher in a New Year. We pray for a good year: for life, and health, and love, and joy, and prosperity, and fulfillment in our labors. And we pray that when, not if, but *when* we encounter the contingencies and uncertainties and losses and the threat of despair that are part of the human territory, we too will hear not only the echoes of the broken notes of the *shofar*. We will hear echoes of the *tekiah gedolah* of that long sustained note which reminds us that we are not alone and, therefore, we can face the future with hope.

I gratefully acknowledge that my thoughts in the last section of this sermon were shaped by reading Genesis, The Beginning of Desire *by Avivah Zornberg.*

CHAPTER 17

The Delight of the Lord is Your Strength

Another year has passed and we gather in this very special way. For me, and I suspect for you, this time is both sweet and a bit sad. Sweet is the gathering of family at home and for worship. Sweet is the impressive grandeur of this full-bodied congregation. Sweet is the liturgy and the music of these days, so stirringly beautiful.

But this is also a sad time for all of us who take this season seriously—who ponder the passing of another year and judge our lives and know the clock ticks by so quickly. There is good stuff in all of our ledgers but we have not done all we hoped to do. We have done some things we wish we hadn't. We are not all we had hoped to be or become. This season highlights our blemishes. These prayers expose our flawed selves.

Oh, this is the season of renewal. Our prayers speak to us of repentance and of change but that message too is often more frustrating than reassuring. We give ourselves the old pep talk and vow to make things different but change and renewal are much easier to speak of than to do. It's so difficult to reshape our deeds, no less difficult to reshape our attitudes toward

_____

Sermon, Rosh Hashanah Eve, October 3, 1986

others and toward ourselves. We want to think well of ourselves, but our egos are fragile, our self-image less sturdy than we often reveal to the world.

This is so desperately true of adolescents: so dependent on the good opinion of their peers, so fearful of being called a *dork*, so easily crushed by the wrong expression on another's face.

As we grow older we should be less dependent on the opinion of others. We should possess mature ego strength, but it's not that simple. Adulthood does not free us from surges of self-doubt. Periodically we say to ourselves "What will I do when they find out I am me?"

Crises of inner confidence are triggered by a bad day at the office, or a stinging remark, the failure to get a particular invitation, or the awareness of what someone we grew up with has done with her life, or when we have tried still another road to peace of mind and discover that our inner demons are very much with us. Or a time like this, which highlights all we have dreamed of becoming and have not become.

How do we respond? We may give up. We stop hearing the message of renewal and change. We assume that what we see is what we get now and forever. We stop making New Year's resolutions. We stop trying to grow, to become different or better than we are. We quit!

Or we insistently, intensely redouble our efforts, determined to grasp the vision. We will become all that we want to become! We make enormous demands on ourselves and each time we fail we grow terribly angry and are personally disenchanted with our lives.

Or we attempt to achieve by illusion what we cannot attain in the real world. We take drugs and alcohol to escape our limited self, a path so very prevalent in our time.

There is another way, a Jewish way. Speaking of this way is an important message for this season. I know that I need it and, judging by my conversations with some of you, you need it too. Go back with me in time to ancient Judea, 2,400 years ago. Ezra the scribe and Nehemiah the Persian-appointed Jewish governor of Judea assembled the congregation of Israel in an outdoor sanctuary of sorts. We read about it in tomorrow's *haftarah*.

This convocation of our ancestors took place on the first day of the month of *Tishri*. It was Rosh Hashanah, perhaps the only place in the Bible where Rosh Hashanah is actually described. What happened that day? The people offered prayers of praise to God. Then Ezra opened the Torah Scroll. Some scholars believe the people had never seen the Torah Scroll before. Ezra and others read from the scroll containing God's commandments. They read the story of how Israel in the wilderness had often failed to abide by those commandments. When the people measured their own lives against the teachings of Torah, they wept.

Instant collective depression overcame the people. They felt so worthless. Then Nehemiah made this remarkable statement: "Don't weep. This day is holy to the Lord. Dress up and eat and send portions to those who are in need so they can eat too because the delight of the Lord is your strength."

Nehemiah was saying to the people, don't afflict yourselves because you haven't perfectly fulfilled the covenant. Let God's delight, let God's acceptance of you in your humanness be your strength in this season of judgment. Oh, you can do better. Some change and growth and renewal are possible, desirable, necessary. That's part of the meaning of this season. But remember, we don't fully arrive. No matter who we are, we are always on the way. That is the essence of the human condition.

There is a story of a holy man renowned for his generous heart and many good deeds. The ruler of the kingdom admired the holy man. He commissioned an artist to paint his portrait. When the portrait was unveiled the ruler was shocked. The face in the portrait was not holy but brutish, cruel, even depraved. "This is an outrage," proclaimed the ruler as he threatened the artist with death. But the holy man, who had posed for the portrait and was present for the unveiling, said to the ruler, "No sire, that portrait is true. Before you stands the picture of the man I have struggled all my life not to become."

Even the holiest among us struggles against evil impulses. Even when we act decently we are often disturbed by fantasies that reveal a more primitive self. But that's okay. It's enough of an achievement that we think ugly thoughts without always acting upon them. Even the holiest of men and women may have such thoughts. It is part of the human struggle.

What is true of our attitudes and relation to others is also true of our relation to self. We envisage an ideal of perfect maturity, which someday we will reach. Maturity, a sense of worth independent of peer approval, of what others are thinking about us; an inner consistency in the conduct of our lives; freedom from jealousy or crises of confidence or fits of depression. It's a great profile, but who or where is the completely mature, totally fulfilled person?

Henry David Thoreau was a great American naturalist. From his secluded hut on Walden Pond, Thoreau wrote elegantly about the beauty of nature and the solitary, self-reliant life. His writings on nature and solitude and self-reliance and civil disobedience have had a tremendous impact on western culture.

Recently I discovered something I never knew about Thoreau. When he graduated from college his mother suggested, "Son, buckle on your knapsack and roam around abroad to seek your fortune." What did Thoreau do? He cried. He feared his mother was sending him away from her. He found it difficult to separate from her. When he went off to Walden to build his secluded hut in the woods, he built it only a mile away from his mother's house in Concord, and he went home to visit every day.

Shocking? No. Does that revelation rob Thoreau of his great contribution to our culture and humanity? No. It only reveals that his quest for self-reliance was a struggle, not a perfect achievement. It only records Thoreau's humanness.

One of my favorite American writers is Bernard Malamud. I have talked about him from time to time. Shortly before his death he was working on another book. He was very frail from a stroke but for him to live was to write. When Philip Roth, a younger colleague, visited him, Malamud gave Roth the beginning of his new manuscript to read. Roth read the opening chapters and, as politely as possible, wanted to suggest that this piece needed a lot of work before it could be considered good. So he asked Malamud, "What comes next?"

In a soft voice, suppressing fury, Malamud said, "What's next is not the point!" Malamud, the man widely acclaimed in his lifetime as one of America's premier writers, was angry. He was not angry at Roth for failing to praise the manuscript. Roth, who knew him well, explained that Malamud was angry at himself because after all those years and all those accomplishments, he, Malamud, had still not outgrown the need for external reassurance and praise.

Does that poignant vignette reduce Malamud's greatness? No. It just confirms his humanness. For him, as for us, total maturity, the ideal self, seems always beyond our reach. Still we wonder. Maybe we just haven't uncovered the proper key. We know that redoubling our effort and lots of pep talks won't transform us into fully mature and whole persons. What about psychotherapy? Maybe it can.

One of my dear friends is a very accomplished psychoanalyst. He has helped many towards greater maturity. He has of course been through a complete analysis himself. As we spoke recently in the candor of friendship, he acknowledged his gnawing moments, his lingering crises of self-confidence, moments when he doubts the adequacy of his powers or the significance of his life. My friend reminded me that those moments go with the human territory, with self-awareness, even after psychoanalysis, even if you are a psychoanalyst. Freud himself once said the purpose of therapy is to transform neurotic misery into normal unhappiness. So not even psychotherapy can make us totally fulfilled mature human beings.

What about religion? Can religious faith free us from the residue of immaturity, from our hang-ups, from the gap between how we would like to be and the way we are? I would like to be able to tell you yes. I know people who say their religious faith has given them perfect peace, total fulfillment. My own faith does not. I regard myself as a religious person but my faith does not spare me from periods of anxiety, lapses of confidence and a painful sense that in attitude and deed I am very far from my vision of perfect maturity or wholeness.

When I get depressed by that fact, as I sometimes do, and I wonder about the adequacy of my faith, I remember that wonderful story the rabbis tell of Moses. He was certainly a man of faith. The rabbis tell of the days before Moses' death. Joshua has succeeded him. Moses says to God, "Lord, let me live a little. I don't mind Joshua being in control. I'm not jealous of my successor. I know it's time for me to retire but let me just go over to the Promised Land and observe from the sidelines." God tests Moses and lets him follow Joshua around for a day with Joshua as leader. At the end of the day Moses realizes how difficult it is for him to see Joshua as leader. He is terribly jealous. Moses turns to God and says, "There are times when death is sweeter than life. I'm ready, God, take me."

For all his religious faith and closeness to God not even Moses was fully liberated from the human condition. Not even he was the spiritually fulfilled, perfectly mature man. That is a Jewish perspective. Not even religion perfectly heals or matures us, or makes our life all we might dream. Religious faith does give us the power to move toward wholeness and the wisdom to know we are not yet there. Religious faith does give us the strength for those darker moments in our life and the courage to hope, although the world is not yet redeemed.

And so, at this High Holy Day season of judgment and penitence, the season that will end with a day of fasting, the season which highlights our flaws and shortcomings and unfulfilled visions, the season which bids us to become better than we are, Nehemiah tells us, as he told our ancestors: don't weep, don't despair, don't put on sack cloth as you recite the litany of your shortcomings. Dress up, take care of yourself and those who have less. Strive to grow and move toward spiritual wholeness. You can make significant strides, but keep perspective. Don't expect to burst the bonds of this imperfect world. God respects the rough edges of your life. God does not expect you to play a perfect game. Neither should you.

Let the solemnity and sadness of this season of judgement be tempered by the joy of a very precious awareness: *chedvat adonay maoozchem*—God's delight in your humanness is your strength.

SECTION IV

Rabenu

CHAPTER 18

The Tents of Jacob–
20th Century

I shall not disguise my sentiments at this precious moment. To stand again on the *bima* of my ordination, reunite with my teachers, and contemplate the privilege of addressing my new colleagues on this day of their commission, is surely ample grounds to declare *she'hechee'anu v'kee'manu v'heegee'anu lazman ha'ze*.

My dear colleagues, the hands of ordination placed upon you this day may betoken a sending forth—some might say a gentle shove—from the cloistered *Yeshiva* overlooking Clifton Avenue to your world of promise. From one who has scouted the Promised Land during the past decade, you have every right to expect an honest account of the giants and the honey. Your day of commission coincides with the reading of that portion of the Torah entitled *Ba'midbar*—in the Wilderness. The coincidence seems a bit ominous. Can it be that Dr. Glueck is sending you forth this day, not to a land of milk and honey, but to a barren and forbidding desert?

Be not dismayed by an invitation to the *midbar*. To sojourn in the wilderness is both to move toward the Promised Land and to know that you have not yet arrived. Is this not the classic

Address at Ordination, Hebrew Union College–Jewish Institute of Religion
Cincinnati, Ohio, June 3, 1967

posture of the Jew? We are commissioned to point toward God's goal for man, even as by our presence we stubbornly insist that Creation's promise remains unfulfilled. The wilderness is the natural habitat of a Jew who walks through an unredeemed world, armed with a vision of a distant land.

Nor should we shudder at our kinship with him who was a *kol koray ba'midbar*—a voice crying in the wilderness. On that day when the congregation of Israel hearkens too eagerly to our words, we may conclude: either we have become purveyors of painless unction, or the earth has grown so full of the knowledge of the Lord that we must file for unemployment insurance. The rabbi addresses men and women who like himself, are struggling for faith and integrity in a wilderness where the standards of piety are often blurred and its rewards invisible to the naked eye. Surely we who would guide men and women *ba'midbar* must endure a measure of resistance and loneliness.

This morning's portion describes a census of the tents of Jacob. What would such a poll reveal today? What are these kinsmen to whom we must minister really like? You have just spent five years of your life grappling with God, Torah, Israel. What do these arcane symbols mean to them?

From some, you will not be able to discover the answer. Their tents are sealed. To the portal is attached the clear request "Please do not disturb." But many tent flaps are at least partially open, and if you enter, the initial patronizing courtesy, the awkward silence, and even the defensive spate of small talk may in time lead to unsuspected depths.

You may wish first to discover their relation to Israel, the Jewish fellowship of fate. It has become fashionable to declare that America is an increasingly open society. Indeed, it is. The signs are impressive and welcome. The sons and daughters of Jacob are amply represented in the Ivy League colleges. We are beginning to enter the large executive suites; Sholom Aleichem has "made it" on Broadway. Novels about Hasidic Jews playing baseball win the plaudits of the American literary establishment. There is serious talk of a Jewish Vice President. Can a generation of Jews reared in contemporary affluent America truly feel kin to that motley band who escaped from ancient Egypt, who endured the periodic sting of enforced exile, who savored many false promises of emancipation, who became charnel witnesses to Hitler's final solution, and who in our day taste the bitter cup of the Marxist false Messiah or confront the grim prospect of an Arab holy war?

Dear colleagues, despite the eloquent and glib disclaimers, fate-consciousness has not departed from the tents of American Israel. It remains the most compelling strand in the fabric of Jewish identity. For all but the most obtuse Jew, Auschwitz continues to evoke a private meaning which it does not have for the most liberal gentile even as Hiroshima's significance for the Japanese survivor may not be fully matched by the most empathetic reader of the *Saturday Review*. For even the marginal Jew our secular society remains far more Christian than neutral. At Yuletide, if he is honest, he must admit to being far more of a cultural outsider than the most secular Christian.

Nor has the special sense of Jewish vulnerability faded. Some years ago, when news of the Kennedy assassination flashed across the country, most of your future congregants felt audibly relieved that Oswald was not a Jew. When a rabbi deplores our country's policy in Vietnam, his most sympathetic listeners will feel perceptibly comforted if he takes pains to invoke the support of Catholic and Protestant clergy. They do not wish the Jew to be a lone dissenter.

The racial revolution has also placed the Jew in an ironic crossfire, symbolized by two radically different voices. At the last White House conference on Civil Rights, a self-styled Negro leader exclaimed, "The trouble with this conference is there are too many white people and too many Jews." And last summer in the all-white Chicago suburb of Gage Park, George Lincoln Rockwell drew clamorous cheers when he shouted "Jews are behind the Civil Rights demonstrations." The anti-Semitic potential of social ferment is very much with us. The American Jew has not yet outlived the peculiar burdens of his history.

Nor have our people lost a sense of Jacob's common destiny. The ominous crisis in the Middle East which this day hangs over our heads like a dark cloud, has sent tremors of pain, anxiety, and anger through the body of American Israel. Rare indeed is the 20th century Jew who can regard the peril to Zion with the objectivity of a remote bystander.

Dear colleagues, Jewish fate-consciousness is hardly an adequate pillar on which to rest our ministry. It is an indispensable component of any honest conversation in the dwelling places of contemporary Israel. Many Jews who may not know the meaning of worship or savvy the theological concepts of revelation and redemption, yet know and feel within the depths of their being, that Israel is a small, vulnerable people whose pilgrimage through history is in some special sense their own.

So much for the lingering claim of Israel, the Jewish fellowship of fate. Can we also continue to speak of the binding claim of Torah? In the past, history and Torah were inextricably intertwined. A liberated people acknowledged that shared history yielded special obligation. "Ye were strangers in the land of Egypt," therefore "thou shalt not oppress the stranger."

Does the son and daughter of American Israel acknowledge this claim? Or do they bristle and bridle contemptuously at the hint of special accountability? With all his vaunted affluence, with all his purported defection from the ranks of liberalism, with all the fastidious frippery of the gilded ghetto, the son of Jacob continues to feel the claim, even when he fails to respond to it. Surely, all too often, our people do ignore the claim. This is the anguish of our ministry.

But the echo of pharaoh's whip lingers on in the "collective unconscious" of the Jew, and its mark has not fully been erased from his heart or his life. Most Jews will at least acknowledge the ethical mandate forged on the anvil of our common destiny, "Know ye the heart of the stranger for ye were strangers in the land of Egypt."

Through what other portals does the lingering claim of Torah most persistently enter the tents of our people? Franz

Rosenzweig spoke of the High Holy Day season as "the only remaining coin in an inherited fortune." For us rabbis, Rosh Hoshanah and Yom Kippur remain in a very special sense, Days of Awe. Those are the days when we try too hard to reach the multitude of Jews who make their annual pilgrimage to the House of Prayer. But for those pilgrims too, these remain Days of Awe.

Why has this Torah claim retained its ineluctable grip? The High Holy Days invite the man born Jew to reflect upon the primary experiences of his life. They speak of his fleeting days, his finitude. They speak of his unrealized potential, of the gap between what he is and what he ought to be. They quench his thirst for self-judgement, forgiveness and rebirth. Is it any wonder that even the marginal Jew is drawn to the synagogue in this season? Judaism has no monopoly on the liturgical expression of human need, but a man born Jew feels compelled to live by Jewish time, at least once a year.

The claim of Torah, the fellowship of Jewish form, is most deeply felt also in the other primary experiences of life. Birth requires circumcision or a naming ceremony; puberty requires Confirmation or Bar Mitzvah—which despite its vulgarization remains a way of binding the individual's search for identity to the norms of his elders. Love seeks consecration. Even the so-called secular Jew wishes the blessing to be uttered, the vows spoken, and not only for the sake of the parents. Death remains a time to deny absurdity or oblivion—to recite or hear the *Kaddish* in the presence of the congregation of Israel. Admittedly this paltry pattern of observances falls far short of that all-pervasive regimen which was to enfold the Jew *b'shachb'cha uvkumecha*—from the moment of his waking to the moment of his slumber. But as liberal teachers of Torah, it is more important for us to understand what has been retained than simply to lament what has been discarded.

As we enter the tents of Jacob let us remember. Torah touches our people most deeply at those moments when it provides the form—the sacred scenario—by which to express the grandeur and mystery, the pathos and glory of life.

The consciousness of Israel lives. The claim of Torah is partially affirmed. But what of God—and the fellowship of Jewish faith? Is God ineffable because He surpasses our understanding or is He ineffable because He is dead? The issue is more than a matter of symbols or semantics. It is fundamentally the question of meaning.

Some have heralded the dawn of a new era. In ages past, we are told, men felt a compelling need to ask ultimate questions, those staples of theology and metaphysics: What lies beyond my finite reach, what is the purpose of my life, what is my destiny? But in the age of "the death of God," we are told, such questions press less urgently upon us. This is the age of "psychological man" and Freud is its prophet. In a letter to Marie Bonaparte, Freud wrote: "The moment a man questions the meaning and value of life he is sick, since objectively, neither has any existence." The analyst is the high priest of our age. He binds his subject to no transcendent order of meaning. He defines salvation as a tolerable truce between one's id and super-ego and redemption as the day the patient no longer needs his analyst.

Psychoanalysis is a system of healing which the sons of Jacob have generously patronized, and by which many have been helped to new levels of self-understanding. But the age of analysis has not stilled the age-old quest. To be sure, our generation is technologically *nouveau riche*. We are so mesmerized by the work of our hands that we have lost contact with the source of our being. Our generation lives after Auschwitz. We have witnessed anew the demonic potential of man and the agonizing silence of God. Our generation lives in the secular city. We receive little cultural support for religious sentiments. On a typical college campus only an extra-ordinarily courageous young man will admit that he prays.

And yet, God is not dead. Doubt abounds, but the intimations of transcendence persist. They are not emblazoned on our people's shirt sleeves, or always verbalized, but no sensitive rabbi has failed to note signs of irrepressible wonder at the mystery of being, a throbbing gratitude for unearned gifts, a soul-searing accountability for the quality of one's life, a relentless drive to understand fed by faith in an ordered universe, a trembling trust that man is not alone in his struggle against evil, a stubborn belief in the primal and potential value of existence.

Why do our congregants balk at a rabbi who recites *Kaddish* for God? Is it because they wish not to be denied a pin-cushion for their impious thrusts? Do they fear the reverberations of the gentile world? Not primarily. In the course of many agonizing and exhausting dialogues with devout non-believers you will find that they are at best "atheists with an ache." They want us to win the argument even when they will not permit us to do so. They need someone against whose honest affirmation they may press their doubt and pursue their quest for faith.

Dear colleagues, there are echoes of God, Torah, and Israel still to be found among the tent dwellers of Jacob. But their classic integrity, their oft-vaunted interdependence, has been corroded by the acid of modernity. God, Torah and Israel are no longer *mitkashrin zeh ba'zeh*, inextricably bound up one with the other in the covenant consciousness of the American Jew.

Many who acknowledge the Jewish fellowship of fate see no relation between *seenah* (anti-Semitism) and Sinai, between our history and Israel's Divine vocation. Many who acknowledge the special ethical burden of the Jew, or who live in part by Jewish time, do not consciously fulfill *mitzvot* in response to a Divine demand. Many who experience personal intimations of transcendence feel few if any links with the God Israel encountered in Egypt or at Sinai.

Surely it is your task to sustain the spirit of *kol yisrael arayvin zeh ba'zeh*, "All Israel stands responsible for one another." Surely it is your task to array the full weight of Jacob's legacy against the dehumanizing forces of our age. Surely you would wish to extend the jurisdiction of Torah and encourage a thirst for the living God.

But the unique and most demanding challenge of your rabbinate in this day and at this time remains to *reunite these scattered sparks of Jewish self-consciousness and rekindle the full radiance of the*

covenant. There were times in our past when Reform embraced
God but reneged on Torah and Israel. There are those who
would now cultivate Torah and Israel but forfeit God. If we
would be true to our calling we must remain bearers of a three-
dimensional covenant. We must rear Jews who *find in the classic
interdependence of Jewish fate, form and faith the key to their fulfillment
as persons.*

Dear colleagues, may you rear a generation which will experience the inner history of the Jew as the sign and price of our
Divine witness in an unredeemed world, a generation that will
acknowledge Torah as *mitzvah*—as God's unrelenting summons
to serve Him in all our ways. May you rear a generation whose
sons and daughters will feel personally addressed by the words
of today's *haftarah.* "And I will betroth thee unto me forever. Yea,
I will betroth thee unto me in righteousness and in justice, in
lovingkindness, and compassion. And I will betroth thee unto
me in faithfulness and thou shalt know the Lord." Amen.

CHAPTER 19

The Legacy of Classical Reform

I note that this is my first opportunity to address the College-Institute family since Alfred Gottschalk, my dear schoolmate and friend, assumed the Presidency of our alma mater. That in itself invests this evening with special personal meaning. It is a high privilege to share this occasion with my teachers and future colleagues. I heartily congratulate tonight's recipients of academic honors. This degree-granting milestone must remind members of the student body that ordination itself is not an eschatological hope, but an appointed and calculable hour.

Almost eighteen years have elapsed since my class was granted the corresponding honors. For us it was the time of ordination. Thirteen of my eighteen years since that day have been spent in a congregation where Kaufmann Kohler, Emil G. Hirsch and Louis Mann preached the message of radical Reform, a congregation which to this day holds a Sunday morning preaching service.

Sinai Congregation, like so many others, has undergone changes in recent years. The Sunday liturgy bears the unmistakable marks of a weekday service. A Sabbath morning men's

Address, Hebrew Union College–Jewish Institute of Religion
Cincinnati, Ohio, December 5, 1974

minyan of worship and textual study has attained significance. Hebrew is a required subject in the Religious School. Men and women are called to read from the Torah and Israel's Independence Day is liturgically celebrated.

I warmly endorse some of the new Reform trends emerging in our time: the emphasis on the worshipper as participant, the recognition that Reform is not only the freedom to discard—but the freedom to reclaim, and the sense of ministering to a generation less impelled to prove its Americanism, more driven to rediscover the depths of a millennial heritage.

Yet I am troubled by the tone of some Reform revisionism. The time is ripe for a more balanced assessment of our "classical Reform" legacy. Such reassessment will, I trust, be deemed an appropriate use of this privileged forum tonight. Consider this, if you will, my modest response to Rabbi Brichto's invitation to join "the great debate."

In this week's Torah portion, Joseph files a *deebah ra-ah*, an evil report on his older brothers. Rabbinic commentators do not hesitate to convict Joseph of slander. He imputed to his elders sins of which they were not guilty. T'was as if he sought to establish his own grandeur at their expense.

Some current discourses on the sins of early Reform offend my sensibilities. Why the snide posture toward our Reform elders? Why contempt for a movement which sponsored our entry into the ranks of professional Judaism? Let us rather acknowledge that we are striving to meet the needs of our time as they sought to meet the needs of theirs. Instead of discrediting them, should we not admit that we are standing on their shoulders?

As far as I can discern not even the most fervent neo-traditionalist among us is anxious to surrender the freedom to wend his own way through the labyrinth of *halacha*. The early Reformers struggled to establish the authenticity of non-Orthodox Jewish options. That battle is not yet fully won. Must we now say to Reform's detractors, "You were right in condemning our elders, but we are different?" To regard classical

Reform with such condescension is not only unbecoming, but unwise.

Judaism has held in creative tension the dialectical themes of life. Let us regain that elemental wisdom as we reassess the relation between the classical Reformers and the neo-traditionalists in our midst.

Our Reform elders conceived of Judaism more as a legacy of ideas than a richly symbolic style of life. They regarded rituals as a *seeyig layahadut*, a means of holding the vision in protective custody. The vision was primary, the ritual observances secondary. To articulate and bear witness to the message of "ethical monotheism" was the "mission of Israel."

We live in an age when lifestyle is more compelling than conceptualization; an age of body language and sensitivity training; of proclamation by demonstration, of folk song and dance more than formal oratory; an age to celebrate the mystery rather than demythologize it. A rabbi today is more inclined to choose for his Confirmation text "The Jewish Catalogue" than a volume entitled "What the Jews Believe." We seek to teach our children how to *live Jewishly* rather than *talk about* Judaism.

And yet even as we respond to the new *zeitgeist* let us not surrender its counterpart. We Jews also remain today what our Reform elders said we were: stewards of a message, a vision, an understanding of God's relation to man and man's place in God's world.

Judaism remains both *halacha* and *agada*—doing the deed and telling the story, observing laws and clarifying values, action and reflection, lifestyle and theology.

In a world where Jews are confronted by the gospel of an evangelical Christianity, the mysteries of Eastern gurus, and the allure of a new paganism, it is not enough to offer *kashrut* as the alternative to organic foods, or the *havdalah* candle and spice box in lieu of incense, or blessing the *challah* as an alternative to communion.

We have not outlived the need to conceptualize and defend the faith, to appeal to the mind as well as the heart. It may well be that we must go beyond such slogans as "ethical monotheism" and transcend the apologetic thrust of a Hermann Cohen or Leo Baeck. If so, let us grope for more appropriate images.

As students in this seminary we would do well not only to discover the style of Jewish observance we shall make our own, but also to probe for the vision, the stance, the *agada* underlying the *halacha*. We must still search for idioms in which to communicate the "message of Israel."

The effectiveness of our ministry will depend not only on the *mizvot* we commend, but on the compelling images of the covenant we form and express. As we seek to revitalize worship let us not minimize the importance of preaching.

Sensitive to both text and culture, the preacher within us will continue to perceive the human scene through the prism of our faith. Consider for example Judaism's concept of the sanctification of life. How contrary to the sanctification of life is daredevil Evel Knievel's brazen wooing of the Angel of Death for a multimillion dollar purse while millions of mortals watch in reverent or diabolical fascination. How stark the contrast as we consider Judaism's obsession with *pikuach nefesh*—the saving of life—and its repetitive counsel against courting danger. To a culture in which thrill-seeking in all its varieties is a desperate antidote to boredom and emptiness, the Talmudic dictum responds, "Do not seek out a dangerous place and expect a miracle to save you."

Life is too precious, too sacred, to be imperiled frivolously or in a vain effort to confirm one's manhood. Such feats Judaism regards not as high courage, but *mishigas*. We can picture the little Jewish man greeting Evel Knievel on the other side of the canyon with the words "*Nu, vos is der chochma?*" (So, what's the sense?)

Saul Bellow has insisted that contemporary man "feels peculiarly contentless in substance and without a proper story." A proper story would express man's "intuition that his own existence is peculiarly significant. The sense that his existence is significant haunts him, but he can prove nothing. And the business of art is with this sense precisely." We might add: it is also the business of religion, and no tradition has more effectively or vividly proclaimed a sense of human significance than our own. More than ever we are called to tell the story of a covenant which casts man as a partner with God charged with the sanctification of life, summoned to help heal the brokenness of the world.

Dear colleagues, if we have discovered in recent years that message is no substitute for lifestyle, you will also discover as teachers and preachers in Israel that lifestyle is no substitute for message. Even in this post-modern age we Jews remain stewards of a truth to proclaim, a story to tell in the tents of Israel and beyond.

That brings me to a second theme: the enduring tension between particularism and universalism, between the image of *am l'vadad yishkon*—a people who dwells apart—and *brit l'amim*—a covenant open to the world.

Surely our teachers in this very room have introduced us to this tension in Biblical and Talmudic sources. The fact is that our Reform elders reformulated the issue for our time. At the risk of oversimplifying, we may say they minimized the image of a people dwelling apart and accentuated the concept of a world-embracing covenant. They experienced a need to prepare the Jew for a different quantity and quality of interaction with the world.

We are chastened liberals of a post-Holocaust world. We have staunchly reappropriated the image of the Jew as an isolated, beleaguered people and of the world as "enemy camp." The polarization of the '60s and the new ethnicity support such a view. The anti-Semitic comments of a General Brown,* and the reception accorded Yassir Arafat tend to reconfirm it.

Nevertheless, sobered though we be by the events of the 20th century we must not surrender too lightly the universal thrust of our Reform elders. They perceived a world in which *it*

Ed. Note: Brown, Chairman of the Joint Chiefs of Staff at the time, made an arguably anti-Semitic remark in public.

is not enough to build boundaries without also building bridges. Even as we recognize anew that we are a people dwelling apart, we ought not forsake a covenant truly open to the world.

Toward that end our Reform elders have left us an enduring legacy based on the universal trends within Judaism itself. What is that legacy? It includes a liturgy which has made God's concern for all His creatures an *explicit* theme. I do not regard as gratuitous such Reform emendations as: "It is good in Thy sight. O Lord, to bless Israel *and all the peoples* with strength and peace."

I hope none of us regrets the new prayerbook's continued omission of the phrase "Praised be Thou O Lord, who has not made me a Gentile." Nor do we regret that the new Haggadah omits the phrase "Pour Thy wrath upon the Gentiles who knew Thee not."

We Jews are offended by demeaning references in Christian liturgy. Must we not also struggle against an ethnocentrism which breeds suspicion and even contempt? I am reminded of Hermann Cohen's High Holy Day experience in a Polish synagogue. He observed the Cantor weeping as he sang "My house shall be called a house of prayer for all peoples." Cohen mused: how touching that the Cantor is so moved by the universal vision that he weeps at its proclamation! After the service Cohen confronted the Cantor and sought to confirm his hunch. "Why *did* you weep?" Much to Cohen's chagrin, the Cantor replied: "How can I help but weep when the place of our holiness and glory may someday be filled with *goyim*?"

Our Reform elders believed that not only our Jewish liturgy but our approach to converts should reflect a world-embracing covenant. The suspension of the requirement for adult circumcision was designed to remove a major obstacle to conversion for many a Western man. Our readiness to regard as Jewish the child of a Christian mother and a Jewish father if that child is raised as a Jew has also expanded the bounds of the covenant.

And yes, I am prepared to grant that those Reform elders and contemporary colleagues who officiate at mixed marriages are prompted in the main by a desire to reconcile the concrete universalism of love with the particularities of our peoplehood. Although I do not officiate at mixed marriages and have chosen to draw the boundary and the bridge in another way, I do not impugn their motives or their concern for the survival of Judaism in an open society.

In any case, though the 20th century has painfully renewed our sense of Jewish isolation and vulnerability the universalism of our Reform elders ought not be cavalierly discarded or disdained.

A third major thrust of our elders deserves reassessment. *Cheeyuv hagolah*—a positive view of Diaspora—was a trademark of classical Reform. Indeed they hastened to link the destiny of the Jew to those countries in which we had struck roots.

In a post-Holocaust world we would, of course, regard as absurd a return to the anti-Zionist vision of a Kaufmann Kohler or an Isaac Mayer Wise. We cannot say that Berlin or even Cincinnati is our new Jerusalem. Indeed, yours is the first generation of Reform rabbinic students whose very educational program empowers you to feel the magnetism of two poles of Jewish existence. You have known at firsthand the unique joy and burden of living in a land where Jews are the establishment, and I presume most of you are drawn to maintaining a vital Jewish presence in a society which remains more Christian than neutral. You have experienced the delight of observing festivals in a land which lives by Jewish time, but you have also discovered the *elan* of belonging to a creative minority in this land. You know the joy of being a Jew among Jews and the privilege of being a zealous Jew among Gentiles.

In other words, yours is a generation which can appreciate the bi-polarity of Elie Wiesel. When he was asked where he felt more at home, in New York or Jerusalem, he replied, "In Jerusalem, when I am not there."

Even in the age of Israel Reborn most of us, I presume, intend to live and labor in the American ambience. To be sure, we feel less prone than our elders to demonstrate a perfect congruity between Judaism and Americanism. Nor are we endowed with their balmy optimism. As veterans of the 20th Century we know that the worst imaginable not only can happen but often does.

Alas, if the Holocaust cremated the complacency of Diaspora Jewry, modern technology has rendered obsolete the old Zionist notion of Israel as Jewish security blanket. From our American perch we, history's charter refugees, tremblingly proclaim: the world has become too small. There is no place to run.

Let us then unabashedly adapt the earlier Reform credo for our time: our deepest fears and our highest hopes are now mortgaged to both Israel and Diaspora. Moreover the destiny of this the largest Jewish community in the world will be shaped not only by the culture of modern Israel, but by the spirit, the ferment, the harmonies and discords of America.

And what of our agenda in this land? The old liberal model of a colorless neutral America has collapsed. The special interests and passions of all peoples in this land cannot be ignored. We may no longer be expected to draw the image of the ideal American in the colors of a white Anglo-Saxon Protestant.

But neither can we Jews (or any inhabitants of America) afford to sulk, glare at, or ignore each other from behind physical and psychic ghettos. The time is ripe for a new form of group encounter in this land. If this society is to be sustained and renewed as we approach our Bicentennial year, we must seek ways to affirm both our distinctness and our commonality. As Jews let us discover new ways by which the taste and texture of our heritage may enrich us and others even as we renew our commitment to this society of freedom under law which makes it all possible.

Dear teachers, colleagues and friends, in an age of neo-traditionalism we need not and must not repudiate the basic legacy of classical Reform. At best we ought sustain the tension between their major thrusts and those of our generation. In so doing we shall be faithful to the dialectical character of classic Judaism itself.

A liberal Judaism which has rediscovered *halacha* must also continue to proclaim the *"message of Israel."* Even now lifestyle is no substitute for message, *halacha* no surrogate for *agada*.

In an age which has reminded us that we are a people dwelling apart who must draw strength and comfort from the tribal solidarity of the community of Israel, we must not forget that we are also intended to be a covenant open to the world. Let us be concerned not only with boundaries but with bridges.

In an age when we have thrilled to Israel's rebirth, trembled at its perils, and affirmed our common destiny with our Israeli brethern, let us boldly reaffirm our positive view of the Diaspora and acknowledge our very special stake in the future of America.

In this week's Torah portion Joseph is guilty of a slanderous report against his brothers. Later Joseph languishes in a dungeon and is himself wronged by a cup-bearer guilty of gross ingratitude. In the rabbinic mind the two episodes are linked. It is as if Joseph's irresponsibility returned to haunt him.

As we struggle for a valid understanding of liberal Judaism today (and you, my dear colleagues will be part of that struggle) feel not compelled to file an evil report on classical Reform, nor imagine their legacy is expendable in our time. We are at our best when we hold up both the vision of our elders and the vision of the neo-traditionalists among us and rediscover with some humility and grace "these and these are the words of the living God."

CHAPTER 20

Rooted in Reality:
In Defense of Agada

Long before I envisioned becoming a rabbi, my love for *agada* was sedulously nurtured. My first private Hebrew tutor introduced me to Bialik's anthology. As a pre-teen I was entranced by these strange narratives, these curious embellishments on the Biblical saga in which God carried on an extended, often impassioned dialogue with men—and especially with Jews. I knew that these were "fables," but I did not ask in what deeper sense they might be vessels of truth. My inchoate faith was not consciously mediated by the language of Jewish God-talk.

Only after ordination did I come to appreciate that *agada* is far more than homiletical ornamentation; it is the primary language of Jewish faith. Mathematical equations symbolize a relationship between quantitative terms, or, at times, various parts of the physical world. The stories of *agada* give symbolic expression to the relationship (i.e., the covenant) between man and God. More specifically, the term *agada* is used here to encompass Biblical, rabbinic, and contemporary narratives through which we seek to express and confirm the reality and meaning of the people Israel's relation with God.

Article, CCAR Journal, Central Conference of American Rabbis, Summer 1975

I

As rabbis we conduct a substantial part of our vocation in the currency of *agada*. Public worship is essentially an occasion when Jews openly proclaim the fellowship of Israel in covenant with God. The prayerbook is *agada* in liturgical form. Its words are designed to evoke, express and confirm that we individual Jews—with all the personal agendas and histories which distinguish us from one another—share a common story that is the key to the primary meaning of our life.

The epitome of liturgical *agada* is the Passover *Haggadah* (the name is, of course, hardly coincidental), which presents the stirring scenario of Israel's bondage and liberation from Egypt. Through such liturgical drama we seek to evoke a continuity between past and present and between the individual Jew and the covenant community of fate and faith.

Agada is also the language of preaching—the invocation of the stories of our past to illumine the contemporary human scene. That is precisely what the ancient agadist was doing when, for example, he cited texts from Jeremiah to explicate the exile of Judah under Rome. I would go even further: whether or not he actually quotes the Biblical story of Moses' confrontation with Pharaoh, the rabbinic preacher remains an agadist if he declares (or implies) that oppression must yield because there is a transcendent Presence active in our time, as in ages past, to make men free. Much of our preaching in the Civil Rights era of the early 1960s was precisely in this mode.

The agadist differs most from the editorial writer or TV commentator when he explicitly declares that the God who challenged, loved, and judged our ancestors addresses us, too. Essentially, the preacher retells old stories with new names and places.

Agada remains not only the language of worship and preaching, but of consolation as well. It is the story we tell to confirm faith in life's meaning, even in the midst of suffering and death. The *Book of Job* and Beruriah's parable on the meaning of the death of her sons are, respectively, Biblical and

Talmudic instances of *agada* as a literature of reassurance. Whenever a rabbi offers a eulogy he tells a story which sets forth the abiding significance of a human life in the face of its end. His listeners' primary expectation is reassurance that, in spite of death, the human adventure is not absurd.

II

Agada is the language in which the rabbinic defender of the faith seeks to respond to the boundary questions of human life: Who am I? What is my task? What difference does it make? What can I hope for? *In the Magic Mountain*, Thomas Mann argues through one of his characters that a human being is one who "consciously or unconsciously . . . seeks the final, the absolute . . . meaning in all his efforts and activities." If his culture responds to such questions with "hollow silence," a certain "laming of the personality is bound to occur."[1]

Robert Bellah, the distinguished American sociologist of religion, contends that "somehow or other men must have a sense of the whole if they are to live; they must have something to believe in and commit themselves to. Religion . . . is an imaginative statement about the truth (the worthwhileness) of the totality of human experience." The focus of such belief is unavoidably a reality transcending what can be scientifically verified. Men need to speak of such a reality, whether that speech is "religious in a traditional sense or not."[2]

Agada is Judaism's "imaginative statement," a collection of stories that embody the Jew's perception of a life ordered and purposeful. These stories tell of God's creation of the world, His covenant with man, and His particular covenant with the children of Abraham. Within the *agada*'s symbolic framework, the born Jew, and all who would embrace the covenant, are invited to experience a world endowed with promise and an individual life imbued with abiding worth.

To ask about the future of *agada* is to ask about the future of a religious orientation to life in general and of Jewish faith in particular. As long as man's affirmation of life's transcendent meaning persists, and as long as the Jewish expression of that meaning retains some recognizable kinship with its past, the agadic form will endure. Let us consider the unique symbolic power of *agada*.

Through a great religious story, our individual lives are linked to life's ultimate drama. Our little sojourn is invested with larger scope and significance. When the love of two persons is consecrated by liturgical *agada* they are invited to apprehend that their intimate bond stands at the heart of life's intended meaning. The wedding benedictions begin by proclaiming that God is Creator of the world and of man, the Source of the sustaining bond between man and woman, and the Giver of a heritage which this couple will transmit to the next generation: "May they establish a home in the midst of the people Israel worthy of praise."

Through liturgical *agada* each of us receives the Torah anew whenever it is read in the synagogue ("Praised be Thou, O Lord, Giver of the Torah"). In a special sense the *Bar Mitzvah* child and the Confirmand become partners of Moses in receiving a sustaining truth. Through *agada*, moments in the lifecycle are acted out on a stage that is larger than our individual lives.

As we encounter the yawning gulf between man's soaring vision and human frailty, we are threatened by a sense of powerlessness and futility. Moved to labor for the realization of values in our personal and social life, we always know that the goal exceeds our grasp, and we fear that our puny gestures are doomed to oblivion. In the midst of this unique human condition, *agada* evokes the primordial trust that we do not labor in vain. Through God's grace, our efforts count; they are not futile posturings. Our nobler impulses are implanted by One who is the Conserver of value and who "establishes the work of our hands."

To clarify the role of *agada*, we might contrast it with the mass media presentation of the "News of the World." In print and film we are deluged by daily images purporting to tell the story of our lives; and yet, for all the wizardry of electronics (hidden tapes, live battles via satellite, and the like), the mass media have not replaced the sensitive storyteller as the chronicler of the human adventure.

In defense of his art, Saul Bellow has observed that the weekly yield of *Time*, *Newsweek*, or the *Sunday New York Times* does not speak to man's depths: "He feels peculiarly contentless in his public aspect, lacking in substance and without a proper story. The proper story would express his intuition that his own existence is significant. The sense that his existence is significant haunts him. But he can prove nothing. And the business of art is with this sense, precisely."[3] Substitute *agada* for art and we have an eloquent articulation of the role of the religious story. At its best, *agada* embodies man's intuition of his personal significance.

Agada also enables this intuition of significance to be shared by creating and expressing a consciousness of true community. The durability of great religious stories is a measure of their power to transform deep, private sensibilities into common experience and collective memory. A great story transcends the generation gap, class differences and diverse levels of sophistication. It enhances the attentiveness of all assembled. Great stories may be repeated again and again without losing their power to move us. Moreover, a special dimension is added when such stories are told orally in a group. All these observations call to mind the evocative power of the *akedah* on Rosh Hashanah morning. To be part of a community is to respond to stories which hold the community in a common grip.

It follows from these observations that worship is most "successful" when liturgical *agada* tells a recognizable, moving story we share with others in the same space. Each of us can recall such worship experiences. Let me cite several.

A service following the assassination of President John F. Kennedy drew a full sanctuary of persons who came not to hear a repetition of the TV or news account, but to share anxiety and, in some way, to reconfirm hope. The weekly liturgy gave common voice to our individual yearnings, and this patent congruity of liturgy and experience lent special power and beauty to that hour of worship.

I recall vividly the year of Chicago's last blizzard. Most of us could not get to the regularly scheduled services. A few could and did—each with a story of braving the elements. Each of us felt that the service took place because of us. We felt needed. Reciting the customary prayers affirming Israel's witness to God, we felt on that occasion most poignantly the burden resting upon us. That service depended on our being there. The blizzard we had braved offered its own symbolic addendum to the *agada*'s story of Israel's witness to God in a turbulent world. How fragile and how precious is the Jewish vocation.

The moments of worship that are most compelling are those which effectively evoke and express a sense of community by relating the symbols of faith (the words of liturgical *agada*) to the soulful experiences of our lives.

Agada also possesses the unique power to bridge the gap between reflection and experience. C. S. Lewis, a great storyteller and lay theologian, once asked himself why the narratives of a religious tradition are so much more durable than its formal theology or philosophy. Lewis offered this answer:

> Human intellect is incurably abstract ... Yet the only realities we experience are concrete—this pain, this pleasure, this day, this man. While we are loving the man, bearing the pain, enjoying the pleasure, we are not intellectually apprehending Pleasures, Pain or Personality.... This is our dilemma—either to know and not to taste or, more strictly, to lack one kind of knowledge because we are inexperienced, or to lack another kind because we are outside it.... You cannot study pleasure in the moment of nuptial embrace nor repentance while repenting, nor analyze the nature of humor while roaring with laughter.[4]

Lewis proceeds to suggest that "in the enjoyment of a great myth (*agada*) we come nearest to experiencing as concrete what can otherwise be understood as an abstraction.... Myth is the isthmus which connects the peninsular world of thought with the vast continent we really belong to."[5]

The Einstein formula $E=MC^2$ symbolizes the ordered unity of the universe. The *Genesis agada* enables us to apprehend and "taste" that unity. The oneness of humankind is an abstraction we cannot directly experience. Frank Borman, James Lovell, and William Anders perhaps came closest to doing so when in December, 1968, they orbited the moon and saw planet Earth from an angle never before accessible to mortal man—and the astronauts' view was transmitted to our home TV screens. Even fortified with technical vision, however, we needed the aid of poetry and *agada* to apprehend and truly experience our common destiny as citizens of the Earth. Indeed, the most effective commentaries on the event were those of the poet Archibald MacLeish and the astronauts themselves.

MacLeish observed that we have now seen "the Earth as it truly is, small and blue and beautiful, in the eternal silence where it floats." We had seen ourselves "as risers on the earth together. Brothers on that bright loneliness in the eternal cold—brothers who now know they are truly brothers."[6]

And the astronauts' commentary? They read aloud the first chapter of the *Genesis agada*. "In the beginning God created the heaven and the earth...." No other words could have exceeded the allusive power of that *agada* at that moment in human history.

III

Classical *agada* is not a confining straight-jacket, but a malleable medium for the message of Jewish faith, aptly reflecting the diversity of human temperament and the variety of religious experience. Nowhere is this flexibility more in evidence than in the *agada*'s grappling with the "problem of evil." There were those in Israel who saw exile as divine retribution, others who accentuated God's own sense of banishment, still others who regarded the undeserved suffering of the righteous as the price for being God's servant in an unredeemed world, and still others who maintained an ongoing lover's quarrel with the God of the covenant—all on account of the problem of evil.

Similarly each generation not only inherited but reshaped

its agadic legacy. Maimonides' God-talk differed substantially from that of Rabbi Isaac Luria, though each inherited the Biblical-Talmudic framework and each prayed basically the same liturgy.

In our own time there are those who feel impelled to speak of God in images of a technological world (energy, force) instead of the anthropomorphic imagery of earlier generations. Even those among us who have found the traditional imagery eminently viable must acknowledge that each generation has made, and can make, idiomatic or substantive changes without necessarily undermining the agadic framework.

Are there no limits to *agada*'s resiliency? Are there no ground rules for agadic reform? Beyond what boundaries, to paraphrase Alfred North Whitehead, do we revise our symbols to the point of blatant irreverence?

For all its flexibility, the agadic framework did not countenance the verdict that life is absurd. The rejection of a moral order ("there is no justice and no judge") may be a way-station, but it cannot be a Jew's final resting place. The underlying function of *agada* was to help the Jew struggle for and re-appropriate the gift of meaning. Even the Jew's arguments with God reflected a primordial faith in quest of reconfirmation. Through all its permutations, the *agada* spoke of a God who calls a cosmos into being out of chaos, creates man, reveals a way to him, and sustains his hope.

Similarly, the *agada* is rooted in the reality and interrelatedness of God, Torah, and Israel; one cannot speak agadically of the meaning of Jewish existence (Israel) without speaking also of God and Torah. Bold doubt is no stranger to the world of *agada*, but Israel, if it remains Israel, must never cease to wrestle for its birthright of transcendent meaning. A synagogue whose liturgy reduces God to an anachronism has trespassed the bounds of agadic legitimacy.

Finally, I would suggest that responsible agadic reforms will justify symbolic change by appealing not only to contemporary insights or new revelations, but to basic motifs within the tradition itself. For all his radicalism, Mordecai Kaplan has observed this principle in his reconstruction of Jewish God-talk.

IV

We come to our symbolic heritage as travelers through the labyrinth of modern self-consciousness. Far more than our ancestors, we know that "the Torah speaks in the language of men." It speaks in symbols which we create. Moreover, we analyze in psychological or sociological terms the very rituals and symbols we are bidden to embrace and respond to with the fullness of our being.

An analogy may clarify the problem. Before the age of Freud, Masters and Johnson, Drs. Ruben and Comfort, the dynamics and mechanics of human sexuality were less fully understood but more spontaneously encountered. It may well be that our peculiar form of sexual self-awareness enables us to cure certain forms of barrenness, frigidity, and impotence, but excessive analysis may also impede spontaneity, total involvement, and joyous immediacy.

This dilemma informs our religious quest as well. Harvey Cox observes that "the problem is how to reconcile a critical degree of self-consciousness with a burning desire for experience which is not spoiled by too much self-analysis. . . . We want to be coolly sophisticated, yet not lose the simple directness we think is vital in human life."[7]

Beyond all defenses of Jewish God-talk stands our need to re-experience the evocative power of the ritual dramas and the great stories and legends binding the people Israel to its eternal God. To this end, agadists through the ages have reminded us that when God offered the covenant to Israel, they responded, "We shall do and (then) we shall hear." An impoverishment of Jewish experience impedes our responsiveness to the interpretive framework of our faith. To put the matter otherwise: *agada* is a barren thistle when it is uprooted from the soil of *halacha*.

Clearly discernible among us is a renewed awareness of the sanctifying power of Jewish observances and the importance of relating ourselves responsibly to the discipline of Jewish law. That is all to the good, but let it not lead us to ignore a deeper encounter with our agadic legacy as well.

All talk of religious crisis in our time brings us back inevitably not only to the erosion of Jewish deeds but to the problematics of Jewish belief. *Halacha* focuses on the terms of the covenant, *agada* discloses its reality and meaning. In re-appropriating one, we cannot afford to ignore the other. As long as the Jew survives as Jew, he must continue to tell stories which illumine the depth of his life and affirm that beyond the mystery there is meaning.

NOTES

1. Thomas Mann, *The Magic Mountain* (New York: *Vintage*, 1969), p. 32
2. Robert Bellah, *Beyond Belief* (New York: *Harper and Row*, 1970), pp. 206 and 244.
3. Saul Bellow, "Machines and Storybooks," *Harper's Magazine* (August 1974).
4. C. S. Lewis, "God in the Dock," *Essays in Theology and Ethics*, ed. by W. Hooper (Grand Rapids: *Eerdmans*, 1970), pg. 65f.
5. *Ibid.*
6. Archibald MacLeish, "Bovage to the Moon," *New York Times* (July 21, 1969).
7. Harvey Cox, *Feast of Fools* (Cambridge: Harvard University Press, 1969), p. 144.

CHAPTER 21

Reform Judaism and Jewish Law

It is good to be here for two reasons. First, whatever the auspices, visiting Amsterdam is a pleasant experience and participating in a convocation with fellow liberal Jews from other countries is a privilege.

For me personally this is also an opportunity to reflect, if only briefly, on an aspect of Jewish tradition which is not generally my first topic of study. My own temperament has inclined me more to the well-spring of *agada* than the labyrinth of *halacha*.

I have been drawn more to the rabbinic question: why did God create one man first when it was presumably within His power to create many, than to the question: what percentage of a substance must be impure to render the entire substance ritually impure?

All considerations of temperament aside, I would certainly acknowledge the importance of both kinds of questions to an understanding of Judaism. *Halacha* is the literature which governs a Jew's behavior. It is the *mitzvot*, the commandments: it is

Address to World Union for Progressive Judaism Conference, Amsterdam, Holland, July 7, 1978

Jewish law. *Halacha* literally means "walking." It defines the way a Jew should walk through life. *Agada*, which literally means telling a story, includes primarily the stories in which Biblical and rabbinic sages described and understood their faith in God and God's relationship to man. *Halacha* is law. *Agada* is lore. *Halacha* is concerned with behavior. *Agada* is concerned with belief or faith. The Torah tradition reflects an interplay of *halacha* and *agada*.

Let us illustrate: when I think of going to Amsterdam I think of Anne Frank's house. In her diary we read that Anne kindled the Chanukah lights during the time she was hiding from the Nazis in the attic. The primary *agada* of Chanukah is the story of the cruse of oil which was intended to last one day but lasted eight. This *agada* has become a metaphor of the miracle of Jewish survival despite the harrowing odds of history. Meeting in Amsterdam, a city once under Nazi occupation, a city in which Anne Frank once lived, lends special poignancy to that *agada*.

The *halacha* of Chanukah raises such questions as: where shall the *menorah* be placed? The Talmud replies: it should be placed in a prominent area in order to "publicize the miracle." But what if we are in hostile territory and the discovery of light would endanger our lives? Then surely, according to *halacha*, one need not set the *menorah* in a prominent place. If lighting the candles endangers one's life, one need not light the *menorah* at all.

Early Reform Judaism rebelled against a traditional view of *halacha*. Indeed if the Reformers had not dissented from the *halachic* tradition, Reform never could have been born. Why? According to *halacha* the laws of the Torah and Talmud derive their authority from God. If you were to ask why must a Jew keep *kosher* the ultimate argument is that the observance of the dietary laws is clearly stated or intended by the Torah, and the Torah is the will of God.

Reform could not and cannot accept this view of Torah. We contend that the Torah bears witness to an ongoing relationship between God and the people Israel over many centuries, that

God inspired the sages and writers of the Torah and in that sense God is the giver of Torah. But the Torah is not so much the word of God as man's response to the presence of God. The Torah is, in part, a human and hence a fallible document.

A second assumption of traditional *halacha* is that a law cannot be abrogated. God's legislation, unlike that of a human legislator, is eternal, perfect, immutable. Thus, for example, if according to Jewish law only a man may initiate a divorce and the man has disappeared with no testimony that he has died, the woman is in marital limbo. She cannot remarry.

Reform could not and does not live under this restriction. The Reform principle of "progressive revelation" affirms that we may be granted new insight into God's will for our time. We accept as sacred the principle of sexual equality and mutuality from which we derive the norm that men and women exchange vows and either can initiate a divorce. In fact, Reform has taken the matter of a divorce decree out of the domain of rabbinic jurisdiction. The rabbi counsels the couple, but the civil authority issues the divorce decree.

A third assumption of traditional *halacha* is that if Jewish law is to be radically reinterpreted it can only be done by recognized rabbinic authority. The catch is that only those who accept the traditional view of Jewish law will be recognized as rabbinic authorities. In practice, for example, the Israeli rabbinate does not recognize the legitimacy of either Conservative or Reform rabbis.

Reform Judaism contends that the ultimate authority in Judaism is vested not in a rabbi or group of rabbis, but derives from the informed Jew's dialogue with the tradition. In this dialogue the rabbi serves as prominent teacher and guide, but no rabbi or group of rabbis are the source of an ultimate decision from which there is no appeal.

Let me not overstate the case. While Reform emancipated itself from the authority of the *halacha* even the early Reformers, for all their revolutionary zeal, showed respect for the tradition. Thus when they did make changes in practice they felt the need to justify those changes by finding precedents within the tradition. When they introduced the German vernacular into the worship service they pointed out that the Talmud itself declares you can recite the *Shema* in the language you understand. And when they excised the prayer for the return of all Jews to Israel the early Reformers pointed out that the Talmud suggests that the Jews were scattered amongst the peoples not as punishment for sin, but in order to promote and spread the message of Judaism. Therefore we need not pray for the restoration of all Jews to Jerusalem.

The early Reformers also maintained the basic structure of the Jewish worship service and the Jewish calendar. It would be fair to say of them what Dr. Freehof says of us: "The Jewish common law ... does not ... rule (but) it continues to shape the life of the average Reform Jew."

In religious school we teach our children about lighting Sabbath candles, observing Passover *seder*, building *sukkot* and the like. We still permit the traditional *halacha* to impose some limits on our life. No Reform Jew will expect a rabbi to perform a wedding at 2:00 p.m. on Saturday afternoon, or permit bread to be served in the synagogue during Passover.

Our members ask rabbis questions of Jewish law. They assume that the rabbi's response reflects his attempt to come to terms with it in some way. We will be asked, for example: is it required that I arrange for the burial of my mother at my father's side, though none of us children lives in that city any more, and my mother did not request it? At what point shall I return to work after my father's death?

In truth then, no Reform Jew can live an authentic life without raising questions of *halacha*. As Dr. Eugene Mihaly put it: "in its broadest sense, *halacha* is the imperative, the *mitzvah*, the commandment that an aware, committed Jew feels and hears and experiences in the specific situations of his life."

In recent years there has been a growing interest in *halacha* within the Central Conference of American Rabbis. More emphasis is being placed on ritual observance and some have felt that it is time to provide congregants with more definite guidance, or even with a code of Reform practice.

In 1971 the issue "do we need a Reform guide" came to a head with a vigorous debate over a proposed Sabbath manual. The opponents of the manual argued that we were leading our congregants down the path to Orthodoxy. A guide, they warned, early hardens into a code and we shall lose that freedom of conscience which is a cornerstone of Reform. The champions of the Sabbath manual saw it as a test of our movement's serious intent to come to terms with tradition and promote more observance in the life of Reform Jews. After the debate a vote was taken. The Sabbath manual was accepted.

When the document passed, its champions embraced each other in glee and its opponents acted as if a nail had been hammered into the coffin of Reform Judaism. At the time I could not get overly excited over the debate, but felt that both those that feared the guide and those who heralded it were each guilty of extravagant expectations. Now, seven years later, the guide has in fact neither destroyed our Reform movement nor radically altered the lifestyle of most Reform Jews.

The guide is helpful but not obligating. At one point, for example, the manual states that it is a *mitzvah* to refrain from certain kinds of activity during some part of the Sabbath day. "Athletics, hobbies and other leisure activity should not be pursued during Shabbat worship hours." Seven years after the publication of the manual those who choose to play tennis on Saturday mornings, or hold dinner parties on Friday nights (much to the chagrin of rabbis) still do so with impunity, while those who are looking for some guidelines for meaningful Sabbath observance may turn to the manual for guidance.

Incidentally nothing is said in the guide restricting a tennis game on Saturday afternoon. Until recently I regarded such afternoon play as part of my *Oneg Shabbat* (joy of the Sabbath). Lately, however, I recognize the competitiveness of the game and the disgust at my poor "performance" is inconsistent with the need for Sabbath rest and relaxation. Accordingly I now feel personally addressed by the *mitzvah* "you shall not play tennis on Shabbat afternoon." But the Shabbat manual published by the Central Conference of American Rabbis was not sufficient to shape my conduct. My behavior in this matter, as in others, was shaped by the interaction between the guidance of *halacha*, the perception of my personal need, and my conscience.

The key for a Reform Jew is individual freedom. The CCAR or individual rabbis may guide and help inform my conscience, but no rabbi or group of rabbis may be permitted to decide authoritatively what shall be Torah for me. That leaves at least one question: how do you guard against the abuse of such freedom? Are there no guidelines within which I would endorse the Reform exercise of conscience?

Yes there are guidelines and the analogy I have often proposed, though it is out of season, is that of a quarterback on a football team. In the Reform version of the Jewish game, the quarterback calls the plays and perhaps no two quarterbacks will call the same combination of plays, but the quarterback has been trained by the coach and exercises his options with the knowledge of the plays shared by his fellow teammates, and a commitment to the goals of the game.

Any quarterback who calls plays consistently which seem calculated to lead the team to the wrong goal post—any liberal Jew who so exercises his freedom as to weaken his bond with God, Torah and the people Israel, must be judged irresponsible.

What are the parameters within which the liberal Jew will exercise his freedom to determine his *halacha*, his Jewish way? Let me list my five guidelines: First, a responsible liberal Jew will seek conscientiously to live by Jewish time. He will observe the significant calendar events of our heritage in a recognizably Jewish manner. He will not permit Passover or the Sabbath or Chanukah, etc. to be just like any other days of the year.

Two: A responsible liberal Jew will sanctify the significant moments of human life (birth, coming of age, love, death), in a recognizably Jewish manner. He will respect the Jewish lifecycle.

Three: A responsible liberal Jew will seek ethical guidance

for his life within the tradition. He will ask: what does my heritage teach about what is right and wrong in this situation?

Four: A responsible Reform Jew will make personal choices with due regard for membership in the total community of Israel. He will, therefore, seek occasions to make public witness as a Jew by identifying with the Jewish community in worship and in matters of common Jewish concern such as Israel, the plight of Soviet Jewry and the like.

Five: A responsible Reform Jew will continue to study the tradition throughout the days of this life. He will base his personal judgments on a continuing encounter with his heritage. He will cultivate an informed conscience.

Within these parameters I feel very comfortable with the principle of Reform freedom. Note that there is an allowance for individual differences in the nature and extent of observance. You and I may not observe Passover or Shabbat or mourn our dead in an identical manner, but while we may not be on the very same path, we will hopefully be traveling on the same Jewish landscape.

It was the great Jewish thinker of the 20th century, Franz Rosenzweig, who used the term "landscape" in this symbolic way: "Once there was a road for all Jews, the universal road with cloverleafs and bridges and towns. But the single road is gone. It has not existed for one hundred fifty years. Now it is only one among many roads, no longer the highway. So we must trust to the landscape . . . all our little personal roads (of *halacha*) are real preparation for the future way."

Let us hope that we shall use our freedom responsibly. May our personal way, our individual paths place us on the landscape of covenant faithfulness and draw us closer to the One whom we liberal Jews also acknowledge as "Giver of the Torah."

CHAPTER 22

Torah
and Life

My colleagues, your families, friends. The year was 1960. It seems not very long ago. Sidney Regner informed me that I, a young rabbi in Flint, Michigan, was being given the privilege of handing out prayerbooks at the CCAR Conference in New York City. Joan remembers that I was very pleased by this first assignment.

It seems like only a few years ago that Vice President Leon Feuer invited me to address this body for the first time during a symposium on covenant theology at the Conference in Philadelphia. I remember being very pleased and intimidated by that assignment. Tonight, I stand before you entrusted with the highest privilege it is in your power to bestow. I stand here gratefully, yet with humble recognition that even at best, the interval between the dawn of one's rabbinic vocation and the approach of evening is indeed *k'hegeh*, like a moment.

I address you as colleagues within the Reform movement and in the context of a Conference program that will probe the promise and problematic of religious liberalism. In his monu-

Presidential Address to Central Conference of American Rabbis, Seattle, Washington, June 1990

mental history of our movement, Michael Meyer reminds us "the German Reformers spoke repeatedly of integrating two elements: *Lehre* and *Leben*—Torah (the teaching) and the life led in the modern world." Tonight I want to explore with you a number of ways in which *lehre* and *leben*, Torah and life, are integrated for us and by us.

I speak as one who has done my share of Reform self-scrutiny, sometimes with painful awareness of the impoverished Jewish lives too many live under our banner. Yet my primary word this night is not apology but reaffirmation. I entered the rabbinate under the aegis of our movement and I continue to carry the banner with pride.

Our detractors accuse us of letting the vagaries of life (*leben*) totally enthrall us. We are cast as the great accommodationists, supinely bending to the rage of the age. In truth there have been two countervailing trends in our people's life. We have viewed the world as an enemy camp and ourselves as *am l'vadad-yishkon*, a people who must dwell in protective alienation.

But we have also seen ourselves as *brith l'amim*, a covenant embracing the world. And our historians remind us that what we have been able to give the world has been enhanced by what we have permitted ourselves to receive from it. As the Jewish calendar attests, our Israelite ancestors borrowed and transformed a rich legacy from the Canaanites. The Pharisees appropriated from the Greco-Roman world a new sense of individualism, a new method of parsing texts and a new appreciation of *chachma*, wisdom literature.

In our time the Reform movement appropriated Confirmation and transformed it into a Sinai-covenant renewal ceremony even as we adopted contemporary idioms for our synagogue music. Under the influence of the social gospel movement we embraced social action as a way of reclaiming prophetic values in public life. And yes, prodded by the modern feminist movement, we redefined the role of women in Jewish life. Must we apologize for such openness to the world? Hardly.

The real challenge in every age is neither to embrace undiscriminatingly nor reject mindlessly the wisdom of those around us. The challenge was and is to respond creatively with respect for the core truths and the sacred texts of Torah.

Some of our significant departures from traditional *halacha*, some of our redefinitions of what is or is not permissible derive not from so-called alien streams but from the living waters of Torah. Consider for example the principle of *k'vod habriot*, respect for the dignity of God's creatures. Out of concern for human dignity one is permitted to violate the prohibitions of Torah. The Talmud tells us of a sage who was walking on Shabbat with a fringed garment from which some of the tassels were missing. Should he be reminded on the street that his garment is a forbidden Sabbath burden and must be removed? No. And why not? *Mipnay k'vod habriyot*, out of respect for the dignity of God's creatures.

Centuries later Moses Isserles performed a marriage ceremony in his house on Friday night. The groom's parents had tried to cancel the betrothal because the bride's family could not honor the dowry. The couple apparently eloped. In justifying his marrying them on Shabbat, Isserles said: *ki gadol k'vod habriyot*—"for the honor of people is great."

Colleagues, when you and I permit a non-Jewish spouse to be buried in a family plot in our congregational cemetery we too are saying *mipnay k'vod habriyot*. To be sure, what remains an exception and is at times a minor theme in traditional *halacha* we have lifted to centrality in Reform responsa. *Halacha* grants an agitated male a momentary exemption from the obligation to recite the *Amidah*. We lift such personal circumstances to the level of norm. In defining the *mitzvah* to mourn our dead we recognize some persons will need more extensive mourning than others. We allow for much individual choice and legitimate diversity in ritual observance.

Yet we know there can be no freedom without boundaries. Indeed there are a cluster of "boundary *mitzvot*" within which most of us would validate our personal choice. Living in Jewish time is a boundary *mitzvah* which includes, of course, observing

Shabbat. Oh, we eschew a definitive enumeration of Shabbat do's and don'ts. We reject the implication "that the more closely you adhere to the *Shulchan Aruch*'s list the more authentic is your observance." But who among us teachers of Judaism would fail to include Shabbat as a boundary *mitzvah* (and this results in more than not officiating at weddings or funerals)? We define as our norm a Shabbat which embraces *oneg* (the joy of celebrating God's gift of life) and *menuchah* (physical rest and renewal); *tefillah* and *Talmud Torah* (spiritual renewal) and *karuv mishpacha*, family togetherness. Thus we have published *Gates of the Seasons* to guide us in our observance.

Yes, there are a large number of our constituents who accept the boundary *mitzvah* in principle but do not try to live within it; those for whom Shabbat is just another day in the week. There are also many self-defined Orthodox Jews who do not live by their more structured norm. Those who take Judaism seriously, be they Orthodox or Reform, will not only acknowledge boundaries but seek to live within them.

Periodically, we as a movement deal with boundary issues. Our debates and resolutions on mixed marriage and patrilineality have been efforts to define or redefine boundaries. We are now grappling with another such boundary issue. Shall we or shall we not formally validate the homosexual rabbi? We do well to ponder all boundary issues prudently and deliberately. We do well to root our stance in texts, concepts, principles derived from Torah even as we take seriously the knowledge we derive from our time and our life. I believe the report of the Ad Hoc Committee which will be presented for your acceptance at this convention reflects that kind of responsibleness.

Some lament that we are an untidy movement. We assert majority positions and grant respect to minority dissents. We draw our boundaries at different points and have not imposed sanctions on those who deviate from the declared norm. I, for one, am not scandalized by the fact that we expel a colleague only for flagrant violation of our ethics code or non-payment of dues. The *herem* motif, the use of banishment as a mechanism of religious control does not provide the brighter chapters in Jewish history.

And even when our movement has tilted excessively toward universalism, in time we have managed to correct our course. Our embrace of Zionism and our reclamation of the day school as a Reform option are instances of such correction and rebalancing.

Some wistfully yearn for a tighter act. If only we could stop validating so much diversity and so much freedom of choice. If only we could return to the traditional *halachic* framework. But most of us cannot. We can play at being *Hasidim* only for a weekend. As far as I can discover not even the most fervent neo-traditionalist among us is really anxious to surrender the right to wend her way through the labyrinth of *halacha*. And why is this so?

First because of what we believe to be true. We believe in revelation but for us the texts of Torah were filtered through the human soul and pen and mind-set. There are times when we must declare with Buber "I believe the prophet Samuel misunderstood God."* We distinguish the eternal from the time-bound even as we ask, what does the God of Sinai require of me in this time and place?

Yes, there is the danger we will become overly accommodationist, but then each movement has its demons to contend with. For us the danger of being prisoners of the dominant mind-set of this age; for our Orthodox colleagues, the danger of rigidity and timidity. For us, the danger that freedom of choice will lapse into a lack of seriousness; for them the danger that piety will lapse into fanaticism and intolerance.

We choose one set of dangers over another and, at best, we choose because of truth and temperament, because of what we can and cannot believe about Torah and because of how we feel about living our life. There are those who feel most at home if

---

Ed. God rejected Saul for not carrying out the command for total extermination of the Amalekite nation, the command transmitted by Samuel.

their life is meticulously structured, and there are those of us who require a tolerance for ambiguity and the leverage of greater personal choice.

We ought not be triumphalist. We can say "these and these," but neither should we be self-denigrating or over-apologetic. The best of our Jewish models compares quite favorably with the alternative, and the worst within each camp do our covenant and our future no credit. At best we live in a creative tension between Torah and life. We continue to ask and answer the question posed by all the generations before us: What is Torah? What is the teaching for me at this time, this place?

II

The relation between Torah and life is more than a matter of processing a *halachic* claim in my world. It is also the burden of bearing witness to the teaching in my life. Since we are rabbis of a movement that has accepted the primacy of the ethical, that burden may weigh even more heavily upon us. Recently, I revisited the first words I formally addressed to my peers. It was student trauma time. The HUC equivalent of trial by ordeal—the Junior year chapel sermon. My text *Kedoshim Tihyu*—"You Shall Be Holy."

Thirty-five years ago most of us lived in the dormitory—with daily housekeeping service, two served meals, linen napkins, in-house laundry. Despite the amenities, we were not a contented crew. Eager for cosmic profundities, we were served a lethal dose of Weingreen grammar. Pre-selected for our assertive egos, we were living in close quarters and survival demanded great ego restraint. Faculty and administration were often cast as the enemy, and the yearning for the day of ordination assumed messianic proportions.

In the interval, our behavior toward each other, indeed our behavior in and beyond the dormitory, fell at times considerably short of the norms we would be preaching and teaching. It seems as if we were permitting ourselves one last binge of irresponsibility before we had to assume the vocational burdens of the rabbinate. And implicitly or explicitly we rationalized our lapses from *kedusha* by citing a stressful environment and bad institutional structures.

That Shabbat I told my peers that "for us students at the college it is all too attractive to postpone the test of *kedusha* until after ordination ... to assume that ordination somehow marks the transition from the bourgeois to the classless society." I parsed the text *k'doshim tihyu*, "you shall be holy," to mean:

> We must criticize social institutions and structures here and elsewhere which tend to impede *kedusha*. We must strive to create structures more in keeping with its demands. But the 20th century has driven home with tragic impact that we have not yet found a master plan which will eliminate the ethically profane ... throughout our rabbinate we shall find a multitude of conditions detrimental to *kedusha*. Nevertheless, *k'doshim tihyu: Within the existing life situation there is always a margin of ethical possibility and the test is always now, in this place, in this time.*

Three and a half decades later I would not revise that message substantially. Though, after years of experience in the "field," I am now much more personally aware of stresses and temptations and of our vulnerabilities. Indeed there are moments when the dormitory may seem like a protective womb, a veritable Eden. Today I have a much greater respect than ever for the *yetzer hara*, a much deeper appreciation of all the ways we can and do stumble and fail. Such recognition is very humbling.

I shall never forget the night twenty years ago when I rode in a trolley car in Munich. Earlier that day a colleague and I had visited Dachau. We had just come from a Munich beer hall very much like the one where Hitler got his start. How often during those days in Germany I had been plagued by fantasies of these people going about their business while Jews were rounded up, interned and murdered. How often I had preached on the words *lo tuchal l'hitalaym*—you are not permitted to hide, to pretend you are not involved and that you have no responsibility.

That night on the Munich trolley we saw a drunken man sitting in his seat, obviously an *auslander*, one who came from a neighboring country to work in the prosperous German economy. At one point the man began to retch uncontrollably. The ticket collector shouted at him. There was contempt in her voice as she told him retching in a street car was against German law. The scene was unpleasant and the voice of authority encouraged distance. The riders standing in the street car instinctively moved away from where the *auslander* was sitting. I did too. A German woman approached the *auslander* and wiped his face with some tissues.

That episode on the trolley and my own act of distancing myself from the *auslander* in Munich, in *democratic West Germany* was disturbing. Even more troubling was the question: how would I have acted in Munich if I were a non-Jew during the Hitler era?

With the passing years, the *al hayt* confessional becomes ever more poignant each Yom Kippur. So does the theme of my brokenness and my need for God's forgiving grace. To be sure our heritage does not expect us to be saints. It does not proclaim an ethic which (like Jesus' sermon on the mount) assumes the imminent dawn of the kingdom. As we have so often preached, Judaism proclaims an ethic for those who would strive to be not saints but decent human beings in a world that is unredeemed.

Still we do proclaim accountability. We do teach there is no forgiveness without *t'shuvah*. And we know that the test of *t'shuvah*, of repentance, is how well we act the next time under similar circumstances, or as Rabbi Judah said: "same person, same season, same place." The truth remains: we who teach Torah cannot simply model our fallibility. The link between *lehre* and *leben*, the teaching and our life, remains the most exacting standard of our authenticity and the tests are *yom, yom*, each day.

We are forever tested by the sensitivity with which junior and senior colleagues in the same congregation treat each other. We are tested by the way we integrate our role as rabbi with our role as spouse and parent. During a pre-marital interview, a yuppie couple asked me, "Rabbi, in your life, how have you made time for your family?" We are tested in timing our retirement:

do we take into account the congregation's need, or only our own? We are tested in our preaching: do we credit the sources of our wisdom? We are tested by the *tzimtzum*, the ego-self-restraint we show when we are cast as the introducer and not the main speaker—or when generally it is another's turn for a place in the sun. We are tested when we change a local *minhag*. Do we show a concern lest the old-timers become total strangers in their own home? We are tested by the way we respond to those congregants who have the power to help and hurt us and by how we respond to those who have no power over our lives.

Yes, God is found in the details and so is *kedusha*. The *yetzer* is stronger than we had ever imagined and appears in so many guises. Our need for *hesed*—God's steadfast love and forgiveness is more amply understood with each passing year. *Still we are both chastened and validated by the manner in which the teaching we proclaim is embodied in the life we live.*

III

There is one more relation between *lehre* and *leben*, Torah and life, I must mention. Torah frames all human experience in relation to a God who is my creator, my teacher, my redeemer. But very often my *life* does not seem to be living that story. I speak now not of those great crises of faith when life appears to mock the teaching, but simply of those long intervals between the "peak experiences," those very substantial segments of life when there is no *gillui shechinah*, no palpable sign of the Divine Presence. Indeed, responsible living means keeping our human covenants during those moments when there is no lightning and thunder at Sinai, no bush that is unconsumed and no bells ringing. Responsible living requires that there be tolerance for much prose punctuated by moments of poetry, periods of quiet love punctuated by moments of intense passion.

Oh, there are those who would redefine transcendence so that we and our people might see everywhere burning bushes that are not consumed. My own inclination is to cultivate in myself and encourage in others the capacity to live with a God who is both hidden and revealed. We teach fidelity to the covenant of one's marital life *between* those moments when love attains passionate intensity. We teach fidelity to the covenant at Sinai even at those times we do not feel the presence of *Adonai*, my creator, my teacher, my redeemer.

But because of our vocation we are also uniquely positioned to witness and name the moments of exquisite grace when the teaching is not elusive abstraction or fading memory or messianic hope, but vivid truth; those moments when *Torah* and *life* are transparently one. So many times a pastoral visit is professional duty or even a matter of pursuing our rabbinic survival, but there are those moments when our awareness of being needed by another person is a sign of God's need and our response to that person is our response to God's call. Those are the awesome moments when we hear *ayeka*, where are you? And we answer, "here am I."

There are times we turn to the Torah text for authority and feel that the connections we make between Torah and our life are strained and even artificial. But there are those times of Talmud Torah when thoughts leaping into our minds, thoughts filtered through the Torah text, or rabbinic commentaries and our own sensibility have the mark of God's revealing presence, of Torah, and you and I stand at Sinai and there is a coming together of *Torah* and *life*.

There are times when we preside at the passages of life and despite the rhetoric there is no *gillui schechina*, no sense that God is in this place. But there are times, at a wedding or a funeral, or a Bar Mitzvah, when the story of Torah and the story of our life are transparently one.

The Bar Mitzvah boy in my congregation that Shabbat had read of a Joseph no longer able to conceal his identity, or his love for his brothers *v'lo yachol l'hitapek*. "Joseph was unable to control himself." Quickly he sent the Egyptians out before breaking down and crying loud enough for all Egypt to hear, "I am Joseph, your brother."

Joshua, the Bar Mitzvah that Shabbat, had written a talk

expounding the portion. He spoke of his extraordinarily close bond with a brother eight years older who was seated with the family on the bimah. Joshua treated that bond with a light touch and the congregation responded to his playing it cool. But then, as Joshua made an additional reference to his brother, he choked up and sobbed quietly. *V'lo yachol l'hitapek.* "He could not control himself." At first all felt compassion for a 13-year old who stood emotionally overexposed in the public domain. Joshua recovered his composure and completed the talk and each of us knew we had witnessed a singular moment when Torah and life became one. God was in that place and we knew it.

Dear colleagues, our burden and our *zechut* is to help our generation parse the relation between *lehre* and *leben*. As Reform rabbis we acknowledge the creative tension between Torah and life and we help our people renegotiate responsibly the claims of the teaching in their lives. Now as always our credibility derives ultimately from how well the teaching is embodied in our life. And most precious for us and our people are the moments when Torah and life are transparently one. At such moments we are moved to proclaim: *ashraynu, ma tov helka-ynu ...*" Blessed are we, how good is our portion, how pleasant our lot, how beautiful our legacy."

SECTION V

---·—·—·—·—·—·—·—·—·—·—·—·—

A Perfect
Healing

CHAPTER 23

Life's Traumas Bless Us with Faith

Several weeks ago during an electrical storm, our house was struck by lightning and caught fire. Within an hour and a half it was virtually reduced to rubble. My wife and I escaped unharmed.

The next day, foraging through the ruins, Joan and I recovered some precious family albums, some books (which the firemen had labored valiantly to save) and some personal effects. But what had been our family nest for almost twenty years was gone.

More than a few of my congregants seemed shocked to learn that their rabbi had no special immunity from such hazards of existence. We were presumed to be decent and, after all, I devoted my life to the service of God; yet of all the homes in the neighborhood ours alone seemed targeted for a direct strike.

The obvious response is that we clergy have no greater claim on God's providential care. People I know, Jews, Christians and others, whose lives have borne more eloquent testimony to the service of God than mine, have endured tragedies that make ours pale by comparison. Why then should a rabbi and his family be spared life's misfortunes?

Houston Chronicle, Op Ed, January 1996

Still, a happening such as this cries out for some theological response. There are at least two kinds of religious answers. The early rabbinic sages speak of a world that "pursues its natural course." Not even God can give us a world of nature without limiting the divine power to control all that happens in the world.

A rickety ladder may cause a bad or good boy to fall to his death. A virus does not respect human character and lightning will destroy what it strikes directly, especially when the fire's sparks fall on a flammable structure on a windy night.

According to this view, my family was not targeted by God. Our home was just in the wrong place at the wrong time. God weeps with us over the pain we mortals endure.

A second view declares that God is Lord of nature and therefore ultimately in control. I may not be able to fully understand God's purposes, but I must trust that beyond the mystery there is meaning. Though our home and many of our possessions are gone, our personal survival remains dramatic testimony to God's power and goodness.

Whatever perspective one chooses (and I have often alternated between them) I do believe God has been with us through this ordeal and is present to help us heal and move on with our lives.

How do we heal? Most crucial is the experience of love. My wife and I have been moved to tears by the outpouring of love from family, friends, congregation and the community-at-large. As a caregiver, it is so much easier for me to give than to receive. From this trauma I am learning how to acknowledge my neediness and to gratefully receive the love of others.

Humor is also critical to healing. The week before the storm I played tennis. When one of my shots hovered and then rolled improbably over the net my partner and our opponents all shrugged and grimaced as if to say, "What can you do when you are playing with someone who has a special 'in' up there?"

My response was, "Remember, I am really in sales, not administration." After the storm my tennis partner came up following Sabbath services and declared, "You were right, you really are in sales, not administration."

From life's traumas we emerge never fully the same. When I am asked where do Joan and I plan to make our permanent residence, I mentally place the word permanent in quotation marks. As the poet Wallace Stevens wrote: "We live in a place that is not our own." Our real home is the frail, vulnerable, *sukkah* (booth) which Hebrew Scripture enjoins us to dwell in during the Feast of Tabernacles.

There is such a thin line between homeiness and homelessness, order and chaos, having and losing, life and death. Therefore we need to value all the more what we are loaned, what is ours to enjoy—for how long we do not know.

From our own vulnerability, from our own knowing the heart of the stranger we are bidden to be even more compassionate toward others who experience the pain of God's world. The Campaign for the Homeless reminds us of those who are not blessed with the marvelous built-in support system we have experienced. They are the truly needy ones.

For every event my tradition teaches me there is a benediction of blessing to recite. The sages instruct us that when you experience an earthquake, lightning, thunderstorms or the like, one should say, "Blessed is the One whose power and might fill the world." And when we have survived a dangerous event or a perilous journey we should say, "Blessed are You, O God, who bestows blessings on a person even beyond his merits and has dealt graciously with me."

In recent days I have recited both blessings with a gut-wrenching "Amen."

CHAPTER 24

Ⴔ Prisoner Cannot Ⴔree Ⴔimself

This Holiday season is upon us. Chanukah, Christmas, the secular New Year—all are times of good cheer and organized celebration. At this season of the winter solstice we kindle lights of hope and gladness.

But for some of us these are days of depression and utter loneliness. In the midst of our good cheer we need to be alert to symptoms of human pain and not become so distracted by our festivities that we miss the subtle call of another for comfort and reassurance.

This is a season to recount miracles. One of the greatest of God's wondrous acts is that He has endowed us with the power to become His messengers of comfort. A Talmudic story tells that when Rabbi Yohanan was ailing, Rabbi Hanina came to visit him. Hanina asked, "Are your sufferings dear to you? Do you accept them as chastisements of Divine love?" Yohanan replied, "Neither they nor their reward." Whereupon Hanina took Yohanan's hand and healed him.

At a later date Yohanan switched roles. He who now felt well visited an ailing colleague and offered the hand of healing com-

Houston Chronicle, Turning Points, 1994

fort. The Talmud then asks, "In each case, why didn't the ailing rabbis heal themselves?" The answer: "A prisoner cannot free himself from the prison." We need the help of another. When we are ailing in body or spirit we aren't helped by telling our troubles to ourselves. We may be helped by telling our troubles to a caring, responsive other—by feeling another's hand.

Normally even if we are clergymen schooled in the art of ministering we may have grave doubts about the adequacy of our powers. A retired colleague, Rabbi Jerome Malino told a number of us of an incident in his early rabbinate.

A crash on the Pennsylvania Turnpike killed instantly a father, mother and child. Rabbi Malino vividly remembers the three coffins set before him as he stumbled through the funeral service. A short time thereafter he met with the mother of the man who had died in the crash. She welcomed him to her home and led him to an alcove in the living room. They sat facing each other. The rabbi tried to speak but no words came. The woman cried. After some time the young rabbi excused himself. All the way home he reproached himself for being a total failure.

A week or so later he returned to the woman's home. This time he had rehearsed the words he would speak. She ushered him in, led him to the same alcove and they sat. He opened his mouth and the words failed him. She cried, he cried and they held hands. After a brief interlude he excused himself, once again feeling so woefully unsuccessful as a comforter. During subsequent months the Rabbi saw the woman in synagogue periodically and each time remembered his faltering efforts.

Months later, after the unveiling of the tombstone the family gathered at the woman's home. For this occasion the mother of the woman killed in the crash had come in from out of town. Rabbi Malino overheard the two grieving mothers talking in the kitchen. The mother from out of town said, "Today was the first time I heard or recited prayers since the funeral. I just haven't been able to go to synagogue or even pray at home." The local mother replied, "I understand. I'd feel as you did if it weren't for the wonderful comfort I received from my rabbi." Overhearing this testimonial the young rabbi's eyes welled up with tears of gratitude.

One of the great miracles of life is our strange and mysterious power to be God's agents of comfort and healing. Now, as in the days of Rabbi Hanina, that comfort may occur not only by the words we speak but by a silent and loving presence.

CHAPTER 25

The Reality of Forgiveness

Kol Nidre, that haunting melody has once again pierced our souls. We gather here on the most sacred night of the Jewish calendar.

We enter this place to confirm who we are, to explore what we may become. We bring to this place the realities of our personal world and that of a larger world to which we belong.

And alas, one of those larger events we cannot ignore on this night of nights, is the death of a man who was once an enemy of our people, but who became a friend. The assassination of Anwar Sadat has stirred the world and affected us deeply. We are saddened. We are anxious about the future.

When life's troubling realities intrude upon us we draw close to each other as a community of fate and faith. We need to transcend the vagaries of the moment, the shrill headlines of the morning newspaper. The Kol Nidre melody, sung on this night for centuries, symbolizes the anchoring, stabilizing quality of our heritage. Here, in this room, we seek to place the threatening realities of our life in manageable perspective.

It is ironic. The last time Anwar Sadat compelled me to

Sermon, Yom Kippur Eve, October 7, 1981

revise a Yom Kippur sermon was 1973. That was the year of the Yom Kippur War, when Egypt, under Sadat, chose the holiest day of the Jewish year to launch a surprise attack on Israel. Sadat was not mentioned honorably in the synagogue on that day. Now, eight years later, on Yom Kippur, Anwar Sadat is mourned in synagogues from Houston to Jerusalem to Cairo. We remember him respectfully and fondly as a remarkable man who dared to make peace with Israel.

Who among us will ever forget that day when the TV screen flashed the picture of an Egyptian airliner taxiing to the terminal at Ben Gurion Airport. In Tel Aviv, Sadat, casting away thirty years of war and hatred, deplaned, listened to an Israeli band play the Egyptian national anthem, walked over to Golda Meir, kissed her on the cheek and said, "Madam, I have waited a long time for this moment," and there was not a dry eye among us.

Later in the Knesset of Israel, the leader of forty million Arabs once pledged to Israel's destruction, spoke these words before the eyes and ears of the world:

> We have been rejecting you, and we had our reasons for that. Yes, we refused to meet you . . . but I wish to tell you today, and I proclaim to the world: we accept to live with you in a lasting and just peace.

That was a day many of us dreamed of, but did not really think possible in our lifetime. We saw Menachem Begin and Anwar Sadat embrace and transform enmity into partnership. We have since seen Egyptian men and women who once regarded Israel as a curse word, greet Israelis with a warm embrace and a *"shalom."* And we have seen Israelis, who once regarded Sadat as a curse word, drink a *l'chaim*, a toast, to his life and health. What a spine-tingling transformation in our time. What a stunning, if fragile achievement!

Anwar Sadat liberated the seeds of national reconciliation and forgiveness in the lives of two hostile nations. For that alone he would merit mention on this night of reconciliation. The spirit of his journey to Jerusalem created a new and beautiful reality. We pray tonight that his spirit will abide and that his work of reconciliation will continue as the ultimate tribute to his life and memory.

But on this night of nights, my friends, we inevitably turn from the global and the political to our personal world, for that is still where the major struggles of our life occur. Most of us are not directly engaged in the struggle to reconcile nations, but we do confront the possibilities and difficulties of forgiveness and reconciliation in our interpersonal lives.

The Kol Nidre theme holds forth the promise of forgiveness, atonement with ourselves, with each other, with God. The introduction of the Kol Nidre proclaims: "We are all transgressors ... all in need of healing, forgiveness, and reconciliation. For what we have done, for what we may yet do, we ask pardon."

And yet outside this room, we don't often talk or act, as if we really believe in divine forgiveness or in forgiving each other, or in forgiving ourselves. And the three are more interrelated than we imagine.

During my rabbinate in Chicago, I came to know and counsel an elderly mother and her middle-aged daughter. They were deeply estranged from each other. The mother insisted (with great scorn and hurt) that her daughter had been a problem as far back as she could remember. The daughter, terribly hostile and resentful, blamed her mother for all her problems and lost no opportunity to hurt her.

Once, in tears, the mother complained to me, "I have been a religious person. So what? Look, if I let her get to me she would destroy me." I said to her, "I am sure you have tried to be a good mother, but have you ever considered that maybe, wittingly or unwittingly, you contributed to your daughter's problems and her attitude? What would happen if next time you didn't say 'how could you do this to me?' What would happen if you said to her, 'I may have wronged you, maybe in ways I am not even aware. And if I have wronged you, I am sorry. I want, I need your forgiveness.'"

There was a stony silence, a total rejection of that idea (and of me), a firm reassertion of defiant innocence.

On another occasion, the daughter had told me how terrible her mother was. I asked her, "Is it possible that you are the cause of some of your problems? Maybe you expected more from your mother than she could offer and punished her more than she deserves. Can you imagine what would happen if you turned to your mother, hugged her, and said, 'We need each other's forgiveness?'" Again there was stony silence.

Mother and daughter rejected any notion of asking for or granting forgiveness, and I believe that each rejected any conscious responsibility for failure in the relationship, because to do so would have left them in an unacceptable trap, a guilt trap. You see they believed in the reality of guilt. From time to time they felt it, but they had no real experience with granting or receiving forgiveness. They refused to accept any responsibility because they didn't believe in forgiveness.

The daughter went from therapist to therapist and some years later took her life. The mother died an embittered woman. From time to time I have wondered sadly, "if only."

On this night of nights "when named heart is revealed to the hiding self," can we remember many occasions (any occasions) when we received or bestowed a monumental gift of forgiveness? Our power to forgive is terribly underdeveloped. We are so much better at nursing wounds. We are better at signaling "don't fail me because I am not good at forgiving." Even if we want to forgive, we find it awfully hard to do so.

I counseled with a couple who love each other, feel their marriage is basically good, but there was a crisis. He had been involved in a brief affair. He felt genuinely remorseful. She felt betrayed. They planned to save the marriage. She *wanted* to forgive, she knew he needed it, but she could not bring herself to forgive him.

We find it hard to forgive not only others, but ourselves. Oh, we talk about "you must forgive yourself," such talk is fashionable, but it is easier said than done. That is especially true when we have wronged a loved one who is no longer living. Oh that terrible indictment which I have heard so often: "I let her down, rabbi. I didn't do all I could or should while she was alive."

Our counseling strategy is to soften the matter. We say, "All relationships are imperfect. She wasn't perfect to you and don't be so hard on yourself, you were fine and you are fine.... " Yet, despite all our tempering allowances, he knows in some ways he really did let her down. He needs to forgive himself, but this is so very hard to do.

There is another sense in which we find it hard to forgive ourselves: when we have failed to become what we feel we ought to have become. I know a solid citizen, a really successful man by my standards, who is haunted by a sense of what might have been; if only he had not abandoned the ambition, the dream of his earlier years. He feels that he sold out to financial expediency, that he took the line of least resistance. He didn't "hang in there" and remain faithful to his dream. Periodically he can't enjoy who he is and what he has because he can't forgive himself for what he might have, but did not become.

We are bad not only at forgiving others, but we are just as bad, or worse, at forgiving ourselves. And so many of us walk through life with burdens, with baggage we try not to face, but from which we are not easily relieved.

Oh, there may be no dramatic acts of failure, no monumental betrayals in our personal kit, but an accumulation of little ones: those times we were so preoccupied with making it that we were unavailable physically or emotionally to our family; the times we catered to those who wield power over us and were insensitive to those over whom we have power; the times we pretended to care and should have cared, but knew we didn't give a darn; the times we put down another person only to make ourselves look good or conceal our jealousy; the times we realized we were not as noble as we appear or would like to be.

We don't think of these as "sins." We don't use the word, but the weight of failure is very real and the cumulative feeling is like a low-grade infection which may not keep us from functioning but takes its toll. It is part of the baggage of nagging regrets in all our lives.

But why is forgiveness so often unavailable or inadequate?

Why is it so difficult to forgive others or ourselves? I think I know. We may not speak of "sin." We may or may not formally declare our belief in God, but we do live under a sense of judgment. We feel, however dimly, accountable to a power greater than ourselves or our parents. We may not view an old man sitting on a throne of judgment up there but we do feel, to use Saul Bellow's beautiful phrase, "bonded to the eternal." We feel judged by some transcendent standard and that impels us to judge others and ourselves.

Only if we experience forgiveness on the same scale as we experience judgment, only if we experience forgiveness as part of the very structure of the world, as God's good gift, can we more easily forgive others and ourselves.

Normally we are far more attuned to the weight, the anguish, the guilt of judgment than we are to the balm of God's forgiving love. So we find it much easier to judge than to forgive. But that is why this night, this day is so precious and so special.

For somehow, beneath the lip service we give these prayers and the casualness of our outward appearance, we sense (however faintly) that what we Jews proclaim on this day of prayer and fasting is what we need and come for and what we want to believe in. We sense the truth of the prayer: "And in Your love, O Lord, You have given us this Day of Atonement that our sins may be forgiven."

Somehow the symbolism of this prayerbook, the Kol Nidre chant, the white vestments, the image of cleansing and purification get to us. Many of you have told me that by the time you leave the synagogue late tomorrow afternoon you feel strangely comforted and at peace. I think it is more than a matter of esthetics. On this day, if on no other occasion, we permit ourselves to acknowledge and receive the fantastic gift of God's forgiveness. We feel strangely comforted, relieved by this day's triumphal assertion:

> "It's all right. I am not trapped by the past entries in my book
> of life. It's all right. So I didn't become all that I could have
> become. So I let her down in some ways. I didn't do all I could

have or should have done. So there were times when I wasn't the husband or wife, son or daughter, the brother, the sister, I could have, or should have, been. It's all right. I can admit my brokenness, my failures. I must, wherever possible, seek to make amends. I can, wherever possible, ask their forgiveness. But I am not caught in a guilt trap, because I am not only judged, I am also forgivable and forgiven. And the Lord said, "I have pardoned in response to your plea."

This day is so special because on this day we not only pray for pardon; we somehow experience the healing power of God's grace. If only we could carry beyond this day a new sense that the power of God's forgiveness is greater than the power of God's judgment, that the one who judges also bounteously forgives and therefore we who judge can also forgive each other and ourselves. If only we could believe this, how different our inner-life, our life with each other could be.

"And the Lord said, 'I have pardoned in response to your plea.'" Lord, Lord God, merciful and gracious, on this night of nights, help us to understand that we are not only judged but forgiven. Help us to forgive one another and ourselves. Praised be Thou, O Lord, abundant in mercy and forgiveness.

CHAPTER 26

Who Shall Live
and Who Shall Die?

This week a Houston dateline appeared in news stories around the world. David, the "bubble boy," died after twelve years in a totally germ-free environment. He had a radical immune deficiency which rendered him vulnerable to deadly disease.

Medical technology made it possible for him to live those twelve years. Medical technology tried to normalize his life with an experimental bone marrow transplant. The procedure failed to normalize or extend his life. Was it right to perform that experimental surgery on David?

"Baby Jane Doe" is the infant girl born with a most severe form of spina bifida. Her skull is too small to let her brain develop. Her spine is open. Were her parents wrong in withholding consent for experimental surgery which could extend Baby Jane Doe's life by an estimated eighteen years?

Elizabeth Bouvia is 26. She is a quadriplegic, cerebral palsy victim who has been judged of sound mind. Elizabeth has decided that her life as a total invalid, dependent on round-the-clock care by others, is no longer worth the living, but she cannot even actively put an end to her life, so she wants the court to compel the hospital to help her die. Should that wish be granted?

Sermon, February 24, 1984

In such agonizing situations we face the question: "Who shall live and who shall die?" We think of this as a High Holy Day theme. Each year we acknowledge that our lives and destinies are dependent upon a power greater than our own. But our sages also believed that when we are seriously ill we should not assume it is our imminent destiny to die. We are called to be co-partners with God in sustaining and enhancing life.

Not so many years ago there was very little medical science could do to alter the course of a life-threatening illness or to repair a chronic disability. Until a relatively short time ago our sole reliance was prayer—prayer that the power greater than our own would heal, or at least extend life.

But even in those days, indeed even in ancient times, our sages realized that under some circumstances one is not sure what to pray for. Shall we pray for extension of life (even under conditions of gross indignity and severe suffering) or pray for death, for the release of the person to *Olam Habah*, that other world of perfect peace and communion with God?

The Talmud tells the story of Rabbi Judah who lay dying. A group of rabbinic colleagues gathered outside his home in a continuous prayer vigil. They hoped their prayers would extend Rabbi Judah's life, but the Rabbi's housekeeper sensed the hopelessness of his situation. She loved him deeply and could not stand to watch him suffer. She refused to join the disciples in their prayers. In fact she took an earthen jar and threw it on the courtyard to interrupt their prayers. She wanted God to take Rabbi Judah's life. And the Talmud records the housekeeper's action with approval. Yes, our tradition teaches that there are times when it is proper to pray that God will relieve our loved ones, or us, from a prolonged dying.

A RESPECT FOR TWO TRUTHS

Praying that *God* grant the peace of death is one thing; our facilitating, our precipitating, our actively hastening death is another. Life is sacred. Life is a gift. Judaism teaches we are not permitted to take our own life (suicide) or another life except under two conditions. We cannot take another's life unless that life threatens our own. Self-defense is permitted. And we may expose ourselves to death rather than betray all that we hold sacred. Martyrdom is permitted.

But what of the limbo, that living which is only a prolonged dying? What of the case of Rabbi Judah whose housekeeper interrupted the prayers of his disciples? May we do more than pray that a person who is dying shall die?

The *Shulhan Aruch*, a 16th century law code, addresses that question. We read:

> It is forbidden to hasten the death of a dying man. If one has been moribund for a long time and continues to linger on, we may not remove the pillow or the mattress from under him . . . for in the process of touching the patient we may move him and thus hasten his death. . . . However if there is anything external which prevents his release from his death pangs, such as a clattering noise near the patient's house, or if there is salt on his tongue, and these hinder the departure of the soul, it is permitted to remove them because there is no direct act of hastening death, for one merely removes the impediment (to dying).

Obviously the 16th century rabbis' knowledge of medicine is archaic by our standards. In our minds removing the pillow hardly constitutes an act of hastening death, nor does a clattering noise prevent the terminally ill from lapsing into death, but the principle is clear. Rabbi Moses Isserles, a 16th century Rabbi, explains: "We must not actively hasten death, but we may remove that which hinders death." That is the distinction we now know as passive and active euthanasia.

The line, of course, may seem very thin, but what the rabbinic tradition sought to establish is a respect for two truths in tension. The first truth—a reverence for human life. We need to guard against any act which diminishes the sanctity of life.

In a contemporary vein we must be wary of determining that the quality of a certain life fails to meet desirable standards and ought not to be sustained. After all, in some ancient cultures, infanticide was practiced. Some infants were put to death because they did not meet certain standards, including a particular gender. In our own time Hitler judged the mentally defective, and yes, the Jews, as not fulfilling a quality of life worth preserving. Judaism is understandably wary of "quality of life" arguments. The sanctity of every human life needs to be respected. One affirms this principle by not actively precipitating death. A physician is bound by the Hippocratic Oath "to heal and not to harm." A Jewish physician is also bound by the Torah to affirm the sanctity of the gift of life.

But there is a second truth in tension with the first. Prolonging the process of dying, intervening to prevent the peace and release of death, is a violation of the dignity, the sanctity of the person—and of God's intention for that person.

How live with these two truths? How distinguish between actions which affirm the sanctity of life and acts which merely assault human dignity and prolong dying? The question is hard enough. Our situation is far more complex and more agonizing than that of our medieval or ancient forebears. We live in an age of high medical technology.

Technology may not conquer death, but it can prolong the process of dying. Heartbeat and breathing can now be sustained even in a person whose brain has deteriorated to the point of liquefaction. Daniel Maguire says: "Death has lost its medical and moral simplicity. We know it more as a process, not a moment, and we have the means to extend or shorten the process." Rabbi Judah's housekeeper could interrupt prayers. We can unplug respirators. Is it ever right to do so?

Many modern rabbis have argued that in cases of terminal illness there may well come a moment when removing the respirator or not refilling the bottle with intravenous nutrients is comparable to removing the salt from the dying person's tongue. It is merely removing the impediment which prolongs dying. I would agree.

A JEWISH PERSPECTIVE ON BIO-ETHICS

Decisions in "biomedical ethics" are often difficult. Let us apply the principle of the two truths in tension to some situations we have mentioned earlier. Remember that affirming the sanctity of life is our duty; prolonging dying is not our duty.

This week David, the "bubble boy" who lived alone in a sterile room or in an insulated space unit for twelve years of life lost his battle for life. David's twelve years were a special gift made possible by the miracle of medical technology. A few decades ago David would not have lived to think, speak, read, play, laugh or love.

Then came a momentous decision. He didn't want to stay in a cage all his life. He and his parents were apprised of an experimental procedure, a bone marrow transplant, which if successful would give David the freedom of a near normal life. Its failure could precipitate death. The family and David chose the additional intervention. We are sad that it failed, but there are no unresolved moral issues here (at least none in the context of the principle we have been talking about tonight). Reverence for David's life and the concern for his dignity were sustained. The story of David is the story of our bold but at times unsuccessful battle to help God repair the brokenness in creation.

But what of the first "Baby Doe" case in Bloomington, Indiana in 1982? An infant with Down's Syndrome was permitted to die of starvation when the parents refused a well-tested, surgical procedure to repair a defect in the infant's esophagus. That surgery would have permitted the infant to receive nourishment normally and to live. The quality of that child's life was not deemed sufficient to warrant its survival and sustenance. Was such a judgement consistent with the sanctity of life?

We can empathize with the parents. What anguish they must have felt, but don't we all know Down's Syndrome persons who are loved and loving and who even live productive lives? Are such children, once born, not to be protected? Should parents make the decisive judgment in determining whether such children should have the right to life? Or ought there be some independent judgment in these matters?

Before attempting to respond let us move on to the case of "Baby Jane Doe." Here, the child was born with an extreme case of spina bifida with gross complications. The parents were told that without surgery she might live as long as two years; with surgery, as long as twenty years. But she would, in all likelihood, be bedridden, could not think normally, or speak, or see. She would be incontinent and in constant pain.

The parents, with the consent of the attending physicians, agreed not to perform the surgery. They see that their child is nourished physically and emotionally and that she is treated for infection, but they have avoided medical intervention which is experimental, offers no cure and appears to give the child a prolonged living death rather than life with some dignity.

With trepidation (and I hope some sense of the anguish involved in both decisions) I find the judgment of the physician and parents in this (the "Baby Jane Doe" case) morally justifiable. Whereas the decision made by the parents and physicians in the Down's Syndrome case in Indiana I find much more difficult to justify. In one, death was precipitated by starving a Down's Syndrome child. In the second, one could argue that surgery would only prolong a living death.

In all such cases I cringe at the thought of politicians actively intervening in the process, as the present administration is doing in the "Baby Jane Doe" case. Such decisions are best made not by political appointees, or even courts of law, but by a soul-searching collaboration among attending physicians, family and clergyman or ethicist. There ought to be a hospital review board by which such decisions can be evaluated. The courts should be a last resort. And we who participate in or judge such decisions must do so with a maximum of medical knowledge, reverence, awe, humility and compassion.

What of Elizabeth Bouvia, the quadriplegic, cerebral palsied, 26-year old who wants the hospital to help her die? Any person who determines that life under given circumstances is not really worth the living ought to be encouraged to find a reason for living. But ultimately no person can decide for another that life is worth the living. If such a person takes his or her life, it is time not for our judgment, but for our humility and silent sadness.

A civilized society, however, cannot encourage doctors or hospital administrators to violate their commitment to heal and not to harm. If a friend were to become an accomplice and help an Elizabeth Bouvia fulfill her death wish, such a person ought to be removed from legal liability. Society's laws must not formally sanction "mercy killing" or helping another person take his or her life. But, after the fact, courts of law should (and generally do) treat such persons with great understanding.

These are awesome issues, hardly to be disposed of glibly in a Sabbath Eve sermon. We raise them on Shabbat, the anniversary of Creation. We know that life is a sacred gift, and we know that, at times, death is a blessing. The question—who shall live and who shall die—is often reducible to another. When are we partners with God in affirming life, and when are we primarily denying a person the dignity of that ultimate release we call death?

There is no simple, standard formula which can be applied mechanically to each situation. May the Creator of a world of life and death, of joy and pain, may the One who empowers us to share in enhancing life, help us to use our unprecedented power with wisdom, justice and compassion.

SECTION VI

L'Dor Va Dor— From Generation to Generation

CHAPTER 27

We Are
Bound

"And he (Abraham) bound his son, Isaac, and placed him upon the altar above the firewood." And he bound his son. From this phrase the story gets its rabbinic name, the *akeda*, the binding of Isaac.

That physical binding on the altar which could have cost Isaac his life and Abraham his only son, was the fruit of a more primal binding. Isaac was bound to Abraham as son to father.

Can a story rooted in the binding of the generations, a story which really tells how children are bound by and to their parents ever grow stale? We sons and daughters discover that *akeda*, that primal bond in a thousand ways: in a cry in the night, in a moment of embrace, in a child's fear of abandonment, in the joy induced by a parent's praise and the guilt induced by a parent's anger.

Oh, we are bound. In a way our very life may be described as a working through, a coming to terms with that parental bond. World literature is full of sons and daughters struggling to work through that *akeda*, that primal bond, from Isaac to Kafka to Philip Roth.

Sermon, Rosh Hashanah Morning, September 29, 1981

The hero of Roth's new novel is a writer named Nathan Zuckerman. Like Roth himself, Zuckerman has written a scandalous and successful book which is regarded as autobiographical and is not generally favorable to his parents. "How could a nice Jewish boy write such things?" is what they are saying. And Nathan Zuckerman's father apparently agrees: "How could he?"

At the end of the book Zuckerman's father has suffered a major stroke and is dying. He receives a visit from his son. The father looks up at his son and in his parting word whispers, "Bastard."

How does the son respond to his father's parting comment? We are told he feels liberated; he feels unbound: "He has become himself again. He was no longer any man's son. Forget father ... He is released. Over, over, over. I've served my time, he tells himself. . . . "

But is he really unbound? Are any of us ever unbound, even after our parents die? Remember Robert Anderson's film, *I Never Sang for My Father*. We are told: "Death ends a life, but it does not end a relationship which struggles on in the survivor's mind toward some resolution which it may never find." In that film, after the father's death, the son says, "What did it matter if I never loved him, or he never loved me, but still, when I hear the word father, it matters."

The story we read from the Torah this Rosh Hashanah morning reminds us of one of the most elemental realities in our life: we are bound. How we come to terms with our bond to our parents will affect how we, in turn, are bound to our mates and our children.

For some among us the parental bond is an intense, radiant and uncomplicated love. For a few, alas, it may be a bond of hate. For many, perhaps most of us, it is a bond of great love qualified by the normal range of ambivalences. We are bound to our parents by a complicated web of love and judgment.

As a precocious teenager I recall sitting in the kitchen of my house with my closest friend. It was late at night and my parents were sleeping upstairs. With adolescent smugness, we began cataloguing the foibles of our respective mothers and fathers. We were in a judgmental frame of mind that night. Suddenly, in an unusual flash of insight, I turned to my friend and said, "I wonder if someday our kids will be sitting here doing the same thing."

We are all bound to our parents. The question is: how may we be blessed by that bond? Is there any more crucial question than that?

A fundamental clue is found in the great fifth commandment: "Honor (respect) your father and mother." Notice we are not commanded to *love*. We have little control over our power to love our parents, but to *respect* them is commanded.

It is all well and good to say they must earn our respect, but the burden of demonstrating the case to the contrary belongs to us. And when we punish our parents too much for real or imagined wrongs, we punish ourselves. By virtue of the parental bond, because they are our parents, they are owed certain gestures. That bond imposes obligations. Translating that general sense of obligation into a pattern of acts which expresses respect is an individual task and struggle. It varies from culture to culture and from person to person.

In the Biblical world of 2000 B.C.E. Isaac shows respect for his father by promising to maintain his father's covenant with God. Isaac shows respect for his father by agreeing to marry the woman chosen by his father's servant Eliezer. That latter gesture would not go over big in the Jewish community of Houston today.

There are acts we sons and daughters cannot do. We may need to set boundaries. A parent, for example, may never see enough of a son or a daughter, or they may wish to dominate our lives; we must lead our own lives.

But somehow, with all the boundaries we set, if we are to experience blessing, there must emerge a pattern of credible acts which signals our respect for the paternal bond. I know it has been fashionable to ridicule the parentally imposed "guilt trip." But there is another side of the coin. We do owe something to our parents for being their children. And unless we come to terms with those obligations of respect our primal bond can never be a blessing.

■ ■ ■

Let us probe further. Again we ask, how shall the *akeda*, that bonding of parent and child bless us? There is a Jewish concept, *zechut avot*—the merit of the fathers (the merit of the parents). According to this concept we ask for God's blessing upon us by invoking the merit of our ancestors. We proudly call to God's attention the merit of Abraham, of Isaac, of Jacob, of Sarah and Rebecca, of Rachel and Leah—and say: dear God, remember them and be kind to us.

In a somewhat different sense, I suppose, we too must be able to take into account, to invoke and affirm the merit of our parents if our binding to them is to be a blessing.

For some persons I know, their parents, it seems, can do no right. And there may be some of us who idolize our parents, who believe they can do no wrong. In truth, our parents need not be perfect or without blemish for us to invoke their merit.

Even Abraham for whom the very concept *zechut avot* was coined, even Abraham was not perfect. Oh, he is generally considered a man of unqualified merit who trusted God so much that he took his only son to Mt. Moriah. Abraham is a hero in our tradition. But there are stories, even about Abraham, which are not so heroic: such as the time when Abraham and Sarah were wandering in Egypt and they encountered an Egyptian pharaoh. Abraham was so fearful that this Egyptian ruler would kill him in order to take Sarah for his harem that Abraham pretended Sarah was not his wife, but his sister. This was not Abraham's finest hour, and I don't think you recall reading it about it in Sunday School. One must be selective even if one is invoking the merit of father Abraham! But oh, how important it was for Isaac to invoke the merit of Abraham and for Jacob to invoke the merit of Isaac and for us to be able to invoke *zechut avot*, the merit of those to whom we are primally bound.

As a child, from time to time, I remember resenting my father's pampering of me. He squeezed the orange juice each morning before I went off to school or dropped off my boots at school if the weather changed suddenly (God forbid his son should be unprotected). I was embarrassed in the presence of my peers. Later, I recall resenting the fact that my father seemed to invest too much in me, to live through me—to expect me to be and become what he could never be or become. I resented his living through me.

But my bond to my father could be a blessing only once I was able to understand and affirm that, despite his foibles and flaws, he deeply cared for and loved me, and much of my deep loyalties as a Jew and much of my love for classic Jewish stories are derived in no small measure from my father.

We can be blessed by our *akeda*, by our parental bond only if we are able to move beyond the morass of negation and ambivalence and find merit in our mothers and fathers.

■ ■ ■

As we look back on our life with our parents we discover that certain events have become imprinted indelibly and involuntarily on our consciousness. Sometimes it is difficult for us to judge immediately the impact of a certain episode, vignette or encounter. Only years later we discover what effect a particular event or encounter with a parent had on our lives. Whether our *akeda*, our primal bond is a blessing may hinge on the quality of those memories that still dominate our consciousness even in later life.

And if we are fortunate, each of us has such sustaining memories we can invoke. Senator William Cohen of Maine recalls such an episode. His father, Reuben, was the town baker in a small town in Maine. His father was a sports enthusiast and had once been a great athlete. He delighted in his son Bill's athletic prowess, and when Bill became a high school basketball star his father would interrupt his delivery truck route in order to stop by at the gym and cheer his son on at practice and yell at him when he made a mistake.

Bill was embarrassed by his father's presence and the other teammates asked that his father quit coming. "Dad," said Bill one day to his father, "the other players don't have their fathers come to our practice, and it makes it difficult for me when you stop by."

The father was hurt. Bill could see it, but it was too late. The father pretended that it didn't matter, that it wasn't of any great interest to him. He just happened to be driving by in his truck and that was the only reason he stopped. No big deal. The son knew better.

For weeks the father didn't come by the gym. One day, during a bad snowstorm, Bill Cohen was dribbling the ball down the court in practice when he felt some eyes upon him. It was dark outside, but the lights from the gym picked up a silhouette outside the window. Bill turned, and there he was. Outside the window stood his father, with his hand cupped around his temples, wearing a snow-covered hat and watching his son practice.

That vignette became a dominant image by which a child perceived his *akeda*, his bond to his father, and it has been a blessing. That memory lent a special poignancy to the occasion when, some years ago, Bill's father came to see his son take the oath as a United States Senator.

Surely the scene we read in the Torah this morning must have been the dominant image in Isaac's consciousness. How could it have been otherwise? The rabbis try to understand how it was that Abraham took him up to Mt. Moriah and yet Isaac was not totally alienated from his father for the rest of his life. Granted, the father was showing his faithfulness to God by going up to Mt. Moriah with his son, but the rabbis ask, did Abraham at any point in that journey reveal the depth of his love for Isaac?

According to the rabbis, when Isaac was physically bound on that altar, he asked his father again, "Father, where is the lamb for the offering to God?" And Abraham said to his son,

"You are the lamb." And as Abraham spoke those words, he broke down and cried bitterly and Isaac understood and comforted Abraham: "Don't worry father. It's all right, do what you have to do!"

Abraham's bitter weeping signaled Abraham's love for his son. It expressed Abraham's anguish at being commanded to take that journey with his son. At that moment Isaac knew that his father loved him. And, say the rabbis, the memory of his father's weeping, that tell-tale symbol of his father's great love remained with Isaac as the decisive image and made his *akeda*, his bond to his father, a blessing.

There is a primal bond between the generations, between fathers and mothers, and sons and daughters. Zuckerman may have declared he was unbound, but in truth neither estrangement nor death completely sunders the bond.

With its rewards and deficits, its joys and its pain, the *akeda*, the binding, is real. The great question is, will that bond strengthen or threaten, enhance or diminish us? If we are fortunate, there is a great and radiant love between us and our parents. If we are fortunate, despite any ambivalences which may qualify that love, we are children who have learned to accept and live by the commandment: "Honor (respect) your father and mother."

We have translated that commandment into acts of respect. We have opened ourselves to and discovered that there is merit in our parents, and there are imprinted in our minds images and memories from past encounters which are sustaining and nourishing.

On this Rosh Hashanah, when we read the *Akeda*, when we confront anew the elemental reality of our lives, the binding of the generations, what more important prayer can we offer than this: May those to whom we are bound in life and memory bless us.

CHAPTER 28

Witnessing a Grandson Accept the Torah

This is one of those peak moments, a very special Shabbat in my life. I have often said that the most compelling consolation for growing older is not wisdom or experience, but the gift of grandchildren. Another is the awareness that what is precious to you will be carried on by your children's children.

That is why grandparents are especially moved as they stand in front of the Ark for that symbolic ceremony of transmitting the Torah from generation to generation. And even members of the congregation who don't know the Bar Mitzvah or Bat Mitzvah family of the week, report being genuinely touched by that transmission.

One of the precious perks of being a rabbi is the privilege of being both participant and officiant at such life cycle events. A first grader at Shlenker asked me the other day, "Rabbi, at your wedding, did you do your own rabbi-ing?" I replied that I was strictly the groom at my wedding.

But I did get to name and bless my infant daughters and be both father and rabbi at their Bat Mitzvahs and bless them at their Confirmations and walk down the aisle with them and then

Sermon, December 4, 1998

officiate at their marriages under the *chuppah,* and be both grandfather and rabbi at the *brit* or naming of my grandchildren.

So this Shabbat offers me another precious perk: to both stand as a grandparent in the Torah transmission line and to preside at my oldest grandson's Bar Mitzvah. The transmission of Torah in a rabbi's family is not something to be taken for granted. Sometimes in order to establish their own space (especially with strong parents) "RK's—Rabbi's Kids" have been known to distance themselves from that which is precious to their parents, including their Judaism. My Christian preacher friends tell me that "PK's—Preacher's Kids" manifest a similar syndrome at times.

So it is a special delight to see the Torah heritage which, after all has become my life's vocation, being received through at least five generations in my own lifetime: from my grandparents to my parents, to me, to my children, to my children's children. I don't take that reality or the privilege of being here to witness it for granted.

As a student of Jewish history I am only too aware of the monumental challenges to what we now call Jewish continuity. Transmitting the heritage, even sustaining the very life of its bearers has never seemed a sure bet. We remain an exceedingly small people and our journey through history has been quite a trip.

No wonder when Frederick the Great asked his advisor to show him a miracle, the advisor replied without hesitation: "The Jews." Jewish history is filled with so much drama and saturated with so much bittersweet irony. Irony is an event contrary to expectations. Our survival as a people has been both wondrous and ironic.

So many times the story could have ended if—that fateful "if"—if events had unfolded in a predictable way. The story could well have ended when the Assyrians exiled the ten tribes of the northern kingdom of Israel in 622 B.C.E. Ten tribes were lost forever. The story could have ended when in 586 B.C.E. the

Babylonians destroyed the Temple in Jerusalem and exiled the remaining two tribes.

It could have ended when the Romans destroyed the second Temple in the year 70 of our era.

Coins minted at the time were inscribed with the words: "*Judea capta*—Judah is vanquished." Alas, the obituary was a bit premature. A rabbi named Yohanan got permission from the Romans to start a little academy for the study of Torah and the ordination of rabbis in a tiny village called Yavneh. That seemingly trifling concession by a proud victor to a lowly vanquished people paved the way for the survival of Judaism, and in a way made possible the transmission of the Torah we witnessed tonight.

Some years ago I personally experienced another dimension of that particular irony of Jewish history. I was visiting Rome on my way back from the State of Israel. There it was, across from the remains of the Roman Forum, the Arch of Titus. As I walked through the Arch, having just come from Israel, I remembered that the arch had been built to commemorate the triumphal procession of Roman soldiers carrying booty—including the *menorah* from the destroyed Temple in Jerusalem, and I remembered the coins that had been minted declaring: "*Judea capta*," and I couldn't help smiling.

Of course the story almost did come to an end in our time when Hitler vowed to rid the world of Judaism and Jews. The Holocaust decimated us. And Hitler not only sought to destroy us physically; he sought to desecrate the Torah. So many Torah scrolls were confiscated and burned or the sacred parchment was used as patterns in the manufacture of parachutes for Nazi Luftwaffe pilots.

But contrary to Hitler's plans and expectations, we as a people are still here passing the Torah from generation to generation. Josh's paternal grandparents came to America as refugees from Hitler's murderous wrath, which of course lends added poignancy to Josh's father, Robert, handing him the Torah this night.

Speaking of post-Holocaust ironies, I will never forget the time in 1970 when the United States Government invited me to conduct a Torah Convocation for Jews in the Armed Forces stationed in Germany. What could be more bitterly and sweetly ironic than for us to gather for the study of Torah and for Jewish prayer at Berchtesgarden, the very place where Hitler had his Alpine retreat and plotted the destruction of our people. The lodge where we stayed was commandeered by the United States Army and renovated. It had been the place where Hitler's entourage would stay when they visited the Führer. Standing on that spot and leading this Jewish congregation in reciting the *Sh'ma* as I held the Torah in my arms and as we sang *"Am Yisrael Chai*—The People Israel Lives"* was a spine-chilling experience I will never forget. What could be more ironic?

There are so many ironies connected with the Holocaust and its aftermath. A young Jewish lad named Henry Grunwald and his family fled from their native Vienna in 1938 just in time to save their lives. Henry's father, Alfred Grunwald, had been one of Austria's leading creators of musical comedy and operettas.

Hitler reduced him and his family to terrified refugees. Father Alfred could never transplant his career in this country, but son, Henry, achieved the great American success story. He rose from an office clerk to become Editor-In-Chief of Time-Life Publications. President Reagan appointed Henry Grunwald as America's Ambassador to Austria.

Imagine returning as American Ambassador to the very city from which you were forced to flee as a child. During Ambassador Grunwald's tenure his father's operettas were performed again for the first time in many decades. A plaque honoring the memory of Alfred Grunwald was placed on the apartment building where the family had once lived. The city of Vienna named a park for their once famous citizen. After the dedication ceremony a Viennese newspaper made this editorial comment: "In a sense he (Alfred Grunwald) never left Vienna. It was Vienna that was absent for a while."

In her new book, Rabbi Naomi Levy tells us a story which reveals another irony of that period. Each year Louis, a Holocaust survivor, makes a pilgrimage to the little German town of Seeshaupt. Why that town?

In 1945, a cattle train carrying Jews bound for an extermination camp stopped abruptly in that town. The Nazi guards ran frantically into the woods to escape the United States Army and its tanks that had just reached the town. Louis was one of the survivors of that train and he returns to the site each year.

One of Louis' most poignant and painful memories of that horrendous era was an earlier train ride when he and his mother were being transferred to a labor camp. As they got off the train, Dr. Mengele, the infamous Nazi medical officer, dressed in his starched uniform waved a baton directing those haggard passengers this way or that way.

While standing in line, Louis' mother saw another mother trying desperately and unsuccessfully to comfort her frantic infant. Louis' mother took the child and tried to soothe it. Just then Dr. Mengele waved Louis' mother and the infant she was carrying and the infant's mother to the left and Louis to the right. He never saw his mother again.

Louis emerged from the Holocaust not just a survivor. He emerged with a deeper-than-ever reverence for life and a special love for little children, especially babies. He is at services every Shabbat in Venice, California, when he is in town. He has been dubbed the honorary grandfather of that congregation for whenever a little child is crying and about to disrupt the services (including the child of the rabbi herself), Louis rushes to the child, takes it in his arms and tries to soothe it either in the Sanctuary or outside. That is Louis' way of honoring his last memory of his mother.

Such stories encapsulate another irony of that terrible time. Not only has a remnant of our people outlived Hitler's death wish for us, but survivors like Louis have defied Hitler's dehumanization agenda. Louis emerged from that darkest time by loving life and loving children.

Of course one of the greatest ironies of Jewish history is that the transmission of Torah has been imperiled not only by persecution but as much or more in periods when we have been seduced by freedom and the threat of assimilation. There have been breaks in the Torah transmission. Entire families have left us, perhaps never to return.

But wonder of wonders and irony of ironies, there have been those who left for a while and returned. I vividly recall a member of our congregation who had a ceremony of reaffirmation in our Chapel and as he held the Torah in his arms and recited the *Sh'ma* he broke down and cried. And there are those who, though not born Jewish, have found their true spiritual home among us, and they have strengthened us. And yes, some lapsed Jews have returned to Judaism through the influence of a non-Jewish spouse. And yes, sometimes, the chain of Torah transmissions was broken for a number of generations and then surprisingly reforged.

John Ackerman shared his story with some of us at Yom Kippur. John was not born or raised Jewish. His wife, Barbara, a Jew by birth, had gone through a period of estrangement from her heritage. Then both John and Barbara were drawn to Judaism. She re-embraced the covenant. John converted to Judaism and became Bar Mitzvah when their daughter, Jessica, became Bat Mitzvah.

Now all this happened before John discovered that his great-grandfather had been a Jew who came to this country after the Civil War. Speaking of his great-grandfather, John said, "I think he would be proud that his great-grandson returned to Judaism. I know he would. The family story is that he was very frustrated because he couldn't interest any of his children in Judaism. Well, Granddad, you got me."

The ironies of our history and the miracle of our survival! I could fill a book with such stories of breaks in the chain and of re-affirmation just from my own experience as a rabbi over these forty some years. These stories, I admit, have warmed my heart and reinforced my faith that it is God's will that our people endure and bear special witness to the teachings of Torah until the end of time. Is not this the theme of the Torah reading we will be doing in the weeks ahead?

Joseph's brothers came from famine-stricken Canaan to Egypt in search of food. In time, they discovered that the person before whom they stood and were dependent upon for their sustenance and survival was the very brother whom they tried to do in and almost killed. They were terrified he would now take revenge on them. Sensing their fear, Joseph replied, "I am Joseph, your brother, don't be afraid and don't be pained that you sold me here. For it was to save life that God sent me on before you to keep you alive as a great body of survivors."

Oh, we have not been spared the vicissitudes and tragedies of history and surely we can't grow complacent about the special challenge of bearing witness to God under conditions of freedom. But those who prophecy the impending doom of our people will be proven wrong. The bittersweet ironies that add up to the wonder of our survival have not brought us so far only that we might disappear now from the pages of history.

I am mindful, however, of the fragility of the journey and of the breaks in the Torah transmission lines that have occurred over history. And so it is such an exquisite joy to see my oldest grandson who's middle name is Louis (for my father) accept the Torah this night. Indeed, it brings soulfully to my lips those very special words, "*Baruch ata Adonai* ... Praised are You, O God, who has kept us in life, sustained us and permitted us to reach this moment."

CHAPTER 29

Intermarriage and Jewish Continuity

We come here tonight as sons and daughters of an honorable and ancient covenant. At this season, if at no other time in the year, we give top priority to our Jewish selves. No symphony or opera or social occasion—or even business and professional considerations, not even the Oiler-Bengal game on TV—is likely to keep us from being here as we bear formal public witness to our Jewish roots and heritage.

The special power of this season is that we assemble in the synagogue in greatest numbers and declare our Jewishness at a time when our prayers address most explicitly our human concerns, fears and hopes.

There is some inner tension between our Jewishness and our humanness, between the particular and the universal in everyone of us. And nowhere does that tension arise more acutely than in decisions concerning marriage and the family. Especially is this so in an open society like ours where the chemistry of physical attraction and the magnetism of human love may so easily transcend our Jewish particularity. Yes, we want to preserve our heritage—we want Jewish children and grand-

Sermon, Rosh Hashanah Eve, September 8, 1991

children—but we want to be able to fall in love and marry whomever we are drawn toward.

How is this tension being resolved? A new study of American Jews has recently been completed. The results of that study provide the text of my message to you this night. About five and a half million persons in this country regard themselves as Jews, five and one-half million out of two hundred and sixty million Americans.

We are a small community here and we are a minuscule community in the world-at-large. More than half of all our marriages are now interfaith. In a small percentage of these marriages the non-Jewish partner embraces Judaism so they become Jewish marriages. In about half of our marriages the Jewish spouse remains Jewish and the Christian spouse Christian. We call these mixed-marriages. How are the children being raised in such families? Twenty-eight percent are being raised explicitly and unambiguously as Jews. Thirty-one percent are being raised with no religion. Forty-one percent are being raised in other religions, usually Christian.

This summer, some Christian friends in northern Michigan described a wedding they attended in a Catholic Church. The bride was Jewish, the groom was Catholic. A priest officiated, but a Jewish friend of the bride recited some Jewish prayers and there was a *chuppah* in the church. Our Christian friends thought it was done very beautifully. A touch of universalism, a recognition of both religions.

Their description saddened me. First because I believe the symbols of Judaism and Christianity are respected most when they are not intermingled that way, but what really saddened me is the knowledge that those children in that family will not be raised as Jews. The church and that priest were making gracious deference to a tradition that would not be preserved in that family union. It was the graciousness of the victor toward the vanquished.

Am I somewhat comforted when I am told: "Rabbi, we will raise the children in both"? No, that saddens me too, not only because it is confusing to children but because, as I try to explain, a child who is being raised both is really being raised Christian. Christians believe that the Church has its roots in the Hebrew Bible, but once you also teach that Jesus is Savior, you have moved the child from the religion of Abraham and Sarah to the religion of the apostle Paul.

If that movement were to take place among us we would no longer be gathered here on Rosh Hashanah or the Sabbath or any other Jewish occasion. We would not be Jewish. We would be Christian.

Why do I raise these issues this night? I raise them because we are all here and what could be more important to discuss? These issues bear so critically on whether we, or our children, or grandchildren will continue to call this their home. In what spirit do I raise these issues? As a rabbi who has committed his life to the teaching and preservation of Judaism and also in a spirit of love and respect for you my congregation. Many of you are part of the story. All of us are in one way or another. Joan and I have cousins in our family who have been lost to Judaism.

I speak with deep respect and love for those of you I counsel in our Interfaith Couples Support Group who have wrestled and resolved and in some instances continue to wrestle with the conflict between a love that knows no bounds and a desire to nourish children in that particular heritage most precious to you.

I speak with deep empathy for the parents and grandparents who ponder and struggle and come to terms with decisions over which they have no ultimate control.

How may we who want our children and grandchildren to be Jewish nurture the survival of Judaism in our family?

First let me say a word in behalf of marrying someone who already shares your heritage. As many have discovered, there is much to be said for entering a marriage with shared memories of Passover Seders and Rosh Hashanah and receiving your little Torahs at consecration and being Bar Mitzvah or Bat Mitzvah and knowing that you both want this for your home and your children.

And yes, in such a marriage neither partner must give up the privilege of living your heritage and transmitting it to your children. After all, the impulse to preserve a heritage is generally as strong among Christians as among Jews.

Of course, I realize that there have been and will continue to be Jews who marry persons not reared in Judaism. That is the fruit of living in an open society. Some non-Jewish spouses have chosen to embrace our heritage. You have become Jews by choice and many of you are among the most steadfast and deeply committed among us. We have been blessed by your embrace of our covenant.

I know of mixed marriages, many in our congregation, where the children are being raised Jewish. The home is Jewish. The children are in our Religious School or our Shlenker School. There are special sensitivities and delicate issues here. Generally such arrangements work best from the vantage point of harmony in the marriage and transmitting the Jewish heritage when the non-Jewish partner (though not ready to convert) lacks a deep commitment to his or her given religion; or is so appreciative of the church's roots in the synagogue that he/she is genuinely comfortable and content, even enthusiastic about the Jewishness of the children.

But this study attests that in America today the majority of children in mixed marriages are not being raised Jewish. What can we, who are committed to the preservation of our heritage, do?

Let me begin with myself. You know that I do not preside at a marriage unless it is a Jewish marriage. If the partners in a mixed marriage have agreed to raise their children Jewish and they are married in a civil ceremony I will attend the ceremony and speak a religious word to the couple and bless them. I will also offer a betrothal blessing to them at a Sabbath service in our sanctuary prior to the wedding.

Let me anticipate a thought in some of your minds. "Rabbi, if you actually married those couples, wouldn't you be encouraging them more to raise Jewish families? Are you not turning them away?" I have spent hours in counseling with such couples before their marriage and in our Interfaith Couples Support Group. And I know of no instance where the way I addressed the issue drove them away from the synagogue or from raising Jewish children.

The merit of my stance, I believe, is that it is both embracing and respectful of boundaries. It helps the couple recognize that religious realities are not to be avoided or blurred. There is a fundamental and unbridgeable distinction between a Jewish wedding and one that is not Jewish, even as there is a fundamental distinction between Judaism and Christianity.

Incidentally, a recent study of mixed couples has concluded that there is no correlation between whether or not a rabbi will officiate at the marriage and how that couple ultimately decides to raise their children.

What is a critical arena which shapes such decisions? Let's speak for a moment of our congregation and of what we can do better in our schools and programs to safeguard a Jewish future in an open society. We must think boldly. For example, the prevailing model of sending children to Religious School a few hours on a Sunday or a Saturday while parents are on the golf course or on the tennis court, or the shopping mall, or at home cannot compare in efficacy with the model of parents accompanying the children and being with them in shared educational and spiritual experiences. There is much more we can and should be doing within these walls as parent and child.

Of course, the most critical decisions rest with us as parents in our homes when our children are under our care. To be sure, there are no absolute guarantees, but if, as they say, we want to play the percentages, then we will give clear, unambiguous signals to our children that our Judaism is very precious to us. Obviously, words are important but deeds speak so much more compellingly. Our children learn to love their heritage by observing how that heritage is loved and appreciated in the life of the family.

If Judaism is something children only get inoculated with during several hours a week in Religious School, and there is no evidence that Judaism is valuable and valued in the home and in the life of the parents, that, as they say, sends a message.

If you impart to your children that Judaism is just being a good person, that too sends a message. To be sure, the ethical component in Judaism is enormously important, but if there is no context or subtext added to that message, the logical conclusion could be: non-Jews also believe in being good people. If that's all there is, what's the big deal? Why be Jewish?

And yes, if because of parental decisions your child experiences only being overwhelmingly in the minority in school and neighborhood with hardly any social support from other Jews, that's a very tough burden for an adult. How much the more for a child! Parents should be aware of this when you decide where you live and what schools or camps or colleges your children attend.

We do not want ghetto-ization. We cherish the freedom to be fully integrated participants in the American society, but in our parental decisions there should be balance and wisdom. We need to provide situations beyond the two or three hours a week in Religious School when a Jewish child can feel peer support from other Jews.

Let me offer a word to the children raised in our congregation who are now adults and must make the fateful decisions. If you do become seriously, romantically involved with someone not of your faith, be true to your visceral feelings. If it matters to you that your home be Jewish and your children be Jewish, say so. I have known instances where a non-Jewish partner could easily have converted to Judaism (they were distanced from their family's religious heritage or were not really raised in a church), yet the Jewish partner never signaled that building a Jewish home together really mattered.

If your future spouse does embrace your heritage, that's an enormous gift. Appreciate it. You have a responsibility to help your partner find meaning and at-homeness in the Jewish religion. In other words, you have a responsibility to make Judaism a more vital and active part of your own life. I have known converts who returned to their former religion because they discovered no real support for Judaism from their Jewish spouse.

If yours is destined to be a mixed marriage (with no conversion) and it is important to you that the children be raised Jewish—say so. I have known non-Jewish spouses who would have agreed that the children be Jewish if it really mattered to their mate, and if the Jewish spouse was committed to taking the major responsibility for their Jewish up-bringing.

And yes, if in the courting phase, after honest expression of personal feeling, it turns out that you and your future mate are each very close to your respective families and religious heritage and each really wants the children given your own particular heritage, that, I am afraid, is a sign that though you love each other, you ought not get married—for each other's sake and for the sake of your children. The reality principle teaches that love is a necessary but not sufficient basis for building a viable marriage.

On this night let me address a special word to parents whose children have intermarried and who have faced the reality that their grandchildren will not be Jewish. Most of you have wisely responded by embracing your son and daughter and their spouse and your grandchildren. You have responded in love to those to whom you are bound in love. You have been grateful if your son or daughter married an honorable, loving mate and if your grandchildren, though not of your faith, are accessible to you for hugs and spoiling and love, and you have drawn even closer to your Judaism for strength and support.

You have wisely and sadly concluded that life does not always present our first choice scenarios, and when all has been said and done we Jews need not deny that there is power and beauty in a religion other than our own. Our sadness is not that our grandchildren are Christian, but that they are not Jewish.

The statistics I have shared with you tonight were reported in *Newsweek* magazine with the headline: "*A Gloomy Study Leads Jews to Fear For Their Future.*" A measure of fear can be constructive if it quickens the mind and the heart. I am deeply concerned but not despairing. Nor should you be. After all, for centuries we have confounded the odds. Our very survival to the 20th century has been deemed a vast improbability, but we are here and, please God, many of us, our children and grandchildren and great-grandchildren and many generations to come will gather in sanctuaries like this to reaffirm our faith as sons and daughters of the covenant.

In this matter as in all else—we must begin where we are and do all within our power. If we really want our children and grandchildren to be Jewish, and we are still able to make decisions that will affect that outcome, then let us be sure we act in a way that can fulfill these words of the prophet Isaiah: *"Yesh tikvah l'achareetayich*—There is hope for your future." So may it be.

CHAPTER 30

The Election, the Covenant, and the Mission of Israel

I

During the late Bronze Age a group of Hebrew slaves united under the leadership of Moses and escaped from Egyptian bondage. In the wilderness of Sinai this "mixed multitude" learned the meaning of its liberation. Fate became faith and the people Israel was born.

> The Lord called to him from a mountain, saying, "Thus shall ye say to the House of Jacob and declare to the children of Israel, 'You have seen what I did to the Egyptians, how I bore you on eagles' wings and brought you to Me. Now then if you will obey Me faithfully and keep My covenant, you shall be My treasured possession among all the peoples. Indeed all the earth is Mine, but you shall be to Me a kingdom of priests and a holy nation.'"[1]

To be a son of the covenant is to remember that mixed multitude's liberation from Egypt as "that which the Lord did for me." It is to share the experience and accept the obligations of that people whom *Yahveh*, the Nameless One, redeemed and consecrated to His service.

Chapter from the book, Contemporary Reform Jewish Thought, *edited by Bernard Martin.*

When he asks, "What mean *ye* by this service?" the wicked son of the Passover *Haggadah* is guilty of faithlessness to the covenant. He fails to identify with his people's sacred history. He denies the actuality or, at least, the personal relevance of Israel's escape from bondage and God's redemptive act.

The modern world has created a fifth son. He accepts the enduring relevance of his ancestor's bondage and liberation but is unable to celebrate those events as "that which the Lord did for me." He may feel himself addressed in some special way by the injunction, "you shall not oppress the stranger" and nod approvingly at the words, "for ye were strangers in the land of Egypt." He shares his people's fate and some of the values forged on the anvil of its common destiny, but he cannot respond to that sacred alchemy by which fate became faith and values became Torah. He acknowledges a covenant with his people, but it is a covenant in which God is at best a silent partner.

For this secular son of Israel, Egypt's Pharaoh may be paradigmatic—an ominous portent of Nebuchadnezzar, Antiochus, Titus. Torquemada, Hitler, Stalin. He does not deny that Auschwitz addresses him, a Jew, with special significance. Indeed to be a Jew is to be refused the privilege of forgetting that Egypt may not be too far behind. To be a Jew is to be a member of a particularly vulnerable minority in an imperfect world.

Let two contemporary Jewish writers speak for this fifth son. "Whatever the distance that separates me from a certain part of Jewry in the world," writes Albert Memmi, "I know that we are living a similar experience. What touches them, what affects them, may one day touch and affect me. They must suffer the same apprehension I do, the same expectation, the same ordeals."[2]

Albert Memmi writes out of his experience as an Algerian refugee. Bernard Malamud's vision has been tempered by the placid breeze of a free society. He remains nonetheless Memmi's covenant kinsman. In a fictionalized account of the Mendel Beiliss case, Malamud describes a Jew who learns that he cannot easily escape the "burdens of history." Unable to acknowledge a covenant with God, this Jew makes a "covenant with himself"

and accepts "responsibility for those who are similarly entan-
gled" until the day dawns when the Jew will be the truly liberated son of a universal brotherhood.[3]

Is the modern Jew's endurance simply the by-product of the
gentile emancipation's broken promises? Is Jewish self-consciousness merely, as Sartre contends, our defensive response to
a world which insists that we are Jews?

Monford Harris has convincingly argued that the Zionist
movement, even in its most secular form, was impelled by a
Jewish will to survive, an inchoate recognition that the Jews *qua*
Jews ought not disappear from the earth.[4] The American Jewish
parent who exhorts his marriageable son: "We are not religious,
but one thing I expect from you. . . . " offers a Diaspora equivalent of this will to endure. To be sure, the world does remind us
that we are Jews, but we find in this reminder the confirmation,
not the source, of that ill-defined feeling that our Jewish vocation—whatever it may be—has not ended.

According to our sacred history, the Jew's endurance is the
by-product of two forces. The first of these is a God whose love
and providential purpose will not release this people. He may
chasten but will not forsake them. For His name's sake, this people must remain His distinct, if not always steadfast witness until
the end of days.[5] The second factor is Israel's faithfulness to its
vocation. God's experience with the people is not an uninterrupted series of dismal disappointments. Israel has frequently
proved ready to suffer and even die for the covenant. Quoting
Psalm 44, the rabbinic sages affirm anew, "Because of Thee we
are slain the whole day long, we are counted as sheep for the
slaughter."[6] And Judah Halevi's rabbi reminds the Khazar
monarch, "Think of the thoughtful men among us who could
escape this degradation by a word spoken lightly . . . but they do
not do so out of allegiance to their faith."[7]

Surely the contemporary American son of the covenant
does not suffer for his faith, but he does have the option of
escaping through calculated assimilation the still-vulnerable status that his Jewishness entails. That many a "non-religious" Jew

eschews this option is not merely a response to lingering gentile exclusivism but the acknowledgement of a claim which he believes ought not to be betrayed.

II

Yet if the fifth son is to recover the depth of his covenant consciousness, he must regain the posture of Jacob-Israel and truly wrestle with his sacred history. He must explore and seek to understand that call-response through which Israel was born.

Jewish theology is the Jew's interpretation of his history. Whether its monotheistic faith came to it decisively during the period of the Exodus or gradually ripened in the prophetic era, a living people emerged which dwelt in an ideological realm far removed from its neighbors. A people was born which acknowledged the sovereignty of a single, universal, imageless, creative, and moral power, unencumbered by mythological counterparts—the sole Ruler of fate, nature, and history. This God demanded exclusive loyalty from His worshippers, and His will was intended to govern every sphere of their lives.

How did *Yahveh*, the Nameless One, become the God of Israel? How and why was a particular relation (covenant) established between *Yahveh* and this people? The Biblical historian's answer is unequivocal. God took the initiative by revealing Himself to this people as its Redeemer and Lawgiver. God's love was then, at least officially, reciprocated by Israel. The people accepted the sovereignty of the Lord and pledged to serve Him. Thus the covenant was born.

Why this particular people? The traditional answer given in rabbinic literature embodies two diverse strands. The one accentuates the mystery of divine love:

> We would not know whether God chose Israel for His treasure or whether Israel chose the Holy One, Blessed be He. The answer is taught in the following: "And the Lord, your God, chose you." And whence do we know that the Holy One, Blessed be He, chose Jacob? Because it is said, "Not like these

is the portion of Jacob, for He is the creator of all things and Israel is the tribe of His inheritance. . . . " (*Jeremiah 10:16*)[8]

The other, seeking a rational ground for the particular destiny of the Jews, explains that God revealed Himself to other peoples as well but Israel alone accepted the demand and promise of the covenant.[9] Only after the people responded "we shall do and we shall hearken" did God refer to Israel as "My people."[10] Rabbi Jose b. Simon has God remind Israel, "Were it not for your acceptance of my Torah, I would not recognize you or regard you any more than the other nations."[11]

Later covenant theologians also sought to rationalize God's love for Israel. Judah Halevi posited a biogenetic endowment which empowered this people to receive God's revelation.[12] And, much later, Kaufmann Kohler was to speak of "hereditary virtues and tendencies of mind and spirit which equip Israel for his calling."[13] But to speak of biogenetic or hereditary endowments is not to dissipate the mystery. Why was Israel so endowed? Ultimately he who seeks to explain the birth of this unique people must invoke such terms as "ripe historical conditions," "chance," "creative genius"—terms no more compelling or explanatory than the claim of revelation and the mystery of divine grace.

III

Jews of today may feel a duty to survive without understanding the meaning of that duty. How did our forebears interpret the significance of their liaison with God? The people of Israel was born by the recognition of God's role in its history and God's claim (the Commandments of the Torah) upon it. This covenant community actually became a missionary people when monolatry ripened into the full-blown monotheism of a Second Isaiah; then Israel's faithfulness to *Yahveh* became a vehicle for His ultimate dominion over all the children of men.[14] The earlier phase of Israel's existence is represented in the declaration, "Ye shall be unto me a kingdom of priests and a holy nation;"[15] the final phase embraces the promise, "In thee and thy seed shall all the nations of the earth be blessed."[16] But the rabbis knew no historical development: from its very *birth*, Israel was a "light unto the nations," and Abraham was the first Jewish missionary.[17]

Whereas the gentile, according to rabbinic teaching, may fulfill his pre-messianic destiny by observing the Noahide laws, the Jew's greater burden of commandments is commensurate with his special divine vocation.[18] By fulfilling the Torah he bears witness to God and hastens the coming of the Kingdom.

By his observance or nonobservance of the *mitzvot*, the Jew either sanctifies or profanes God's Name in the world.[19] When an Israelite observes the Sabbath he bears witness to God as Creator of the world.[20] Indeed, his recitation of the Sabbath prayer renders him, as it were, "a partner with God in the Creation."[21] Of the Chanukah *menorah*, the Talmud asks rhetorically, "Does He then require its light? Surely during the entire forty years that the Israelites traveled in the wilderness, they traveled only by His light." To which the following conclusion is given: the light of the *menorah*, the publication of the miracle, is testimony to mankind that God's presence rests in the midst of Israel.[22]

The transcendent significance of Israel's faithfulness to the covenant is rehearsed in many statements, the boldest of which is attributed to Simeon b. Yochai: "Scripture declares, 'ye are my witnesses and I am God.' This means, so long as you testify to me, I am God. If you cease to testify to me, I am no longer God."[23]

Significantly, Israel's vocation was not dependent on an active and successful proselytizing campaign. After Rome's alliance with the Church prohibited Jewish missionary work, Jews still believed that by their very endurance as the *mitzvah*-observing people they were in some direct way hastening the day of redemption.

Jewish existence was, however, not solely the instrument of providence. By covenant faithfulness the individual Jew also attained personal fulfillment. What life has greater meaning than that of the man who believes he is needed by, and has the power to serve or betray, the Source of his being? The Pharisees accentuated this personal dimension of Jewish existence. They elaborated what Ellis Rivkin has called a "*mitzvah* system of salvation," whereby the individual Jew believed that his personal destiny in this world and in the world to come was contingent upon his covenant faithfulness. Under the Pharisaic aegis, Rosh Hashanah was transformed from a ceremony celebrating the enthronement of *Yahveh* to a day of personal judgment in the presence of the Creator and Ruler of the world.[24]

The motif of personal fulfillment receives it crispest formulation in Rav's rhetorical question: "For what difference does it make to God whether one slaughters [an animal] from the back of the neck or the front of the neck? Hence, the commandments were not given save to purify God's creatures."[25] The Jew, claims Rav, has received a precious path to self-humanization through which he may attain blessing in this world and in the world to come. To the question, "Why should I be a Jew?" the rabbis thus offered a twofold answer: *covenant existence is both the means to my personal fulfillment as a man who was born a Jew and the way I may share my people's unique vocation in the world.*

Later theologians, reflecting on the covenant, have accentuated one or the other of these dual motifs. In his *Guide for the Perplexed*, Maimonides explains that man's "possession of the highest intellectual faculties, the possession of such notions which lead to true metaphysical opinions as regards God ... gives him immortality, and on its account he is called man."[26] And how does the Jew attain this goal? Maimonides' *Commentary on the Mishnah* portrays God as declaring: "If you will heed my commandments, I will assist you in their performance, so that you may attain perfection in them ... the persons who strive to do the commandments will be healthy and secure until they have attained that degree of knowledge through which they will merit the life of the world to come."[27] Even the messianic age itself, Maimonides claims, is but a tranquil state of earthly existence such as would enable the Jew (man) to cultivate his highest intellectual faculties.[28]

If Maimonides conceived the covenant, with its command-

ments, as a unique and splendid instrument for man's self-realization, Judah Halevi gave priority to Israel's divine vocation in
the world. Israel is a prophet people, the bearer of God's truth
until the time of the world's redemption. Israel's credentials are
certified by its willingness to die for the faith, its steadfast loyalty
despite suffering, its very survival, and its unbroken tradition of
transmitting the Torah from generation to generation.[29] This people is punished and purified through suffering, but the Torah
remains the vehicle for the discharge of its exiled task. Thereby
Israel is able to "cleave to the divine quality in prophecy and states
of mind that are close to it."[30] "Israel," says Halevi, "is the heart of
mankind;" as this organ is afflicted by the diseases of the body, so
too the health of the heart radiates blessing to the entire body.[31]
He speaks also of Israel as a seed "which falls to the ground and
apparently is transformed into earth, water and dung without
leaving a trace," but in reality this seed "transforms earth and
water into its own substance . . . [until] the tree (all mankind) bears
fruit like that from which it had been produced."[32]

The distinction between Maimonides and Halevi must not be
pressed excessively. Whereas one is especially gripped by
the self-fulfilling dimension of Jewish existence and the other
by the mission of a living, suffering, and witnessing people,
Maimonides surely affirmed that the Jews were also custodians of
a unique truth and Halevi regarded the Torah as an avenue to personal salvation as well. But what for them was a matter of emphasis has become in modern times almost a matter of separation.

It may be argued that Jewish liberalism, in its early phase,
defined the covenant primarily, if not exclusively, as the vehicle
of the world's redemption. To Hermann Cohen, the Jew was the
sole bearer of a truth essential for "the religious progress of
mankind." Its elements included the unity and uniqueness of
God, man's direct confrontation with his Creator, the freedom
and moral responsibility of the individual, and the messianic
hope.[33] Cohen's concept of the Jew as a servant of a religious
idea became, for Kohler, a people's obligation to a personal God
Who consecrated it as "the bearer of the most lofty truth of reli-

gion among mankind."[34] Kohler affirmed that past periods of oppression and enforced isolation had caused many a Jew to "lose sight of His sublime mission for the world-at-large," a mission best expressed in the *Ne'ilah* service of David Einhorn's *High Holy Day Prayerbook*: "Endow us, our Guardian, with strength and patience for our holy mission and grant that all the children of Thy people may recognize the goal of our changeful career—one humanity on earth even as there is but one God in heaven."[35] At times, it seems, Jewish religious liberalism was so preoccupied with what the Jew could offer the world that it virtually ignored what living within the covenant could offer the Jew.

This emphasis of classical Reform theology was totally reversed by Mordecai Kaplan's Reconstructionism. "Jewish religion," writes Kaplan, "is that aspect of Judaism which identifies as holy or divine whatever in the cosmos impels and enables the Jewish people, individually and collectively, to make the most of life ethically and spiritually."[36] Whereas Kohler saw Jewish survival as an instrument for the fulfillment of a divine mission among the peoples of the earth, Kaplan has viewed Judaism as an instrument for the survival and self-realization of the Jew.

To be sure, Kohler would not have denied that Judaism humanizes its adherents, and Kaplan, in his later writings, has been drawn to speak of a Jewish vocation in the world. In his book the *Purpose and Meaning of Jewish Existence*, Kaplan contends that "none of the historical religions other than that of the Jewish people is capable of undergoing the reconstruction which is essential to rendering [it] relevant to the urgent needs of contemporary mankind."[37] Thus he who once disdained Reform's concept of a mission for Israel has himself lately assigned a transcendent and unique role to the modern Jew.[38] Whereas Kohler viewed Israel as the bearer of ethical monotheism in its most exalted form, Kaplan's Jew is potentially a unique teacher of the role a de-supernaturalized religion ought to play in the life of man. Nevertheless, Kohler saw Israel chiefly as the bearer of God's word, while Kaplan continues to view Judaism primarily as an instrument for the self-realization of the Jewish people.

IV

One who believes that the Jews have a unique and essential role in the history of redemption must still ask: how shall this task be fulfilled? In the pre-emancipation era all Jews would have agreed that the "yoke of commandments" was the way to fulfill the mission of a holy people. However, with the break-down of the Torah's binding power and the growing self-image of the Jew as a more active shaper of his own destiny (and that of the world about him), the strategy of covenant fulfillment has been reappraised. Let us consider three distinctive answers that have been offered in the modern world.

Negating the exile, Liberal Judaism in its classical form saw the Jew as a creative catalyst for messianic redemption within the land of his domicile. Like Hermann Cohen before him, Leo Baeck regarded the Jew as the potential vanguard of the spirit of ethical monotheism which would, in time, become the cornerstone of a just and benevolent society. In his classic volume, *The Essence of Judaism*, Baeck enjoined: "The good that one practices is the best witness of God that one can give . . . the standard of action thus becomes the following test: will it bear witness for Judaism?"[39] The American Reformers found a soil uniquely hospitable to this witness. In response to the query "why be a Jew?" Emil G. Hirsch once replied:

> Our distinction results simply from the keenest sense of responsibility and the consciousness that whether other men may or may not choose to be slow to do the right, we must ever be quick and exemplify the higher life in the eyes of the world. As individuals or by our social institutions, by our public morality, by our deeds and in the secrecy of our closet even, we must so live that indeed through us God's name be sanctified and the families of the earth be blessed through our influence for the good, noble and true.[40]

The Jew, said Hirsch, must fulfill his divine vocation as "sentinel and soldier of righteousness."

At first, one would hardly regard Emil G. Hirsch and Martin Buber as theological kinsmen. Yet each affirmed that it was the

Jew's task to serve as God's exemplar. Commenting on Isaiah's messianic vision, Buber declared: "Nations can be led to peace only by a people which has made peace a reality within itself. The realization of the spirit has a magnetic effect on mankind which despairs of the spirit."[41] The "spirit of Israel," Buber maintained, is Israel's understanding that man must initiate the creation of a "true community" and its acceptance of the mandate to lead the way: "There is one nation which once upon a time heard this charge so loudly and clearly that the charge penetrated to the very depth of its soul."[42]

Buber thus shared the vision of the classical Reformers: Israel is commissioned to demonstrate, by word and deed, the goal which God has set for all men. But whereas the Reformers saw the Diaspora Jew as an effective witness for prophetic truth, Buber regarded the rebirth of the Jewish community in Palestine, and particularly the creation of the *kibbutz*, as the most fertile soil for the cultivation of the Jewish spirit in the contemporary world. In the Diaspora the Jew all too often merely proclaimed his faith in the Messiah without taking seriously the "preparation of the world in readiness for the Kingdom."[43] In the modern Diaspora the "American of Jewish faith" is apt to neglect or even betray his task through lack of any true communal existence. Israel—and here Buber agrees with Ben Gurion—offers the Jew a unique possibility to fulfill his sacred vocation:

> For only an entire nation which comprehends peoples of all kinds can demonstrate a life of unity and peace, of righteousness and justice to the human race as a sort of example and beginning . . . a true history can only commence with a certain definite and true nation . . . the people of Israel was charged to lead the way toward this realization.[44]

To the question of the content of the Jew's divine vocation, Rosenzweig offered still a third answer that is at variance with the more promethean activism of Hermann Cohen, Emil G. Hirsch, and Martin Buber. The Jew, said Rosenzweig, is at once a stranger in the world and at home with God. By his biological endurance and his continuing response to the commanding presence of the God of Abraham, by bearing children, and by observing the precepts of Torah, the Jew simultaneously anticipates the world's redemption and declares that the Messiah has not yet come.[45] Rosenzweig eschewed the role of the Jewish activist. The Jew is already "with God," the God from whom the world remains estranged. His exile is a sign of the world's alienation. In the pre-messianic age, the children of the covenant have no responsibility for God's world save to endure as a faithful community. The Jew need seek no converts, establish no model communities, involve himself in no social movements, to advance God's kingdom. Thus, Rosenzweig could write without fear of misunderstanding: "Insofar as it has reached the goal which it anticipates in hope (for all mankind) ... its soul ... grows numb to the concerns, the doing and the struggle of the world."[46]

Two fundamentally distinct modes of Jewish witness have thus been suggested. Hirsch, Buber, Cohen, and Baeck all affirmed that what the Jewish people must offer God *is active engagement in the task of transforming the world in His behalf*, whether as proclaimers of truth, "sentinels of righteousness" in the Diaspora, or builders of a true nation in the land of Israel. For Rosenzweig, what the Jewish people offers God is simply its *presence* in the world, a presence which in and of itself proclaims God's sovereignty, casts judgment on all of man's penultimate solutions, and patiently waits for the messianic redemption.

The difference between Rosenzweig and Buber is essentially the distinction between what Sheldon Blank has called the "passive" and "active" mission in biblical prophecy.[47] The "passive mission" is the prophetic claim that God's impending restoration of Israel's glory and Israel's grateful acknowledgement of His grace and power will sanctify God's name and hasten the day of His universal kingdom. *God's* acts are here regarded as the crucial factor. Israel serves Him by receiving and publicly acknowledging *His* benefactions. "I, even I, am the Lord, and beside Me there is no savior. I have declared and I have saved.... Therefore ye are My witnesses saith the Lord, and I am

God."[48] The "active mission," also embodied in Deutero-Isaiah, commissions this people to speak God's word and to share God's work:

> I, the Lord, have called thee in righteousness, and have taken hold of thy hand, and kept thee, and set thee for a covenant of the people, for a light of the nations, to open the blind eyes, to bring out the prisoners from the dungeon and them that sit in darkness out of the prison-house.[49]

Rosenzweig offers a modern equivalent of Deutero-Isaiah's concept of the passive mission. Israel's very endurance is a vindication of God's sovereignty: "wordless evidence which gives the lie to the worldly and all-too-worldly sham eternity of the historical moments of the nations."[50] Buber's vision, on the other hand, is more akin to the active mission of a prophetic people whom God has charged to pave the way and begin the work of redemption.

V

"The teachers of Judaism," wrote Abba Hillel Silver, "almost instinctively rejected a formula of either-or in assaying religious values. They avoided all sharp antinomies, all irreconcilables which lead to a spiritual impasse."[51] Let this wisdom guide us as we seek to find the contemporary meaning of the covenant. To the question, why be a Jew? let us answer with the best of normative Judaism: *covenant existence is equally and unequivocally the road to personal fulfillment for a man who is born a Jew and his way of sharing the vocation of a people consecrated to God.*

Each man is the offspring of particular parents. Each man inherits a particular history. When a man or people respond to an event with the words, "this is what the Lord did for me," history becomes revelation. Each man turns to his own "inner history" for the meaning of his individual life. Here, in part, is what continues to separate Christian and Jew. The Christian remembers Bethlehem and Calvary, the Jew remembers Egypt and Sinai.

That sign of God's love which one has found in the

Incarnation, the other has received in his liberation from
bondage and the gift of the Torah. That standard for piety
which the devout Chrisitan finds in the life of Jesus, the Jew
obtains from the teachings of Torah. That forgiving grace which
one derives from a sacrificial death, the other receives from the
God who says, "Am I not like a father unto you, O house of
Israel?" That confidence in God's death-transcending, value-
conserving power which the Christian affirms through the
Resurrection, the Jew derives from his covenant relation to Him
who is the Author of death and the Renewer of life. That
redemptive hope which one finds through Him who came and
will return, the other finds in Him who has been promised and
is yet to come. Those categories of meaning which the Christian
has found in Father, Son, and Holy Spirit, the Jew has discovered in God, Torah, and Israel.

As a Jew, I need not deny that the mystery of Divine love
and grace is present in the sacred history of my Christian neighbor, and I disavow the implication—admittedly present in some
of my forefathers' utterances—that God loves me more than him
who dwells outside my covenant. I believe in the mystery of election but reject the concept of special love. Nor must I deny that
Christian and Jew each has a role in the work of redemption.
But even as the sacred history through which the Christian finds
personal salvation is not mine, the truth to which he bears witness subtly and at times not so subtly diverges from my own.
Each of us anticipates the coming of God's Kingdom; until then
we must wait for the decisive arbitration of our conflicting
claims.

The Christian gospel is derived from God's revelation in
Jesus Christ; the mission of Israel is grounded in the covenant
of Sinai. The key to an understanding of my unique Jewish vocation may be found in *the very structure of the covenant itself, for God's
relation to Israel is the paradigm of His covenant with all men.* He
whom we have known in our history lifts all men to the dignity
of sharing in the work of redemption: "The human world is
meant to become a single body through the action of men them-

selves. We men are challenged to perfect our own portion of the universe."[52]

Man's dignity derives in part from his Divinely appointed task, from his power to transform the world in accordance with a Divine design. This truth is embodied in the conditional dimension of the covenant. Man is commanded and is accountable. His acts are laden with profound consequences. Through Israel, the Nameless One reveals man to himself as a partner of God. But if one dimension of the covenant affirms man's power, another no less dramatically confirms his finitude. The covenant was born when God's power and unmerited love liberated a band of helpless slaves. The people is called upon to judge itself in terms of a transcendent source of value—a standard given to and not created by man. The people bears witness to a kingdom which God alone must bring to pass.

Israel's life with God uniquely reveals a creative tension in all men's relation to the Source of Being. *We live our lives astride accountability and grace, justice and love, forever poised between an affirmation of our significant power and an acknowledgment of our dependence on divine gifts.*

The Jew is called to proclaim a twofold truth for all men: we mortals stand before God "creaturely and creative." Man both receives life and holds it in custody. He accepts Torah and performs significant deeds. He must wait for the Messiah even as he prepares the way for His coming.

For a covenant-affirming Jew the contemporary theological ferment is a two-edged sword. He will respond to the spirit of the "secular city" with one hand that beckons and another hand that repels. When its prophets call on man to accept a significant measure of responsibility for the work of the world, the Jew will give his gladsome approval. When, however, the "new theology" seeks to deny the transcendent power of a God who creates worlds, redeems the oppressed, and reveals value, the authentic Jew will suspect a new idolatry. The covenant does not call man to glorify God by celebrating his own nothingness, but neither does it permit man to create himself in the Divine image.

Twentieth-century man's staggering power lends unprecedented urgency to the prophetic demand for man's acceptance of his human responsibility. An Isaiah reincarnate would hardly counsel reliance on Divine love to prevent the nuclear apocalypse. Our prophetic legacy also impels us to see the plague of racial turmoil as warning and judgment upon all who refuse to "let My people go." Man remains, however, God's partner, not his cosmic successor. Man is summoned to share the work of redemption and suffer the consequences of default, but covenant man will deny that he is himself the Redeemer.

The greatest of commandments is the prohibition of idolatry. To serve the Nameless One is to disarm the numberless claimants to His throne. No cult, ideology, social order, or person deserves our uncritical devotion. Indeed, even our *images* of God and Torah are themselves subject to continuing reappraisal. Man's continuing openness to transcendence is his greatest safeguard against worshipping himself or the work of his hands. Such openness is also his deepest ground for hope.

VI

The very structure of the covenant confirms the Jew in a mission at once "active" and "passive." That dimension of his faith which affirms his partnership with the Divine-summons him to share with all men in the world of the kingdom.

It has been frequently said that we Jews are the "barometer of history." Our fate appears to be inextricably bound up with a nation's response to the issues of justice. When a society in which we dwell fails to build with the plumb line of justice, we who merely *share* in these failures are *singled out* as the most vulnerable victim of the crumbling social order. Is this perhaps the eerie meaning of Amos' prophecy: "You only have I known of all the families of the earth; therefore, I will punish you for all your iniquities?"

When the Jew is tempted to identify with the oppressor or turn a deaf ear to man's cry for freedom, the great weight of covenant responsibility is soon suspended over his head. The Jewish bigot soon discovers that he must ultimately choose between a George Lincoln Rockwell, the neo-Nazi who hated the Jew no less than he did the Negro, and a Martin Luther King.

That individual Jews may betray their heritage, or that many a non-Jew surpasses a son of the covenant as witness for justice, does not compromise, much less invalidate, the primary obligation of a people who first heard the words of the prophets and remain charter witnesses to the divine demand for *tzedek*. That demand addresses the Jew both in the Diaspora and in the land of Israel. If in America we stand especially accountable for the quality and intensity of our involvement in "social action," in Israel we are summoned to build a Jewish state which submits to the judgment of its prophetic legacy. By *tzedek* the prophets meant more than doing justly, but surely nothing less.

What of our "passive" mission? We are history's most illustrious survivors. This in itself lends a unique dimension to our covenant faithfulness. To deny that redemption is here and yet attest that "my Redeemer liveth" is a witness fraught with special significance when borne by history's most time-tested survivor in a world that proclaims "God is dead."

By our Sabbath observance we continue to affirm that life is a purposeful gift, not an accident. The *seder* testifies that the tyrants of history do not speak the last word, for man is not alone in his eternal quest for freedom. Our annual observance of the Feast of Revelation and our weekly reading of the Torah confirm that true values are ultimately man's discovery, not his creation. The Jew who "in spite of everything" joyfully brings his children into the covenant of Abraham thereby denies that life is nothing more than a sick joke or a dirty trick, even as the Jew who kindles the *menorah* and pridefully admits that he is a cultural outsider in the Christmas season most poignantly proclaims that the day to which Israel first pointed has not yet arrived.

By all these "ritual" acts which bind him to the covenant of his fathers, the Jew becomes a member of Rosenzweig's "eternal people," affirming that God—the Creator, the Giver of Torah, the Redeemer of the oppressed—is not dead, though His kingdom has yet to be established upon the earth. By his life as a Jew the son of the covenant "binds creation to redemption while redemption is still to come."[53]

The most formidable task of our time, however, is to develop a generation for whom Jewish history can become once again revelation, a generation able to remember the Exodus as "that which the Lord did for me." Technologically *nouveau riche*, modern man finds it difficult to see beyond his possessions and powers: he feels no compulsion to confess that he is the receiver of divine gifts. Those forces which have corroded modern man's response to transcendence have surely afflicted the Jew with even greater intensity. (After all, is this not what Halevi meant by the price of being "the heart of mankind?")

The staggering enormity of demonic evil in our time has compounded man's incapacity to hear by God's failure to speak. The "hiddenness of God" is responsible for the fifth son among us who affirms Jewish fate without faith. His predicament should engage, not the self-righteous scorn, but the empathy of even the most theologically committed Jew. Anyone who takes seriously God's silence at Auschwitz may be forgiven the occasional thought that perhaps Moses was the only hero of the Exodus after all. Yet surely the goal of an authentic covenant existence is a reunion of fate and faith, of history and revelation. The authentic Jew is *Yisroel*, the one who contends with God but does not deny Him, who argues while he prays, who doubts as he serves, and whose very demands of his Creator betray a primordial trust yearning for confirmation.

Covenant theology speaks of a God who would much prefer to be honestly challenged than ignored. If in this age of God's eclipse, the Jew remains *Yisroel*, dare we not hope that in time fate will acknowledge faith and history, revelation? Then the pre-messianic vulnerability of the Jew will be traced once again to Sinai, and his duty to survive will be experienced as an answer to a claim which is at once an inescapable burden and a precious heritage. That heritage will need no longer be transmitted, that burden no longer assumed only "on that day when the Lord shall be One and His name One."

NOTES

1. *Exodus 19:3-6.*
2. Albert Memmi, *Portrait of a Jew* (New York: Orion Press, 1962), p. 275.
3. Bernard Malamud, *The Fixer* (New York: Farrar, Straus & Giroux, 1966).
4. Monford Harris, in Arnold J. Wolf (ed.), *Rediscovering Judaism* (Chicago: Quadrangle Books, 1965).
5. *Ezekiel 36:20-24; Sifre 35b, 112a.*
6. *Sifre 73a; Canticles Rabbah 1:15; T. B. Gittin 57b.*
7. *Kuzari, Book IV:23.*
8. *Sifre 134b; cf. Deuteronomy Rabbah 5:6.*
9. *Mekilta Bahodesh,* Lauterbach Edition, II, 234ff.
10. *Tanhuma B. Vaera 9a.*
11. *Exodus Rabbah 47:4.*
12. *Kuzari, Book I:95.*
13. Kaufmann Kohler, *Jewish Theology* (New York: Macmillan, 1928), p. 328.
14. *Isaiah 42:6; cf. Exodus 20:3.*
15. *Exodus 19:6.*
16. *Genesis 12:3.*
17. *T. B. Sotah 10b; Genesis Rabbah 43:8; cf. Sifre 134b.*
18. *T. B. Sanhedrin 56a.*
19. *Mekilta Shirata, II, 28f.*
20. *Ibid., Shabbata, III, 200.*
21. *T. B. Shabbat 119b.*
22. *Ibid., 22b.*
23. *Sifre 144a.*
24. *T. B. Rosh Hashonah 16a.*
25. *Genesis Rabbah 44:1.*
26. *Guide for the Perplexed,* Book III, chap. 54.
27. Maimonides, Commentary to Tenth Chapter of *Sanhedrin.*
28. *Ibid.*
29. *Kuzari, Book II:30-44.*
30. *Ibid., I:109.*

31. *Ibid.*, II:44.
32. *Ibid*, IV:23.
33. Hermann Cohen, Lecture to World Congress for Religious Progress (1910), cited in S. Bergman, *Faith and Reason* (Washington, D. C.; B'nai B'rith Hillel Foundation, 1961), p. 33.
34. Kohler, op. cit., p. 323.
35. *Ibid.*, pp. 339 ff.
36. Mordecai M. Kaplan, *The Purpose of Meaning of Jewish Existence* (Philadelphia: Jewish Publication Society, 1964), p. 55.
37. *Ibid.*, p. 310.
38. Compare above with Kaplan, *Judaism as a Civilization* (New York: Reconstructionist Press, 1957), chap. 10.
39. Leo Baeck, *The Essence of Judaism* (translated by Victor Grubehwieser and Leonard Pearl [New York: Schocken Books, 1948], p. 271.
40. Emil G. Hirsch, "Why am I a Jew?" in *My Religion* (New York: Macmillan, 1925), p. 30.
41. Martin Buber, "Plato and Isaiah," in *Israel and the World* (New York: Schocken Books, 1948), pp. 110 f.
42. Martin Buber, "The Spirit of Israel and the World of Today," *op. cit.*, p. 186.
43. *Ibid*, p. 188.
44. *Ibid.*, p. 187.
45. Selections from "The Star of Redemption" in Rosenzweig, *Franz Rosenzweig: His Life and Thought* (ed. by Nahum Glatzer [New York: Farrar, Straus & Young, 1953], pp.292 f.
46. *Ibid.*, p. 339.
47. Sheldon H. Blank, *Prophetic Faith in Isaiah* (New York: Harper, 1958), pp. 143-60.
48. *Isaiah 43:11 f.*
49. *Isaiah 42:6 f.*
50. Rosenzweig, *op. cit.*, p. 340.
51. A. H. Silver, *Where Judaism Differed* (New York: Macmillan, 1957), p. 108.
52. Martin Buber, "The Spirit of Israel and the World Today," *op. cit.*, p. 186.
53. Rosenzweig, *op. cit.*, p. 340.

CHAPTER 31

Sitting on the Mourner's Bench

At this service we remember our loved ones. We single out for public naming those who walked among us last year at this time and who, in the intervening months have departed from our midst. Last year my mother, Reba, was a worshiper among us. It has been hard for me to fully realize that she would not be calling to let me know her flight number, hard to believe that she has not brought the special cookies and the honey cake and the unique blessing for the New Year.

I have comforted many of you in your time of grief. What have I learned as one who but recently left the mourner's bench?

I have learned that the issues I have helped others deal with were suddenly mine. I was not there when Mother died. We were together three weeks earlier and I had planned to return on the day when—as it turned out—we would gather for her graveside funeral. When I learned of Mother's precipitous failing, I rushed home, but only in time to kiss her lifeless form.

We had been in touch by phone daily during those intervening days and she knew I loved her and I would be coming back soon. She was not alone those final days and hours, but I was not there.

Sermon, Yom Kippur Memorial Service, 1990

Oh, I have received the proper responses to my feelings of regret, "You gave her so much *nachus*.... She shared so many wonderful times with you and your family.... You really said goodbye when you spoke and embraced her three weeks earlier.... She, who loved you so, would not want you to afflict yourself with unreasonable reflections.... How could you know? ... Judge yourself by the chronicle of the years.... "

Still the added pain and regret is there. It was not a perfect goodbye which only highlighted the more momentous truth: for all our precious bonding, we did not fulfill all of each other's expectations. Ours was not a perfect relationship. Are there any?

During the time when grief mingled with gratitude and regret, I needed and received the comfort of loving family and friends, the sensitive listening of my mother's rabbi and his fitting tribute to her, borne of genuine fondness and respect for a remarkable woman; the cantor's *el male rachamin*, the Mourner's *Kaddish*, the spade of earth at the grave, and the stories of Mother as we remember her and will remember her, the *minyan* services at her home, the tears and smiles and hugs—all that helped me cope with my loss.

And this Yom Kippur I am most viscerally aware of God's great gift of maternal love and keenly aware of the jagged edges in all our lives and relationships, and of our need of forgiveness from each other and from the One who has taught us to reach beyond our grasp.

From sitting on the mourner's bench I also learned how irrevocably sharp and absolute is the boundary between life and death. At two moments I became most starkly conscious that the boundary had been crossed: when I kissed the pale, motionless face of a woman whose countenance had always radiated such energy, I knew the life force had departed from her. And again death's finality struck me at the cemetery when what was left of that once sturdy frame was laid to its eternal rest. Standing at the grave is a harsh moment which dissolves all strategies of denial. You then know that your beloved is gone.

From my own mourning I learned the wisdom of our tradition: that it is neither fitting nor wise to return immediately from the grave to the stream of life. One needs those days to step aside from the normal routine, to nurse wounds, to begin to come to terms with the new reality. As Murph, my philosopher friend at the Health Club put it, "Rabbi, you ain't no child to anyone anymore." At any age it is not easy to realize that you are an orphan.

Stepping aside from life for a while, as our tradition prescribes, ritually declares something awesome has assaulted you and you can't simply do business as usual. You have crossed a threshold. Things will never be the same.

And yes, I also learned that in its time, after you have stepped aside for a while, the return to one's full burdens and re-committing oneself to life's joys is also healing. In its time the return to work and play is redemptive and liberating.

The last word is that these weeks have taught me not only to come to terms with the finality of Mother's death, but to feel in a new way her abiding presence. As the rabbi at the funeral said, Reba reminded him of a book titled *Saying Goodbye without Leaving*. Reba was the kind of person who is not leaving. In her lifetime she touched me so powerfully that the spirit abides. Anecdotes involving her continually pop into my mind. I see her and hear her. Her favorite expressions now punctuate my speech even more than ever. I don't need photographs or video cassettes, though thank God we have such mementos. Even unbidden, her strong, nurturing and at times brooding presence is as close to me as my breathing.

In a sense then, her soul is not only eternally in God's keeping; her *n'shama*—her life's spirit abides within me to bless me, my family and all who were touched by her earthly pilgrimage. Oh, it is not the same as it was, the loss is real, the pain is real, but so is the vivid presence in mind and in heart. Many of you have lost a loved one and have told me the same. That perhaps is our most precious consolation at such a time as this. Those who have given us life do in some way continue to accompany us on our journey.

SECTION VII

Valedictory

CHAPTER 32

The Peril and Promise of Reform Judaism

Dear friends, there is an inescapable poignancy in this, my last High Holy Days as your senior rabbi. It doesn't seem that long ago when I stood on this *bimah* for my first Rosh Hashanah. Since this is the season for serious reflection, and since this is the time to reach the greatest number of you, I've decided to use the pulpit tonight, tomorrow morning and Yom Kippur Eve to sum up what I have tried to impart during more than two decades as your rabbi.

Today I want to focus on our brand name, Reform Judaism, the movement to which this congregation has belonged for most of its 144 years; the movement to which I committed myself when I entered the Hebrew Union College in 1952. I was not born into Reform Judaism. Why did I choose it for myself? What have I tried to help it mean to you?

As a Reform Rabbi, I take God and Torah very seriously. I believe that God's revelation was filtered through human minds and souls of prophets and sages who grasped eternal truth, but who were also shaped by the time-bound insights and understandings of their own age.

Sermon, Rosh Hashanah Eve, September 20, 1998

We understand some things differently than our ancestors and we must respond to realities they could not imagine, much less anticipate. We share their commitment to our people's covenant and their determination to preserve a vital Jewish presence in the world. But we have felt impelled to re-examine certain boundary issues.

During my rabbinate I've been privileged to be part of re-assessing some of those issues. Ours was the first movement to empower women to serve as rabbis and cantors, even as we expanded the role of all Jewish women in worship. Our movement has sought to affirm the Jewish dignity of those, our children, our grandchildren, our brothers, our sisters, our friends who by fate, not choice, are gay and lesbian.

Our movement was the first to acknowledge the significant reality of inter-faith couples in our community and to reach out to them and encourage them to feel at home in the synagogue and to raise their children as Jews. And since in interfaith couples the father as much as the mother may decisively influence the religion of the child, we regard a child as Jewish if mother or father is Jewish and the child is raised as a Jew.

To re-address these and other issues is not without risk and we Reform rabbis do not always agree among ourselves where to re-draw the boundary. In all such deliberations we need to feel connected to the sacred texts and the spirit of Torah and we need to respond sensitively and compassionately to the challenges of this time and place.

Sustaining that balance is not always easy. What for example shall be the role of the non-Jewish parent and grandparent at a child's Bar Mitzvah? At Beth Israel we encourage the non-Jewish grandparents to sit on the *bimah* and both parents, of course, stand with the child at the Ark. But we pass the Torah Scroll from generation to generation among Jewish grandparents and it is the Jewish parent who embraces the Torah and hands it to the child, because the Torah Scroll is more than a generic symbol of God and universal ethical values: the Torah is the symbol of the particular covenant between God and the

Jewish people and it is this Jewish covenant that is being passed from generation to generation.

One father of such an interfaith couple perceptively declared, "Once you veer away from an Orthodox treatment of such issues and re-negotiate the boundaries and grant some privileges, it is difficult to say 'yes' to this and 'no' to that." I agree, it is difficult, but that is our Reform territory and for all its difficulties it is where I have felt most at home living my life as a rabbi.

Our elders, especially in America accentuated the universal aspects of Jewish faith. "We no longer live in a ghetto," they said. We want to take active responsibility for the welfare of the larger community of which we are a part. As the prophets of Israel taught, we need to be concerned as Jews with issues of justice for all of God's children.

Not by accident then our movement has been the pioneer in joining with other faith communities to elevate the quality of life for all people in our society. We may disagree among ourselves over what it means in any given case to fulfill the imperative, "Justice, justice shall you pursue," but social justice is one of the core concerns of our movement

As Reform Jews we don't delegate to any group of rabbis past or present the right to define in minute specificity what we must as individuals do to fulfill the covenant. We believe that two serious Jews may follow diverse paths to *kedusha*—to Jewish holiness. But, they must remain within our common Jewish landscape. There are boundaries.

So how balance our individual freedom of choice in ritual and other matters with our responsibility to walk on that Jewish landscape? That's a very critical question! Over the years I have formulated six guidelines to ensure that we use our Reform freedom wisely.

First, while we need not follow all the prescriptions of the traditional law codes, it is a *mitzvah*, a sacred obligation to live by Jewish time—to make the Sabbath and the holidays a significant reality in our lives.

It is a *mitzvah* to mark the passages of life in our family from birth to death in a Jewishly significant way. It is a mitzvah to be guided in our ethical decisions by the teachings of our heritage. When we ask under what circumstances abortion is a moral option, we turn not to the *New York Times* editorial page or to the *Wall Street Journal*, but must wrestle with the question "What does Torah teach me?"

That brings us to the fourth guideline, we must study, continually study and seek to be informed Jews. And yes, it is a *mitzvah* to do our praying and studying and Jewish decision-making not only alone but in the midst of a congregation and to affirm our membership in the Jewish community and to feel a special responsibility for the welfare of our people anywhere in the world.

And finally, it is an obligation to be made conscious daily that we are Jews by virtue of some things we choose to do or refrain from doing. For me personally, that happens to mean praying daily in my personal devotions from the *siddur*—the Jewish prayerbook and it means refraining from pork (and more recently, shell-fish) as I venture forth into the world.

I'm not worried about the authenticity of any Reform Jew or the future of Judaism if our people will exercise their individual freedom within those general guidelines. This freedom has led us to discard many prescriptions and prohibitions in the traditional law codes. It has also led some of us to reclaim specific deeds and traditions which earlier generations discarded. You and I have been together long enough to see this happen.

More persons, including some who grew up at Beth Israel, have reclaimed the *tallit* (prayer shawl) and *kippah* for worship. *B'nai mitzvah* children now choose to read or chant their Torah portion; and while we continue to pray primarily in the language we understand, more Hebrew is incorporated in our service; a more intensive Day School educational track which we had earlier concluded was for Orthodox Jews and Catholics is now a genuine option through our Shlenker School.

This reclaiming process has, on the whole, been amazingly

smooth, but it has not been totally without its strains. After I had been here about a year one of the past presidents stood up at an Advisory Committee meeting and noted he was seeing many more covered heads since my arrival and that I should instruct the ushers to ask them to remove those *yarmelkahs*. I found myself replying, "If that is a serious request, I'm afraid you'll have to get yourself a new rabbi." Without missing a beat he replied, "Maybe we'll have to." Fortunately, that sentiment was not shared by others in the room and over the years that past president and I learned to disagree with respect and even fondness for each other.

Why this trend toward the recovery of such traditions in our time? For one thing, even as the world of the ghetto was very different from the world of the western Jew, so our world is very different today from the modern world of our elders only a half century ago. There was more overt anti-Semitism then. Exclusion from neighborhoods and the corporate suites, and opportunities in certain professions—all of which did not encourage a highly distinctive public Jewish profile. One of you who grew up in Houston told me, "We were more uptight about our Jewishness."

Today America is different. Our place in America is different. We are different. A child who graduated from The Shlenker School was applying to a prestigious, predominantly non-Jewish private school. In the application form she was asked to write about a meaningful experience in her recent life. Without hesitation she wrote about her Bat Mitzvah. Seeing the essay, her mother was about to suggest it might be better if she wrote on something more general, less Jewish.

Fortunately, the mother wisely realized she was replaying her own old tapes and she later told me she was very grateful her daughter felt so much more open, at ease and proud of being publicly Jewish than she did growing up. That helps explain in part why we now feel more comfortable reclaiming some distinctive traditions which an earlier generation discarded.

But why do some of our young people who grew up in this

congregation express a desire—even a need—to recover some of those traditions? Again, because we live in different times. Some have called our age post-modern. In America today there is a deep religious hunger. We realize that science and reason alone are not sufficient to satisfy the soul's hunger for meaning. Nor can the seductions and blessings of our secular world give us the ethical and spiritual anchorage we want and need for ourselves and our children. The recovery of some rituals (which, by the way, is occurring in the liberal churches as well) and the desire for more Jewish study is part of the quest for a deeper spirituality.

That quest is reflected in the additional worship services that have emerged at Beth Israel: Tot Shabbat, a healing service, a Shabbat Morning lay-conducted *minyan*, the early Shabbat Eve Service; and it is reflected in Sisterhood Torah Convocations, adult Hebrew classes, more text-based Bible Study groups, the Sabbath Torah Seminar, Adult Bar and Bat Mitzvah and now Confirmation class for adults; and efforts by many of our younger couples to make their homes more distinctly Jewish.

Dear friends, when our Reform founders rebelled against a rigid and overly ritualized Orthodoxy two centuries ago, the question they asked was this: "How can I be uniquely Jewish in a way that does not impede my participation in the modern world?" Our question today is: "In an unprecedentedly open society, how can Judaism be vital enough, distinctive enough, spiritually nourishing enough to be cherished and sustained by our children and our children's children, from generation to generation?"

During the years I have been with you, have we all taken our Judaism as seriously as your rabbi would have liked? No, I can't say that! Have I been as fully effective in creating teachable moments to deepen Judaism in your life? Hardly! But then this season, like life itself, teaches us to be humble. Were it not for the fact that we are not all we are intended to become, we wouldn't be meeting here on Rosh Hashanah.

But this is hardly a time for self-denigration or despair. I take pride in having stood on the shoulders of the Reform rabbis and elders who came before us and I take pride in what you and this congregation have become during my watch. I sense in an ever-growing number of you a genuine desire to deepen and renew your Jewish soul. And many of you, in your own way have embraced eagerly and intensely the heritage you proudly bear.

If over the years we have modeled some of the perils and risks of Reform Judaism's freedom, we as a congregation have also embodied the great promise and fulfillments of Reform Judaism.

Reform is not an alien fruit. It is an authentic branch of Judaism's living tree. It is a Judaism for those like you and me who by conviction and temperament could not find a Jewish home elsewhere. I shudder to think what the American Jewish story would have been like if the Reform option were not available.

We are not yet all we are called to be, but on the threshold of our 24th year together, you and I, standing as members of this great congregation have ample reason to declare "*Ashreinu, ma tov chelkeinu*—Blessed are we! How good is our portion! How pleasant our lot! How beautiful our legacy!"

CHAPTER 33

You're Also Right

There is an old Jewish story my father told me many years ago. A couple with marital problems goes individually to counsel with the rabbi at his home. The man explains his grievances, the rabbi listens and his parting words are, "You are right." An hour later the wife appears and she describes her grievances. The rabbi's parting words are, "You are right." The rabbi's wife heard the parting words to each and confronted her husband, "How can you say she's right and he's right? And the rabbi responded, "You're also right."

For a long time I have felt a kinship with the rabbi in that story for I am drawn to understand both sides of an issue and can often at least partially validate even the point of view with which I must ultimately disagree. For better or worse I have an eye for the grays, the ambiguity, the unresolved tensions in life and in the quest for truth.

We find evidence of this approach to life's most fundamental issues at this very season. Rosh Hashanah is the anniversary of Creation. The rabbis tell us that when God was about to create the world, God decided to create it on the basis of justice

---

Sermon, Rosh Hashanah Morning, September 21, 1998

alone—strict accountability, shape up or ship out; but God realized that a world governed by justice alone could never stand.

So God decided to create and govern the world on the basis of unconditional love. But God realized a world without accountability and boundaries and limits could not stand. So God created the world on the basis of both justice and love, accountability and forgiveness. At this season God is pictured by the rabbis as shuttling between the thrones of judgment and unconditional love.

This tension is embedded in our most fundamental human relationships. Our children need to be held to a standard and judged accordingly, and they also need to be confirmed as persons who are accepted unconditionally.

As a child of immigrants, Alfred Kazin felt the relentless (if sometimes unspoken pressure) to achieve higher and higher levels of success, as if it were his mission to redeem his parents' unfulfilled lives. This pressure did not abate even after his parents' death, even after he, Alfred, had become one of America's most prominent literary critics and writers. This pressure took its toll. In a journal published only a few years before his death, Kazin (a professed agnostic) penned this prayer to God:

> When I pray to You to give me some peace, to cease this endless clamor of anxiety which consists always asking "O Lord, what am I to do next?" I am really asking for relief from my over-strained will, from the determination to do and even do over what is expected of me.

More than a few of us have felt this relentless burden of being on a sloping, ever steeper treadmill of judgment and needing to climb higher and higher. It can be very wearying. On the other hand, I remember the son of wealthy parents still floundering in his late twenties, flitting from one graduate program to another, one therapist to another, one exotic trip to another. Joan and I couldn't help wondering if, in his case, a large trust fund and the lack of parental expectations was not more of a curse than a blessing. This young man might have been better off if he had to work to put food on the table, if he was expected to earn his way in the world. We need both accountability and unconditional love.

I'm in correspondence now with a man I met years ago. He is serving a prison term for a repetitive pattern of writing bad checks and embezzlement. Recently I received a letter from him that made me hopeful for his future. He writes:

> When I entered prison I did so after I lost my wife, my family, my home, my self-respect. I had spiraled so far out of control that had I been allowed to continue I would most certainly be dead by now.... So there is some relief in the fact that the Justice System saved my life. I have come to believe that I must obey laws and rules in order to protect my basic freedom. This freedom is what I have always taken for granted....

This man has discovered there is judgment in God's world, there are rules and consequences for violating them. But even God realized the world could not stand without love, a love that values us even when we do not value ourselves and reaches out to us in the midst of our brokenness.

Therefore, my supportive letters to this man and the letters and expressions of love and concern he receives from some family and friends and my commitment to help him find a suitable half-way house and return to a productive life after his release—all of this is at least as important as the justice meted out to him in making possible his redemption.

I said this tension between judgment and forgiving love is embedded in every sphere of life. Certainly it is at the heart of the very sad drama unfolding in our nation's capitol these days. Discounting the partisan politics and the prurient interest that has fed this story, the fact remains the President of the United States has acted irresponsibly and called into question his moral authority to govern.

Even those who would acknowledge his great political skills and embrace his political vision, and hope that he can finish out his term and believe that is ultimately best for the country, must recognize that this pattern of conduct, now brought to light, allows for no blanket forgiveness that is divorced from judgment and accountability.

Yes, significant judgment has already been meted out in the pain he has caused his family, the humiliation he has endured, the inevitable weakening of his office, the permanent stain on his presidency.

Yet those now entrusted with the President's fate cannot simply put this matter behind them or us without at least some formal censure, without receiving from the President a formal unlegalistic apology, and a commitment to move forward in a spirit of repentance. The re-affirmation of the moral order we profess and teach our children requires no less.

At this High Holy Day season where can one find a more powerful example of the tension between holding even a President of the United States to account and offering the possibility of repentance and forgiveness to a human being who, like all of us, needs both judgement and redemptive love.

This tension between being held to account and being embraced by unconditional love has resonated throughout my life as preacher, teacher, counselor. It will now attain a new meaning as I prepare for what is generally termed retirement. I'm asking for and receiving advice.

Some has come from a rabbinic friend who is retired. He told me the story of his son, the doctor. The son asked his patient who was about to retire, "Jesse, what are you gonna do now?" Jesse reminded his doctor that all his adult life he needed to work two jobs to make ends meet. He would come home from one job and see his neighbors sitting on the porch rocking and shmoozing with each other or just observing the passing scene. Whereas he, Jesse, would go into his house, shower, get a bite to eat, and go to a second job. "What am I gonna do now, Doc? I'm gonna do a lot of sitting on the porch." That's one bit of advice.

This summer in Charlevoix I visited with Harold Bliss now in his 80s, quite frail, long retired from his executive position at Ford Motor Company. And when I asked Harold what he advised as I prepared for retirement, he responded crisply, "Sam, get another job."

Jesse is right and so is Harold. What am I going to do after I am no longer the Senior Rabbi at Beth Israel? My equivalent of sitting on the porch will be lots of stuff I didn't allow myself to do during my work life. I'm going to read the newspapers for breakfast as long as I want to without feeling pressed to get to my desk and get to work before the phone starts ringing. I'm going to wake up at least some days each week and ask, "What would I like to do today?" I hope to see places I haven't seen, to spend more time with my grandchildren, watch more baseball, visit friends without having to make a date a month in advance, take a course rather than give one. Ah, but there is that other part of me that will still hold me to account for doing *mitzvot*, teaching Torah, responding to the needs of others, and continuing to pull my weight in God's world.

You and I know that life's profoundest truths are sometimes most starkly illustrated when we are most severely tested. Being human takes its inevitable toll. We never know when or how our bodies will be assaulted. What happens to this tension, this balance, then?

Some of you may have read that poignant book *Tuesdays with Morrie*. Morrie Schwartz was for many years a popular college professor who earned the respect and love of his colleagues and his students. In his 60s, Morrie was assaulted by ALS, Lou Gehrig's disease. As the disease progressed Morrie was ultimately confined to bed. He became almost totally dependent upon others for his care. That can never be easy. Yet Morrie managed even this stage of life without losing his sense of worth and dignity. As his mind flashed back to his infancy when he had enjoyed being bathed and fed as a sign of love, so at this stage of his life, Morrie allowed himself to be embraced by the love of his caretakers and his family, and he did his best to enjoy it.

But from his bed Morrie also remained very much a teacher to all who visited him. As long as Morrie could speak he taught his former student Mitch Albom who interviewed him for this book, he taught his caretakers, he taught his family, he taught any of his friends who entered that room, he taught those who watched that *Nightline* interview with Ted Koppel, he taught all of us who have read the book so much about how to do our living and how to do our dying. Almost to the end, even as Morrie allowed himself to be embraced by the unconditional love around him, he continued to hold himself to account, he needed to bestow a gift of life's wisdom to others. To the end of his days, Morrie was both a teacher of what it means to be a *mensch* and he was the receiver of unconditional love.

Dear friends, as we gather here this awesome day, we reaffirm that whatever the circumstances of our lives it is our sacred calling throughout our lives, to act, give and touch other lives for blessing. We are held to account for our track record of success and failure. We are also embraced by One who at every point along the way, in our strength and in our weakness, in our triumph and defeat, in our nobility and our sinfulness, in our health and sickness, cherishes us with unconditional love.

This tension between two truths cannot be resolved in logical formulas of the mind but in the act of living day by day. And the One who expects us to be a blessing to others and holds us to account, also expects us to enjoy life's permitted pleasures while we can be a blessing to ourselves.

How fortunate are we to gather here under the sponsorship of a heritage, a Torah, that is so profoundly wise and sustaining. May the God who straddles the thrones of judgment and love be with us and bless us and may we bless each other at the beginning of this New Year.

CHAPTER 34

Experiencing God's Presence

Many years ago psychiatrist Victor Frankl wrote a book titled *Man's Quest for Meaning*. Frankl concluded that the human will to live may not be taken for granted, it is not instinctive; it can be lost. Witness the phenomenon of suicide. But Frankl insisted that this will to live can be sustained under even the most terrible circumstances if something within the mind and soul endows life—then and there—with meaning.

This conclusion was born of grim personal experience. Frankl was a survivor of Auschwitz. He describes one of a series of tortuous marches in frigid icy conditions when death would seem much more inviting than life. What enabled him to cling to life? He and his friend Otto found meaning in the goal of just helping each other get through the day. When one slipped and fell, the other lifted and encouraged him. Frankl was also sustained by a vivid image of his beloved wife who was a prisoner in another camp; and by his hope against hope that her condition was better than his and that they would be reunited. He concludes that the capacity to love and care for another was sufficient to sustain his will to live even in Auschwitz.

Sermon, Yom Kippur Eve, September 29, 1998

Most of us don't encounter, at least much of the time, such extreme circumstances. For us too, however, the will to live, the meaning of life are derived from having some goal or cluster of goals that fully absorb the mind and mobilize our energies. Routinely we don't pause to ask the big question of life's meaning; we're busy pursuing those goals: caring for loved ones, raising our children, striving for success in our business or profession, enjoying life's diversions. But there are times when life intrudes in a way that forces the big questions upon us.

Kirk Bains, successful entrepreneur, risk taker, deal-maker, went for a consultation with Jerome Groopman, a distinguished research and clinical oncologist. Kirk had been diagnosed with metastatic cancer and given a grim prognosis. Dr. Groopman did not challenge the prognosis but he tried an experimental treatment which unexpectedly produced a full remission. Initially Kirk was ecstatic but within days he seemed strangely indifferent as if nothing mattered.

Some months later the disease reappeared. When Dr. Groopman told him the news Kirk responded, "You shouldn't feel sorry, there's no reason to live anyway." Kirk then explained that he used to read three newspapers each morning only for information for deals and commodity tradings:

> I never really cared about the world's events or its people, not deep down inside ... and when I went into remission I couldn't read the newspapers because my deals and trades seemed pointless ... I was a short-term investor ... I had no interest in creating something, not a product in business or a partnership with a person, and now I have no equity, no dividends coming in ... Nothing to show in my portfolio.

Kirk explained to his doctor that he had lived in such a way that he had not really invested in friends or even his wife and children and they would be better off without him. And he added, "Suddenly the remission meant nothing because it was too late to relive my life."

Reading those words I was reminded of Rabbi Eliezer who told his disciples they should make *teshuva*—repentance one day before their death. The students asked the obvious question, "How do we know what day that is?" The rabbi replied, "We don't know, so you should re-examine your priorities and your deeds today."

One of the functions of these High Holy Days which we have shared now for almost a quarter of a century is to help us focus on the larger question of meaning, if only to be reassured that we are on the right track. Or, if necessary, to make some corrections in the course of our life while there is still time.

For over four decades as a congregational rabbi (and not only on the High Holy Days) I have taught that the deepest answer to the question of life's meaning is essentially a religious one. It is found in our covenant with the One who has called us into the world and is the Source of our being, the One who has given us the way we are intended to live, the One who is with us as healing, empowering, loving Presence on our journey.

Being a defender of this faith has been a great privilege and at times an awesome burden. This God of ours does not always make it easy to believe. The Jewish mystics compared God to rays of the sun reflected on the water's surface, radiant, but not graspable, elusive, darting in and out of our consciousness. If we are attentive, we are given many intimations of God's presence but God also gives us the space we need to be persons. That space, that freedom enables us to turn toward God or away from the Source of our being and we have a great capacity to ignore the signs that are daily presented to us. Being a rabbi hardly guarantees that I don't ignore those signs.

Early mornings while I'm swimming for exercise and even while I'm sitting for five minutes to rest after the swim, my mind is too often focused on problem-solving and planning. But there are those special moments. Some weeks ago during my rest interval, I hadn't planned it that way, but I just watched the early morning sun irradiate the tree branches. The sky was beginning to turn blue and the squirrels were playing with each other by running up and down the trees. In that simple vignette I suddenly grasped the wonder of being alive and of life itself.

I became conscious of my breathing and that daily prayer

which I too often recite so mechanically, this time lifted me to that other level of consciousness as I said the words, *"modeh ani l'fanecha*—I thank you God *sh'hechezarta be nishmati*—for restoring my life, (literally my breath), this day. How great is Your faithfulness." Too often I am so goal-oriented that I miss the wonder and the mystery of being. The Talmudic sage Rava said one of the questions we will be asked at our final judgement is, *"hávanta davar m'toch davar*—Did you look beneath the surface?" My Judaism at its best helps increase those moments of deeper awareness of the Source of my being and the wonder of being alive.

For much of my daily life, like you, I do what I am scheduled to do because I am programmed, that's what's expected, it's my job. I give it my all and I generally find much satisfaction in what I do. But occasionally, this level of living is punctuated by moments when I am aware of doing more than just performing my job or meeting the needs of another person. At that moment I feel I am where I am intended to be, I am responding to the Giver of the way, I am fulfilling the purpose of my life. At that moment I feel the power of those traditional words *"l'chach notzarta*— for such a moment as this, were you created."

Hearing this, you may say, "You're a rabbi, no wonder your job is lifted from time to time to the level of vocation and calling. After all, you are comforting mourners or visiting the sick or blessing a baby or teaching Torah." I know we can all have such moments if we raise our level of spiritual consciousness. The insurance adjuster who visited us after fire destroyed our home, the person who draws my blood for testing at the laboratory, and the person who waits on me at the store lifts our encounter beyond the mundane by how they respond to me and I to them. I've seen it happen! Haven't you?

But even if our job never rises to the level of vocation, we are all capable of experiencing such moments in other venues when we devote ourselves to a worthy cause, when we are there for our family and friends in time of need. There can be times in all of our lives when we too feel *"l'chach notzarta*—for such a moment as this, I was created."

Rava said that on Judgment Day we will be asked: "Did you look beneath the surface?" Much of the time, like many of you, I live my life on the surface. When an event goes well I feel good about myself and take some pride in my achievement. When things don't go well, I'm disappointed in myself or in others and try to figure out what I could have done differently.

When I'm struggling in vain for an idea for a sermon or an essay, or to solve a problem, and nothing comes, and then, suddenly things come together, I take it for granted and go on to the next challenge. When I'm feeling well I take my good health for granted. When I face illness I seek all the help I can get from physicians who dispense pills and therapies. When I am healed, if I am healed, I take it as my due.

But there are precious moments when my Jewish faith carries me to greater depths of understanding and gratitude. I realize that my power, such as it is to compose thoughts and communicate them and my power such as it is to bring comfort and healing to another person are God's gifts. I have been energized by a power greater than my own. And the healing interventions of another person in my life and the therapies he or she dispenses to me is also a reflection of the Ultimate Healer.

At such a level of consciousness I am aware, if only for a moment, that we repairers of brokenness, we human healers (and all of us can be healers in other people's lives) are partners of the Divine. Through our prayers we become humbly aware of that Presence greater than ourselves, greater than our human healers. Even when we pray for but are not granted a healing of the body, it is possible to receive a healing of the spirit: the amazing courage and strength to face what we must face and the discovery that God is "even in this place of my life and I did not know it."

Yes, there are times which sorely strain our power to believe, not because we are inattentive, but because there is so much suffering we don't deserve and some of the nicest people we know are assaulted by life's toughest scenarios. I, a defender of the faith, have had my own dark moments of the soul because of what I have experienced, but even more because of what I have observed in the world around me.

Someone has said there is a believer and an unbeliever in each of us. I have done my share of wrestling with God. My life, too, has been an amalgam of faith and doubt. But doubt has been the seed of renewed faith because even at the most difficult moments I have never fully relinquished my faith, and not just because I am a rabbi, but because that faith in God as Source of Being, Giver of the way, and caring, healing Presence remains the only adequate framework for the meaning of my life. While it is not always easy to live with a God who is both hidden and revealed, it is impossible for me to live without God. I agree with Elie Wiesel who said: "A Jew can be with God, for God, even against God, but not without God."

I confess that among the most precious moments of my congregational rabbinate over these forty-some years are those occasions when you or others like you have told me that some word I spoke or some moment of prayer we shared or even some sermon I gave or just my being there helped you re-open your soul to the gift of faith.

But what you may not realize is that we have been spiritual partners. You have helped deepen my capacity to believe the faith I teach. I have come to know so many of you over the years who have experienced the darker side of God's world in full measure and yet you have not allowed the traumas of life to permanently embitter you. You have not abandoned the core faith that life is worth its price, that life is good, that there is meaning beyond the mystery.

I could go on all night telling your stories and how they have touched me but let a very few stand for the very many as tonight I acknowledge my debt to you. I think of a couple who lost a daughter and after you did your deepest grieving you returned to life and reinvested your love in troubled teenagers who needed a temporary home away from the family of origin. You gave these young persons on the verge of despair new life and hope and you reaffirmed your own sense of life's meaning.

I think of a vibrant senior adult who in the course of a very happy marriage was faced with the need to nurse a husband through a long debilitating and terminal illness, and who experienced the death of a young adult son, but you have accepted the all of life without losing your zest for living, your capacity to enjoy friends and baseball and volunteer work. You've not lost your wry sense of humor or your faith.

I think of one of you who in the midst of chemotherapy and its after-effects wore a colorful turban on your head and belted out and led the songs with the kids at last year's Purim *Shpiel*.

I think of the Holocaust survivor who has spent many painful but significant hours telling your story especially to school children in the hopes that your efforts will make it less likely that such a thing will ever happen again. You told us a few Yom Kippurs ago, "Loving mankind and having faith in God is my way of honoring my dead parents . . . and the memory of the six million."

All of you and many more in this room tonight have been sustained by even as you have struggled with that mysterious Presence in the depth of our souls and at the core of the universe we call *Adonai*. You realize that we affirm this faith at times because of what we experience and we affirm it at times in spite of what we experience. I thank all of you who have truly been my spiritual mentors.

If after more than six and a half decades of living and more than four decades as a rabbi I were asked to give the bottom line on the big question of meaning, I would recall the tale told by Rabbi Levi Yitzhak, defender of the faith to a congregation and community in an earlier century, a rabbi who experienced anti-Semitic pogroms against his people in Poland and had his own personal struggles with a God who could permit such things to happen. Yet Rabbi Levi once sent messengers to summon all the people in his tiny village to the village square for a very important announcement. When they arrived, the rabbi declared, "I Levi Yitzhak announce to you there is a God in this world." I, your rabbi, announce to you on this Yom Kippur night there is a God in this world.

SECTION VIII

The Soul of the Rav

The Soul
of the Rav

When we speak of "The Soul of the *Rav* as Teacher" we penetrate to the core of who we are and what is entrusted to our care. I see myself this morning as a *Sheliach Tzibbur*, one called to lead us in a soulful encounter with our vocation. If I fulfill this task with any measure of success it will be because the hopes, disappointments, fears, yearnings and fulfillment I lift to consciousness are not mine alone but ours.

Let us begin by defining the borders of our calling. Our *Bet Midrash*, the place where we do our teaching, is portable. Have Torah, will travel. We teach in the classroom and the sanctuary, in our study and in our people's homes, in the intensive care unit and the family waiting room at the local hospital: sometimes even in the whirlpool of the JCC Health Club, when a Jew probes: "Say, Rabbi, I've been meaning to ask you...."

I teach when I tell children that *Dubner Maggid*'s parable of the diamond with the scratch, or when, at a Torah Seminar, in response to my discussion of Moses' impending death the older members of the group talk about the incompleteness of every human life.

Address, Central Conference of American Rabbis, Grossinger, New York, 1984

I teach Torah as I stand before a bride and groom and describe what happens to *eesh* (man) and *eeshah* (woman) when the letters spelling the word for God (the *yod* and the *heh*) are removed from their love for each other. And yes, I teach Torah when I visit Larry, who knows that he is dying of cancer, and whose mind is alert as he asks, "Rabbi, how do you prepare?"

If our *Bet Midrash* is portable, so was our predecessors'. Many of the rabbis we read about in the *Midrash*, or who are the focus of *Hasidic* tales, were also generally teachers in more than a strictly *halachic* sense. We are their heirs. When I first chose the rabbinic vocation my mother made a point of informing me that I was the direct descendant of Pinchas Shapiro, more commonly referred to as the *Koretzer Rebbe*. My maternal grandmother was born in Safed and lived in Jerusalem until her death. I saw her twice. When I visited in 1954 I was both the oldest grandchild and a Reform rabbinic student. She warmly embraced me as grandchild and conveniently suppressed my vocational intentions. I detected no animus against non-Orthodox Judaism. It was just too incomprehensible to her: a descendant of Pinchas of Koretz, her grandchild, studying to be a rabbi and yet so manifestly unrabbinic in appearance and *minhag*.

The second and last time I saw her, a number of years later, she had somehow managed to integrate my two identities. She gave me a Hebrew Bible and wrote in the inscription "*l'nechdi hayakar* to my dear grandchild—haRav Schmuel Karff." That inscription was her greatest gift to me. It was the equivalent of a weighty blessing.

The *Koretzer* died in 1791. Almost two centuries separate him from us. Yet our need for authenticity requires that we make credible connections between his rabbinic vocation and ours, and this despite our awareness of his *halachic* rigor and our conscientious liberalism. We go beyond Koretz. We ask: what connects us to all the generations of rabbis who preceded us?

Like them, we too are gripped by the passion to do what we do. We read in the Jerusalem Talmud: "more than the calf desires to be nursed, the mother wants to nurse." The high points of our rabbinic vocation are moments when we feel we must—that we are defined by what we do; to be a *Rav* is our intended destiny. At such moments we cannot conceive of ourselves not telling stories to children, not speaking a word of comfort to the bereaved, not addressing a congregation Kol Nidre night.

Oh, there are more than a few moments when I feel otherwise—when I feel what keeps me a rabbi is my unpreparedness for anything else. At times I do covet the presumedly more favored lot of those who are psychiatrists, college professors, physicians, attorneys, entrepreneurs. It is comforting to realize that at times, they envy me as well. And so many of our forebears also had such moments. Pinchas of Koretz was not spared agonizing self-doubt nor was that ancient rabbinic sage who said: "don't lust for the table of kings, for your table of Torah is greater than theirs and the Master will reward you for your labors . . ." (*Avot 6:5*). Sometimes even they weren't so sure of the *yichus* of the rabbinate or its rewards.

True, in that earlier age the *Rav* had another vocation. They said in Rabbi Judah's name: "The earlier generations (of rabbis) made Torah *keva* (a regular pursuit) and their work *arei* (occasional) and both were sustained. Our generation makes work regular and Torah occasional and neither our work nor our Torah is sustained."

For Rabbi Yohanan Hasandlar, the sandalmaker, such words could mean that sandalmaking had pre-empted Torah study. For us it means that rabbinic administrative tasks, committee meetings, Red Cross luncheons, all keep us away from Torah. Yet I do feel most connected to those who went before when my books are strewn across a large table and I am checking out a *midrash* to a particular Biblical text. What is the significance of our connection to the text? What is at stake in bonding ourselves to it and what emerges from that bonding?

Jacob Neusner has argued that the entire thrust of the "exegetical process is to link upon a single plane of authority and reliability what a rabbi now says with what the written Torah says.... Rabbinic tradition makes no systematic effort to distinguish the revelation transmitted to an ancient prophet from ... a Torah teaching of a contemporary sage."

There are moments of study when thoughts leaping into my mind, thoughts filtered through the Torah text, the rabbinic commentaries and my own sensibilities, have the feel of God's revealing presence. Those are the most authentic moments of study. We are neither prophets nor the daughters or sons of prophets, but we are rabbis and the daughters and sons of rabbis and there are moments when our study casts us as instruments, as messengers of the One whose teaching is revealed to us and through us. Neusner boldly asserts the full implications of an oral Torah: "In the rabbis the word of God was made flesh and out of the union of man and Torah—producing the rabbi as Torah incarnate—was born Judaism, the faith of Torah, the ever-present revelation, the always open canon."

How heady are those moments when we seek not only to understand what they said and taught, or what the Torah meant to those who were inspired to record its words, but when we make our personal connections to the text, our little glosses; when we feel something new has been revealed to us. I recall a moment of wrestling with the Jacob and Esau story when suddenly it all seemed so clear. God had to choose between Jacob and Esau, so not even God is spared the dilemma of choosing between less-than-perfect alternatives. God had to choose between a man who desired the birthright so deeply he would cheat to secure it and a man who so lightly esteemed it he forfeited the birthright for a bowl of lentils. Working with flawed human material, God made a difficult but inescapable choice. God decided it is better to care too much than too little. When that train of thought leaped from the pages of the Torah or from the deep recesses of my mind, or from a dialogue between mind and text, at that moment I felt I was quintessentially a *Rav*.

Even more soul-tingling are those occasions (we have all had them) when a text is illumined by our personal experience. After the death of Aaron's sons we read: *Vayeedom Aharon* "Aaron was silent." He did not mourn. Indeed Moses said to Aaron and his surviving sons: "Do not bare your heads and do not rend your clothes, lest you die and anger strike the whole community ... You must not go outside the entrance of the tent of meeting, lest you die, for the Lord's anointing oil is upon you."

Why could not Aaron be encouraged to break down and cry? The favored rabbinic response is that by not mourning Aaron acknowledged the righteousness of God's judgment. Not compelling. Could there be another explanation?

When I presided at the Bat Mitzvah of each of my daughters I was deeply moved, but to all outward appearances remained in control. Whereas at my nephew's Bar Mitzvah in another congregation when I was invited by a colleague to speak a word to my nephew, in the midst of my remarks, my voice cracked and tears flowed. Why the difference? Surely I did not feel more deeply about my nephew than my daughters. Ah, but at my daughters' Bat Mitzvah I was also the officiant at the congregational service, whereas when I spoke to my nephew I felt no such additional burden. I was simply Uncle Sam. The voice cracked and the tears flowed.

Not because he acknowledged God's righteousness was Aaron silent. One can acknowledge the justice of a verdict and still weep bitterly. Why did Aaron keep silent? He deferred his grieving until "the Lord's anointing oil" was no longer upon him, until he was no longer carrying the burden of officiating at the altar. The discovery of such connections between the text and our lives or the lives of our people is our task, our calling.

■ ■ ■

At times the prevailing interpretive legacy does not satisfy us. That is not problematical in the realm of *agada* for the *agada* is intrinsically multi-valent. The precedents of *halacha*, however, are more constraining. Still we exercise a liberal option. We say no as well as yes to the text and we do so with reasonably clear conscience for we believe that the Torah speaks in human language and was revealed through mortal creatures. We do not hesitate to assume that when Samuel heard God order Saul to smite every Amalakite man, woman and child, Samuel "misunderstood God." Of some other *mitzvot* we say they do not address us, or at least "not yet."

However, the strains on the liberal *Rav* are unique. Our *halachically* bound forebears no doubt agonized over their inability to permit what their heart and mind endorsed. We sometimes agonize over the impact of what we do permit on the discipline and continuity of the covenant. *Brit Milah*, the 8th day, even if it falls on Shabbat, or Yom Kippur; that is the *halacha*. But the mother leaves the hospital now on the fourth or fifth day. She wants the circumcision to be done there. How shall we interpret the *mitzvah*? Shall surgery be done on the fourth or fifth day, and the prayer recited at home on the eighth day? Ah, the burdens of being a liberal *Rav*.

Generally, we feel most authentic when we can reclaim rather than discard the *mitzvot* as they have been given, or when even our negations are grounded in some larger textual affirmation. Thus we reject the sexism of our heritage and we may do so by drawing forth the full implications of Adam and Eve's creation "in the image of God." We do feel most the *Rav* when our study of the texts informs our negations as well as our affirmations.

I am drawn more to the study of *agada* than *halacha*, but I can fully ignore neither. If I am away from the texts too long I am assaulted by pangs of inauthenticity. I feel some withdrawal symptoms. A return to primary and good secondary texts is like a fix. It is therapeutic. One must fight for those quiet times, early in the morning before the phone rings, or late at night. And, as has been our *minhag*, long summers where uninterrupted full mornings are routine. Without such extended periods for study I feel drained, empty.

The soul of the *Rav* is nurtured by study. If we are fortunate we have all savored those moments of discovery and insight, the joy of deriving a new thought, the sensuous excitement of feeling gripped by a truth that comes from our past and addresses our present. The *Rav* must study.

Connectedness to the text is one hallmark of the *Rav*; connectedness to the student is another. The *Rav* must teach. We study in order to teach. More exhilarating than the discovery of a great text or a new interpretation is the excitement of sharing it with a responsive other. Redemptive are the moments when what we teach is heard, read, appreciated—and affecting. How exquisite to behold a child's eyes pop in wonder as our story unravels, or hear a person say, "Rabbi, that sermon really touched me," or *shep nachus* as a student, months after class, refers in an appropriate context to the struggle between *yetzer tov* and *yetzer hara*. The lean times in our lives are the moments when they are not there to listen or are there but are not listening, or don't seem to care.

Hillel the elder said: "There are times to disseminate what you have learned and times when the people are so unresponsive that you should simply horde your learning for a more teachable generation." This latter prospect discomfits us. How sad to answer questions no one is asking. How sad to expound with fervor and see glazed expressions or closed eyes.

Take some comfort, my colleagues, in the knowledge that our illustrious predecessors were also not spared dozing students, at least from time to time. We read: "Rabbi (Judah Hanassi) was sitting and expounding and the people dozed." He sought to wake them up by applying rhetorical shock treatment. Rabbi said: "One woman bore six hundred thousand in her womb." A student woke up and asked, 'Who was that?' Rabbi answers: "Yocheved, mother of Moses, because the child she bore was the equivalent in value of six hundred thousand." We may be unimpressed by this rhetorical gimmick but apparently it worked. The students woke up and the problem that rabbi addressed is not unfamiliar to us.

Question: Given the frustrations that so often attend our efforts, would we want to be free of the burden of having to teach and reach our people? Given the pastoral pressures imposed by needy congregants, would we want to be spared such interruptions? Would most of us be content to be left alone to study if we were compensated adequately for doing so? The *Koretzer Rebbe* once told his wife, "If only they would leave me alone. If only I could be free to study and meditate all day." His prayers were answered. For days, weeks, no one came near Pinchas to seek counsel. He felt terribly lonely and unfulfilled. He soon realized he needed to counsel and teach his people as much as they needed him. He prayed that his gift be restored. And when it was he thanked God and said, "A person should not pretend to be what he is not."

Like the *Koretzer* we need to be interrupted. "You know," said the teacher, "my whole life I have been complaining that my work was constantly interrupted until I discovered that my interruptions were my work. . . ." How sad when they no longer interrupt with the words "Rabbi, I've been meaning to ask you. . . ."

We must study and we must teach, but how do we teach? Buber holds before us the supreme challenge when he writes of "holy sparks leaping across the gap. . . . The teaching must not be treated as a collection of knowable materials . . . either the teachings live in the life of a responsible human being, or they are not alive at all. . . ."

We not only teach Torah, we must strive to be a Torah. The *Rav* confronts the burden of bearing witness. That burden is considerably lighter if we confine ourselves to one-night stands, if we dazzle and entrance and then move on to another engagement. The burden is greater if we are rooted in a community; if we teach in the midst of a single congregation day after day, week after week, year after year, for they will come to know us as well as our teachings.

A few may remember if we gave the same sermon every other Rosh Hashanah. They *will* know if we betray our marriage vows, or if we decry materialism from the pulpit and then stridently press each item in contract negotiations. Our tradition itself gives us leverage in such matters. Judaism does not glorify vows of poverty. There can be no Torah without *kemach* (without

dough) and "the greater the person the greater the *yetzer*...."
Still, the *Rav* who teaches must be nourished by what she
imparts. The teaching we embody must appear to make some
difference in the quality of our lives. We cannot only model our
human frailty. Torah must help us tame our *yetzer* (evil impulse).

We model not only *menschlichkeit* but *emunah*—faith. Martin
Marty writes about a blues singer who had "just wailed the bluest
wail one could ever hear." After the sad song an interviewer
talked with him and found the blues singer to be very upbeat
and light-hearted. The interviewer asked the obvious question.
"How do you connect your life with your musical creations?
Were they born of deep personal suffering?" "Oh, of course,"
the singer said. He had gone through plenty of hard times as an
urban black, but those bad days were now gone. Still the people
wanted (needed) sadness and he remembered how to give it.
The singer explained, "I don't live as sad as I sell."

What do we sell? The *Rav* is cast as a master *agadist*, a
defender of the faith. Our people need reassurance that *lamrot
hakol* in spite of everything, life is not absurd, that beyond the
mystery there is meaning. Is this not the bottom line of our
teaching and preaching and presiding? Do we live the faith we
sell? In the matter of religious affirmation we also have a great
deal of leverage. We can model our struggle for faith, confess
our personal doubt and keep company with Abraham, the
psalmist, Levi Yitzhak of Berditchev, all of whom had their
lover's quarrels with God.

So we stand at the grave of a young child whose life was
snuffed out shortly after dawn and we echo the bitter plaint of
her loved ones: "Why? Why? Life is so unfair," we say. But we
also guide the family to the declaration: "Praised be Thou, O
Lord, Judge of Truth." And we lead the mourners in the recitation of the *kaddish* which Elie Wiesel calls "that solemn affirmation filled with grandeur and serenity by which man returns to
God His crown and His scepter."

Let us confess. There are times when we do sell more faith
than we can live. Stationed in the battlefield as God's defenders,

as comforters of life's wounded, we may rise to spiritual affirmations we do not always feel in our souls. Are we then hypocrites? No, we are modeling that very amalgam of doubt and faith that is the price of living with a God who is both hidden and revealed.

And yet our own spiritual nurture and our power to nurture others is enhanced if doubt and struggle are punctuated by moments when we too have experienced the nearness of the Holy One. For we remain like our forebears, not only guides to *halacha* but custodians of *agada*. To us is entrusted the story that life is a covenant. While that covenant may have hidden clauses, beyond the mystery there is meaning.

Paradoxically our faith may be strengthened by the very events which call it into question. And even more paradoxically we who come to teach humbly discover that we receive far more from our students than we may ever hope to give them. By virtue of who we are, we enter, at times, a very special academy where vulnerability, deep need, and trust engender a sharing of the unvarnished meditations of the heart.

Larry was a man in his late sixties. He came to our city to be near his daughter and grandchildren. Suddenly, a malignant tumor assaulted him and despite initial surgery, the destructive process became irreversible. Larry was dying. He knew he was dying. The body was progressively consumed. The mind was still intact. Larry knew he probably would not live to witness his grandson's thirteenth birthday, though he asked, with a thin smile, "Do you think God will let me cheat death until after the Bar Mitzvah?"

Moments later he said he felt the end was near and he asked, "Rabbi, how do you prepare?" I found myself thinking of the rabbinic dictum that we live each day, or ought to live each day, as if it were our last. "Larry," I said, "We prepare all our lives and you've prepared well. You've shown you love and care. You have a proper sense of right and wrong. You've made your share of mistakes like the rest of us. But you've earned a good name and you'll be missed. And maybe this is your finest hour and your greatest gift to your family: you've accepted your dying without bitterness, with great consideration for them, and appreciation for every kindness. Larry, I pray when my time comes I have half your courage and dignity. It's a privilege to know you."

Tears streamed from his eyes. He clasped my hand to his lips and kissed me. I recited the *y'varech'a* and the *Sh'ma* which he repeated after me and I left. Being with Larry was terribly draining. I felt faint as I left the room. Had I encountered my own mortality? But I also felt more privileged to spend one hour with Larry than many hours poring over the texts of Torah. Later I thought of the words of Saul Bellow's character, Mr. Sammler, as he stands at the coffin of his uncle and benefactor Elya Gruner:

> Remember God the soul of Elya Gruner ... at his best ... he was aware that he must meet, and he did meet ... the terms of his contract, the terms which in his inmost heart each man knows, as I know mine, for that is the truth of it, that we all know, God, we know, we know, we know. ...

To be a *Rav* is to offer some assurance to the dying and to their survivors that a human life has not been lived in vain; that what is most important is not ultimately subject to extinction, for God is a conserver of value. More than occasionally the soul of the *Rav* is sustained by what we are taught and teach in such a *Bet Midrash*. To be a *Rav* to Larry is the *massah*, the burden and the *zechut*, the privilege of our vocation. Our souls are nourished by our study and our teaching and our learning from those we have come to teach.

■ ■ ■

When all is said and done, dear colleagues, there is one final paradox: the more we truly succeed in our vocation the more we will be assaulted by fear of failure. The *Rav* never has it made. There is a holy insecurity in what we do and who we are. Those nagging questions never fully disappear: Did I really respond adequately to those who needed me? Whom did I really reach with that sermon? Are my High Holy Day messages equal to the rigors of the hour? Am I worried more about my acceptance or about being worthy of acceptance? What do those Confirmands I've taught possess of Torah and *mitzvot*, and a sense of living as sons and daughters of the covenant? How much do I know of what I am commissioned to teach? Can this ambiguous liberalism I embody really offer sustenance to hungry souls? Can the tradition itself really respond to the needs of our people in an age of laser beams and computers?

No matter how many great sermons we preach, or good classes we teach, or fine counseling sessions we share, such troubling questions don't disappear. We continue to have times of nagging uncertainty as well as moments of blessed confirmation. *L'chach notzarta* (for such a moment you were created). It goes with the territory.

But when we think of all the possible ways of spending that brief interlude between birth and the grave, when we think of what is given to us to be and to do, we have reason to declare with unique passion those words reserved for our morning devotions: "Praised be Thou, O Lord, Ruler of the Universe, who has sanctified us by Your commandments, and commanded us to busy ourselves with words of Torah." Perhaps a special benediction should be added to the *Birchot Hashachar*: "Praised be Thou, O Lord, who has made me a Rabbi to Your people Israel."

Index